# Playing Cards
# of the World

Dedicated to

My Goddess Maat

My Mother Anna

My Father Michael

My Sister Stefka

and My Friends David and Christine

# Playing Cards of the World

## A Collector's Guide

## Kathleen Wowk

 LUTTERWORTH PRESS · GUILDFORD SURREY

First published 1983

## ACKNOWLEDGEMENTS

First and foremost I would like to express my gratitude to Colin Narbeth without whom this book would not have been possible. In addition I would like to thank the following people and firms for their unreserved help in supplying me with information and checking through the manuscript: Sylvia Mann, Roderick Somerville, Joyce Pattison; the members of Stanley Gibbons' Playing Card Department; Margot Dietrich of the Deutsches-Spielkarten-Museum; Dennis Savage; Tony Beale, Hon. Secretary of the International Playing Card Society; Maurice Collett, Caroline Jenkins, David Sebastian Cade, Elaine Fuller, and the firms Ferd. Piatnik & Sohne, ASS and Heraclio Fournier.

The photographs used to illustrate this book are by courtesy of Stanley Gibbons, Sylvia Mann, Somerville of Edinburgh and Brian Kemp.

ISBN 0 7188 2408 3

Filmset by Inforum Ltd., Portsmouth
in VIP Palatino 10 on 12 point; captions 9 on 11 point Palatino bold

Printed in Hong Kong by Colorcraft Ltd.

# Contents

## FRENCH SUIT-MARKS

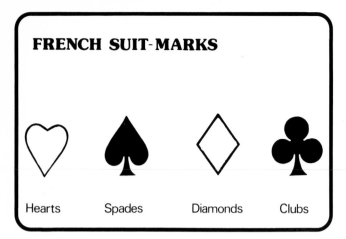

| Hearts | Spades | Diamonds | Clubs |

## SPANISH SUIT-MARKS

| Cups | Batons | Money | Swords |

## SWISS SUIT-MARKS

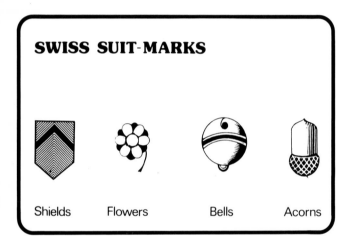

| Shields | Flowers | Bells | Acorns |

## GERMAN SUIT-MARKS

| Hearts | Leaves | Bells | Acorns |

## ITALIAN SUIT-MARKS

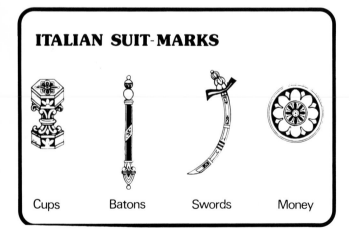

| Cups | Batons | Swords | Money |

## ITALO-SPANISH SUIT-MARKS

| Batons | Cups | Swords | Money |

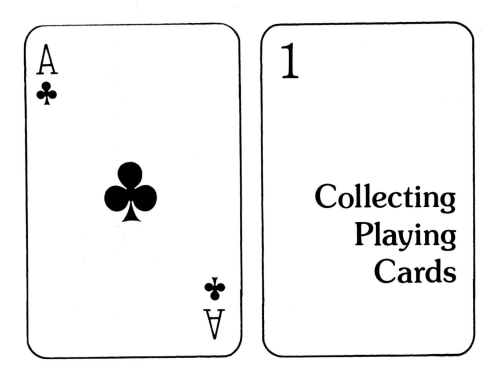

# Collecting Playing Cards

ONE of the fascinations of playing cards is their variety and beauty, coupled with the irony that most people take them completely for granted.

It is always a surprise to discover that in other countries playing cards are produced with unfamiliar suit signs and that packs can range from as few as 24 cards to as many as 384. Equally surprising is the fact that they come in a variety of shapes, sizes, materials and designs and that famous artists have designed packs for the amusement of the rich and even as a method of teaching royalty. Furthermore, from these miniature works of art it is possible to learn about the history of various countries, cultures and something about the different methods of printing.

But as well as being a stimulating educational medium, playing cards pose a lot of mysteries, many of which will never be solved, and there is plenty of room (in fact a necessity) for original research. One of the most puzzling questions is from where did playing cards originate? In the past, many authorities have placed the East as their rightful place of birth, stating that they evolved from existing games such as dice, Chinese chess, or Korean divinatory arrows. A more colourful suggestion is that they were invented by the frustrated wife of an Indian Maharajah in an attempt to occupy both hands of her husband who had the annoying habit of fiddling with his beard.

If cards did originate in the East, how did they reach Europe? Two of the most popular theories were that they were brought over by either Crusaders or gypsies. Both these theories have now been shown to be unacceptable. The first reference to playing cards in Europe is in Italy in 1376, whereas the last Crusades were ending in 1291 and the gypsies did not come to Europe until after the time playing cards are first recorded. It is perhaps more plausible that playing cards came to Europe via eastern traders. It is, however, also possible that they were invented independently in both the East and West. This subject is dealt with more fully in Chapter 2.

Although fascinating, this sort of speculation need not over-concern the new collector. Indeed the only question the beginner needs to ask is what shall I collect? Because the number of packs produced is so enormous, no one can hope to build up a comprehensive collection of the 'world'. Therefore specialization is necessary.

Many people collect the standard patterns of a favourite country. Playing cards bearing standard patterns are the ones produced for the purpose of playing card games, and as such bear uniform designs. This type of collection may seem very simple at first, but most countries did not just employ one standard pattern, but many patterns, each of which is peculiar to a certain region. Some of these patterns are no longer produced, and can be difficult to find. Others have

Russian non-standard 'Anti-Religions' pack by GKM, Leningrad, c. 1935. The spades suit satirizes the Eastern religions; hearts, Catholicism; diamonds, Judaism; clubs, Greek Orthodox.

Costume pack by Gilbert of Paris c. 1850 showing British personalities on the court cards.

survived to the present day. The regional patterns of a country, or even group of countries, often share some of the same characteristics and it is interesting to study their development and to try to trace them back to their origins. One can also acquire examples of the same pattern made by different makers, all of which will differ slightly in quality, artistic treatment and details. Sometimes the design on standard cards was changed to conform to current political or religious views. This happened during the French Revolution when all the French court cards had their crowns and tops of sceptres removed.

The other main group of playing cards is the non-standard variety. These are usually produced with novel designs or subject matter which often give the cards an additional function other than gaming. These, of course, can lead to a thematic collection with a number of interesting possibilities.

One of the most common themes for non-standard cards is education, including geography, geometry, arithmetic, spelling, history, carving, heraldry, and logic. Politics is also a favourite subject, often leading to playing cards being used to propagate various

views and ideals. Many political packs appeared in the midst of, or just after, a war or change of government and either feature the bad points of the opponents or the virtues of the allies.

Closely linked to politics is religion. In England a long series of political packs was produced in the 17th and 18th centuries which had strong anti-Catholic undertones. There are also many packs which feature scenes or personalities from the Bible, while one of the most famous Russian non-standard packs is an 'Anti-Religions' pack of c.1935 which satirizes the world's religions.

For the artistically inclined, there are the costume packs which became fashionable in the 18th and 19th centuries. Beautifully produced, they show the court figures dressed in the costume of different countries, regions, or periods of history. Similar packs were produced showing historical characters from real life, operas, plays or novels. At one time packs were also produced showing the music from operas and popular songs. These musical packs usually have their values indicated by a miniature playing card index in one of the top corners and could either be used for gaming or

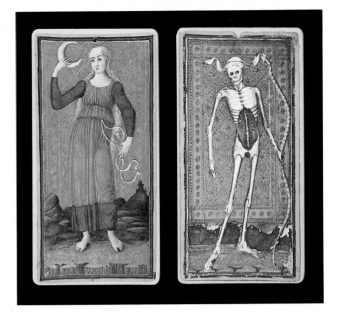

Two trump cards from a reprint of the Visconti Sforza tarot, *c*. 1428.

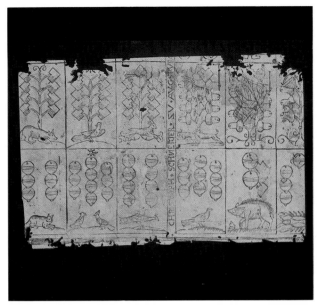

German 16th-century sheet of playing cards found in a book binding.

laid out and used as a music sheet.

Fortune-telling cards are another area for consideration. These too are usually well produced and can range from very simple cards with just a situation picture and a one-word explanation such as 'marriage' or 'sorrow', to cards which show astrological and zodiacal signs, a palm reading, Hebrew letter and a detailed text.

Another fascinating branch of card collecting is the Tarot. Although most people associate tarot cards with fortune-telling, originally they were used for gaming, and still are in many European countries. The 'magical tarot' did not evolve until the late 18th century and, as one might expect with such an emotive subject, many varieties of packs exist. Some 'magical tarots' are very similar to the original standard tarots, while others use Egyptian, Hebrew or Eastern symbolism.

An important point to consider when choosing a theme to collect is the availability and price of playing cards. Because playing cards were meant to be used until worn and then thrown away, many early packs have been destroyed, with the only surviving examples being in museums. Occasionally, one comes across sheets of 15th or 16th century playing cards which, due to a paper shortage at the time, were used in book bindings and so were preserved through the ages. Some other packs have survived bound in book form. In the main, however, collecting only becomes a feasible proposition with the playing cards of the 1700s onwards.

Prices at present are very reasonable. The highest price paid on the open market (at the time of writing) is £10,000 for a Mantegna Tarot pack of *c*.1450. This is, however, exceptional. The packs from the 17th and early 18th century, which are the earliest items most collectors would come across, have all been sold for under £4,000. This is very little compared with other established art forms such as paintings. A fascinating collection can equally well be made from more modern cards and here there is material available within all price ranges.

Many modern standard patterns are beautifully produced and remain faithful to their antecedents, so a person with modest means can still trace the history of standard patterns through modern editions. There

Part of a sheet of 16th-century German playing cards showing two complete cards and half of another.

are also many interesting modern non-standard cards being produced, some of which are made in limited editions of as few as 100.

Various factors influence the price of playing cards. Three of the most important are age, rarity and condition. These factors although seemingly self explanatory can be misleading. For instance, a sought-after pack in excellent condition that was issued in the 20th century in a limited edition of 1,000 can fetch more than a common pack of the 19th or even 18th century. Hence, just because a pack is old it does not mean it is rare or desirable to the collector. Also, it should be remembered that a normal pack is a used pack, and often it is impossible to find rare antique packs in good condition or complete. Obviously one tries to buy the best example possible. But if you come across a design you have never seen before which is a little ragged and has maybe one card missing, if it is within your price range and essential to your collection, then buy it. After all, at a later date if you find a better example you can trade the original pack.

The popularity of a subject or country also affects the price of playing cards, in accordance with the laws of supply and demand. At present Europe and Britain seem to be the most popular areas. Russian and Oriental cards are not so widely collected, but because examples can be hard to find, early material can be quite expensive. In the chapter on Oriental cards I have mentioned many variations for the sake of historical continuity, although many of the packs are only found in museums or are unique items. However, there are quite a few modern packs still being produced which are easily accessible to the collector.

Once it has been decided what to collect, the next question is where to buy one's material. There are various sources. Until recently, because the hobby was relatively unknown, the only way to find cards was either through friends, while on holiday in foreign countries, or by hunting in junk or antique shops. These methods can prove laborious and unfruitful. Also, because expert knowledge is required before one can price playing cards accurately, you may find examples at inflated prices. On the other hand, of course, there is always the thrill of coming across a bargain.

Fortunately, more and more firms have now begun trading in playing cards. They sell both rare antique and modern cards over the counter as well as holding regular auctions. There are also various societies from which you can obtain names of fellow collectors with whom you can trade packs or just correspond for information. Societies hold regular conventions where dealers and collectors give talks on their subject

*Left to right*: two woodblock-printed cards from a 16th-century German pack; the duty ace of spades used from 1862, from a pack by De La Rue & Co., *c*. 1865.

and sell or exchange items.

As soon as a few packs have been bought, thought should be given to housing the collection. This is largely a matter of personal preference and the following can only be taken as suggestions. Because there are so many cards in a pack, many collectors just mount their courts, trumps, or other interesting cards with photo corners on sheets of black cardboard or in stamp albums. The rest of the pack can be stored away. Albums are available with special plastic sheeting that protects the cards from damage and fading. There are also albums with plastic 'pockets' which enable both the fronts and the backs of cards to be displayed. Attractive packs can be framed and used as wall decorations or used to decorate a glass coffee table. It is advisable to do a 'write-up' for each pack acquired. This information may include: where a pack was bought, when and for how much; in which country the pack was made, by whom and when; and any other special features.

Of course, in order to produce a worthwhile 'write-up', one must be able to identify the cards. The most obvious clue is whether the cards bear suit signs, and if so which ones. The various suit signs are listed below, together with their areas of use. During the 1800s, however, many European countries stopped using their own traditional suit signs and adopted the French suit motifs. Unless these packs bear the maker's name or 'indices', they can be difficult to identify at first glance.

Indices are the marks in the card's corners which denote the card's value. Their widespread use first occurred on standard-patterned packs in America in the 1870s, but other countries did not adopt them until some twenty years later. The idea of corner indices was not, however, totally new. Some early Spanish packs are found with indices and the modified designs used on French cards during the Revolution often included indices on the court cards. They are also found in some form or another on many non-standard cards from at least the 17th century.

Initially, these indices took the form of either a miniature playing card in one or two of the corners, or of a letter or number value together with the suit sign in the card's corner. Now all indices are of the latter variety.

In general the following indices (which correspond to king, queen, jack and ace) appear on French-suited cards from the 1900s onwards:

K M B T Bulgaria
K D B Es Denmark
K D Kn 1 or ES or E Denmark, Norway and Sweden
K D B A Denmark, Germany, Austria and occasionally ex-Empire

11

K Q J A England, America and now internation-
ally used
R D V A or 1 France, Belgium, Switzerland and
other small card producing countries
K D K 1 Finland
K R S 1 Finland
B K O A Greece
H V B 1 or A Holland
K D G As Iceland
K D W A Poland
К Д B T Russia

The traditional German-suited cards bear the indices K O U A while traditional Swiss-suited cards feature the words König, Ober and Under.

Once a pack's country of origin is known, the pattern can be identified by checking the pack's characteristics against the descriptions of the various standard patterns in the chapter concerned. *Here care should be taken*, for although the most common standard patterns produced are described in full, it should be noted that many variations of the same pattern were produced in different areas, times, and by different makers. The variations of the same pattern are too numerous to mention, but the most common ones are the way the court figures are facing, what objects they hold, if any, and in which hand. One of the most difficult things to find out about playing cards is their date. This is largely a matter of experience. The following general points to look out for can only be taken as guidelines and usually only enable one to arrive at an approximate date.

1. *Printing Methods*

Apart from the early non-standard engraved cards which were black and white and had illustrations on each card, most playing cards until the mid-nineteenth century were made from wood-blocks and were hand coloured by stencils. Some countries, however, continued to use this printing method until the 20th century. By and large though, playing card makers adopted new printing methods shortly after they

were introduced, including lithography, photolithography, photogravure, etc.

France and England retained plain card backs until the 19th century, whereas the rest of Europe employed back decorations, however simple, from a very early date.

2. *Single- or Double-Ended Courts*

Many European countries adopted double-ended courts in the first quarter of the 19th century. Again, earlier examples are known, and some countries, notably England and the United States, used single-ended courts until after 1850 and Belgium after 1900. Some standard patterns are still produced with single-ended cards, while others are found with both single- and double-ended court and number cards.

3. *Square or Rounded Corners*

Generally, rounded corners on cards were not introduced until the late 19th century. Sometimes the square corners on cards have been rounded through continued use and as an extra precaution when dating, one should note whether the card's frame line (where there is one) also has square or round corners.

4. *Tax Stamps*

Tax stamps appear on cards of all countries. Tax collectors, wishing to ensure that all card makers paid their taxes would stamp one of the cards from a pack. The amount of tax paid varied from country to country and period to period. During times of war for instance, when more revenue was required by the government, the tax went up.

The actual tax stamps also differ. Sometimes they just denote the amount paid and at other times they have a code word or letter for the tax region, plus the date and the amount.

Unfortunately the existing information on tax stamps is very sketchy. A comprehensive study would warrant a complete book to itself and is too specialized for the present work. For further details on the subject, one should consult the various authoritative articles on tax stamps published in The International Playing-Card Society's magazine.

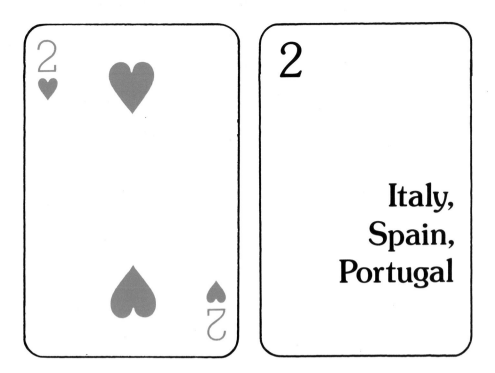

# Italy, Spain, Portugal

IT IS often amusing to read books on a particular subject and ridicule some of the deductions, presented as facts, which in the light of further study have turned out to be completely wrong. This is often the case with the theories on the origins of playing cards, some of which have been dealt with in the first chapter. So it is with great hesitation and some trepidation that I pass on the belief that the 'mother of invention' as far as European playing cards are concerned is Italy.

Unfortunately, as with so many areas of the history and development of playing cards, there is no proof to support even this theory. However, in favour of Italy, it should be noted that the first reliable mention of playing cards in the West is in a decree in the city of Florence forbidding their use. The decree is dated 23 May 1376. After this date, references to playing cards (usually in the form of a ban) can be found in most parts of Europe. Therefore it can be supposed, that, at the time of the Florentine decree, playing cards had only recently been introduced to Europe.

During the 14th century Italy was both the cultural and trade centre of Europe. Her three main commercial cities were Genoa, Venice and Florence, each of which had designated trade routes covering the then known world. For a long time Genoa and Venice, both maritime cities, had almost exclusive trading rights with Asia Minor, the East Indies and the Far East. Hence, if we accept the opinion that Western playing cards were initially inspired by an Eastern equivalent, the chances are that the 'middle-man' would have been a sailor or merchant using one of these two Italian ports.

Florence, on the other hand, concentrated on trade with Northern Europe. Once playing cards had found their way into Italy, it is likely that Florence would have been largely responsible for spreading them to other parts of Europe. After all, if the Florentine decree of 1376 did nothing else, it would surely have shown her merchants and traders that playing cards were a popular and therefore profitable commodity.

Indeed, gaming with cards quickly became so popular in Italy that one of the greatest preachers of his time, St. Bernardino of Siena (d.1444 and canonized by Nicholas V in 1450), took it upon himself to condemn publicly the evil pastime. In his sermon in 1423, conducted on the steps of the Church at San Petronio in Bologna, he moved the townsfolk so much that they lit bonfires and proceeded to burn their games and playing cards.

From the earliest times the Italians adopted the suit signs of: *spade* (swords), *bastoni* (batons), *coppe* (cups or chalices) and *denari* (coins). Initially, it would have been these Italian-suited cards that spread to other parts of Europe. However, whereas most European countries eventually devised and disseminated their own suit systems, Spain and Portugal adopted the

*Left to right*: Geographical pack by Giambattista Albrizzi, Venice, *c.* 1780; biblical cards engraved by A. Visentini in 1748 from drawings by Francesco Zuccarelli; a non-standard pack with suits devoted to American, Spanish, Roman and Arab themes by Felipe Ocejo, Madrid, *c.* 1810.

Italian suits for their own standard cards, although both countries made minor changes to the designs.

Two of the main features of early Italian cards are 'turned-over' edges and designs on the backs of the cards. The turn-over edges were produced by a larger piece of paper being glued on to the back of the playing card and turned over the card's front to form a raised protective border. The backs of cards were usually adorned with allegorical scenes, coats of arms, or small pictures. The illustrations were often the maker's trade mark.

As well as adopted non-standard playing card designs initially produced in other countries, Italy contributed a number of now famous packs herself. One of the earliest of these is a heraldry pack of 1682 entitled *Preggi della Nobilita Veneta abbozzati in un giuoco d'Armi di tutte le Famiglie, Di D. Casimiro Freschot*. The cards (produced in a second edition in 1707) show armorial bearings of Venetian and other ruling noble families. As with many non-standard playing cards, the value of each card is indicated by a figure or letter overprinted on a suit sign in the top right hand corner of the card. In this pack the suits are the flowers: violets, roses, lilies and tulips.

In the same year a card game was issued by the Venetian author Giovanni Palazzi entitled 'Virtue in Playing or Illustrious Daughters of Patrician Families

in Venice'.

In *c.*1780 Giambattista Albrizzi of Venice issued a geographical pack which was concerned not only with Italy, but with the whole world. It was called *Il Giuoco Geografico, in cui si contengono tutti i Paesi, Regni, Provincie, Repubbliche Citta, . . . del Mondo scoperto*. Each suit is devoted to a particular continent: the suit of cups represents Europe; swords Africa; coins Asia and batons America. All of the 52 cards list information about a particular place and their value is shown by a miniature Venetian playing card in the upper right hand corner. The pack contains eight extra cards giving the title and rules of the game. In a later edition of this pack the eight extra cards are numbered in Roman numerals.

About the same time Albrizzi issued another pack named the 'Chronology of the Popes'. Again containing 52 cards it also has six extra cards giving the title and rules of the game. Numbered from 1–52 the order of the suits is: cups, coins, batons and swords. The first card depicts St. Peter and card No. 52 is concerned with the accession of Clement XIV in 1769.

In 1826 P. & G. Vallardi of Milan issued a geographical pack which gives printed accounts of various countries of the world. On each card is a medallion containing a figure in the costume of the land in question. The pack comes with a list of the countries mentioned and a folding engraved map.

A similar pack was issued by Lopes y Cia. of Barcelona, Spain, in c.1875. The courts of each suit show figures representing the different races of the world. The coins represent Asia with Chinese people; cups symbolize Africa, with, oddly enough, Oriental figures; spades deal with Europe; and lastly batons characterize America with Red Indians.

By the same firm is a 48-card pack showing historical people on the court cards. In contrast to most Spanish packs the court cards are king, knight and maid as opposed to king, knight and jack. The coin suit shows the king as *D Taime el Conquistador*, the knight is *D Juan de Austria* and the maid is *Dama de la Corte de Fernando III*. In the same order the cups suit shows: *D Pelayo, D Alvaro de Luna*; and *Dama de la Corte de Filipe IV*. The swords show: *Carlos V Emperador, Gonzola de Cordova*, and *Dama de le Corte de Carlos II*. The batons show *D Pedro el Cruel, El Cid Compeador* and lastly *Dama de la Corte de Alonso XI*.

In 1872 Fulladosa y Cia. of Barcelona issued a pack showing eminent Spaniards from the 15th to 19th centuries on the court cards. Again the pack includes a maid instead of a jack. A little later Fulladosa y Cia. produced a geographical pack, where the four suits represent Asia, Africa, Europe and America.

Returning to Italy, C.B. Marcovich of Trieste made a historical personages pack in c.1880. The cards are French-suited, wood-engraved and stencil-coloured. The kings show: Lear, Louis XIV, Ziani and Mohammed. The queens, sometimes depicted as males, are Spanish, French, Greek and German figures. The jacks are Schiller, Victor Hugo, Byron and Machiavelli.

The Bible was a favourite subject of the Italian card makers and in 1748 A. Visentini made a 52-card pack concerning the history of the 'Old Testament from the Creation to the birth of Christ'. The cards are split up into 4 groups of 13. The groups are lettered: A to NN; O to Z; a to nn; and o to z. The suit signs are: an orange circle; a yellow diamond; a pink heart and a lavender jar. Within each suit sign is a picture such as a candle or bird. The main part of the card's face shows a Biblical scene with Latin and Italian inscriptions above and below. The drawings on the cards were originally by Francesco Zuccarelli. G. Pirotta of Milan in 1815, produced a 48-card pack showing scenes from the life of Christ, with accompanying text. Another such pack was made by P. & G. Vallardi of Milan. On each of the 48 cards is a Roman number and an oval medallion illustrating an incident from the New Testament. The same makers produced similar style packs depicting Greek and Roman history.

Sadly the Portuguese did not produce many original non-standard playing cards, and of the ones they did, few have survived. Like the Low Countries, the Austro-Hungarian Empire, Switzerland and Germany, they adopted a playing card design where the court figures are dressed in hunting or historical costumes while the aces show national views.

# MODERN CARDS

The most important and prolific 20th-century Spanish card manufacturer is undoubtedly Heraclio Fournier of Vitoria. This firm has made a great number of imaginative and high quality standard and non-standard playing cards, and also produces a catalogue of the cards in the Museo de Naipes in Vitoria.

Some of the earliest cards Fournier produced concentrated on the old links between Spain and America, of its discovery, people, cultures and wars.

In 1929 L. Palao designed a pack for Fournier called 'Historical Ibero-Americano Playing Cards' to commemorate the Iberian American Exhibition in Seville and Barcelona. The named court figures show personalities associated with the discovery of America, while the number cards show artefacts, gold coins, chalices, etc. The backs of the cards show the arms of Spain and her provinces – a double-headed eagle with crown and shields. In 1954 Fournier produced a pack called 'Discoverers and Colonizers of America' which was designed by Serny.

By special request from the American Association of University Women, Fournier produced a pack showing symbolic Inca figures and another with Maya figures. The 52 French-suited, double-ended cards are extremely decorative and were produced before 1948.

More recently, c.1960, the firm made the 'Arts of pre-Columbian America', or more simply the 'America' pack. Each of the four suits is dedicated to one of the old American cultures; the spades show the North-West Indians, diamonds – Red Indians, hearts – Aztecs, and clubs – Incas. The jokers show a map of North and South America, and the backs show a god surrounded by snakes. An explanatory booklet explains the history of the various races personified on the cards.

Fournier also produced a pack which had court cards showing leading personalities of the American Civil War against a scenic background. The aces show battle scenes, the two jokers feature flags and weapons, while the four of each suit has military equipment on it. On the backs can be seen an eagle with laurel branches and arrows. This pack was issued in 1961 and designed by Teodoro Miciano.

For the Pavilion of Spain, New York World Fair, held in 1964/5, Fournier issued a pack designed by Carmen Guzman. Containing 48 plus 2 extra cards the Spanish suits are shown in novel colours: coins, gold; cups, purple; swords, blue; and batons, green.

Turning aside from America, Fournier makes playing cards which capture the essence of a number of different countries and eras. His 'Ancient Civilizations' pack is 'Dedicated to the Great Empires of Ancient Times' and again has thematic suits. The clubs show Egypt, diamonds Sumeria, spades Assyria and hearts Persia. The cards are French-suited, double-ended and the court figures appear as though they are the frozen sleepy survivors of past eras embedded in rock waiting to be woken by the player's warm hands. Again, as with most of Fournier's packs, there are two jokers and an explanatory leaflet.

Fournier's 'Classic' pack was designed by Paul Mathison and has court cards showing a god or goddess of the classical world. In the hearts suit we find: Dionysius, Venus and Apollo; clubs, Neptune, Flora and Hercules; diamonds, Jupiter, Juno and Mercury; spades, Pluto, Persephone and Mars. The backs have a marbled effect and the court figures are presented in a modern sketch-like manner.

A particularly beautiful and colourful pack by Fournier is the 'Historic Iranian Designs'. This pack is based on an earlier pack made by De La Rue of England, for export to Iran. In the Fournier pack the spades show the Achaemenian Dynasty of 559–330B.C. (a different design is featured in the De La Rue pack), hearts show the Sassarides Dynasty, 242–652B.C. (featured on the De La Rue spade suit), diamonds the Safavides Dynasty of 1501–1753 (featured on the De La Rue heart suit) and lastly clubs, the Aphars Dynasty of 1736–1749 (the same design is on the De La Rue club suit also). The 52 cards are double-ended and have both French and Iranian indices and two jokers showing the Simong – a legendary Persian bird.

Lastly, one of Fournier's most acclaimed modern packs, made c.1973, features skilfully executed caricatures of world personalities. The cards come in a twin pack so there are in total 104 different personalities, such as: Stalin, Tito, Makarios, Queen Elizabeth II, Harold Wilson, Edward Heath, Haile Selassie, Charles de Gaulle, Mao Tse-Tung, Richard Nixon and the Kennedy family.

It will come as no surprise to learn that one of the most popular subjects for non-standard cards in Spain is bullfighting. These packs feature a bullfighter or bullfighting scenes on either (or both) the front or back of the cards. One such pack, c.1930, has the suits of faces, glasses of wine, swords and banderillas. Containing 40 Spanish-suited cards, the backs carry an advert for *Las España* chocolate with photographs of bull-fighting scenes, while the courts portray the actual bullfighters as children. Another pack was made at the turn of this century by Julio Garcìa (printer) and Pedro Maldonado (author) called the 'New Bullfighting Pack'; which again has non-standard suits. The coins suit shows different cattle brands; the cups have Picadors' faces superimposed on them; while the batons picture Banderilleros, with the darts they use in the bullfight cleverly converted into neckties. Similarly the swords' suit portrays swords with the faces of élitist Maestros instead of hilts. The court cards show full length portraits of matadors either posing or 'in action'. All the personalities featured are named. A similar pack was made by Simeon Dura of Valencia. Called *Baraja Taurina*, the courts are named toreadors and their assistants, while the number cards of the coins suit show either the heads of famous bullfighters or cattle brands enclosed in tambourines or glasses.

Still with sport in mind, a 48-card Spanish-suited 'Boxing' pack was made c.1920 which shows boxing personalities on the court cards, aces and some number cards. Details regarding the weights for different boxing grades are given on the 8 of cups, while the different types of punches and stances employed in boxing are shown on the back of the cards. The Italians also produced an unusual sporting pack in 1978. It was issued by Arti Grafiche Alinari Baglioni, and designed by Costantini and shows historical Florentine footballers in 16th-century costumes. The cards are very attractive and resemble woodcuts. The court figures all hold footballs and the suits are split into various Florentine parishes representing the football teams of: S. Croce for swords, S. Giovanni for batons, S. Spirito for coins and Santa Maria Novella for cups. The Erresei playing-card company also made a pack of football cards entitled 'Juventus' which shows various famous footballers and their signatures on the court cards.

Spain produced a number of modern cards with non-standard suit signs. An amusing one by A. Comas of Barcelona, c.1930, shows the courts as humanized soda bottles and the suits as: bottle tops, glasses, siphons and bottles. The pack was made to advertise *Bebidas Carbonicas*. Another pack by Litografia Industrias Madriguera S.A. of Barcelona, c. 1930, has the suit signs of balls, cups, swords and skittles. The 40-card packs show children playing with the suit signs as toys. The backs show famous footbal-

A twin pack of 'Political' playing cards by Heraclio Fournier, Vitoria, *c.* 1973.

One of 40 cards showing different bullfighters from the 'New Bullfighters' pack printed by Julio García, designed by Pedro Maldonado, *c.* 1900.

---

lers. Children at play is also the subject of the *Baraja Infantil* Spanish-suited pack. Made *c.*1960, the suits are: balls, beets, cones and wooden swords. The cards of this pack were inserted into chocolate packages.

Another pack which was issued with packets of chocolates for Evaristo Juncosa and made by Lit. Baño of Barcelona, has the coin suit devoted to pictures of film stars.

Other packs featuring film stars include the *Cinematografica* pack made by Lit. J.M. Arnau of Barcelona in the 1920s. This 48-card pack shows the famous early film stars on the court cards and coins suit, including: Charles Chaplin, Douglas Fairbanks, Mary Pickford, Harold Lloyd, Buster Keaton and Rudolf Valentino. The backs show scenes from films and they were issued to advertise *Chocolates Jaime Boix*. There is also the film star pack by Fenis of Barcelona of *c.*1920, where each suit is devoted to a particular film personality. The coins show Harold Lloyd; clubs, Buster Keaton; swords, Ben Turpin; and cups, Charles Chaplin.

As Italy is a country with a long history of political struggle and unrest, it is fitting that many of her 20th century playing cards have been devoted to political and military themes. More often than not, these tend to ridicule and satirize their subject matter, such as the *Carte da Giuoco Nazionali* by Istituto Editoriale Italiano of Milan. Designed by Enrico Saccetti in 1915, the kings of each suit are caricatures of the rulers of Bulgaria (hearts), Germany (diamonds), Austria (spades), and Turkey (clubs). Note that Italy is not included! The queens show peasant girls while the jacks are enlisted men.

Another pack, by Dal Negro of Treviso, was specially printed for the firm of Italsider in Genoa and has courts dedicated to the pre-World War One dynasties of Austro-Hungary (hearts), Great Britain (diamonds), Germany (spades), and Russia (clubs). The jokers show Rasputin. These cards are No. III of a series made in 1964 with a print run of 2,100. Pack No. I was made in 1961 with a print run of 2,500 and pack No. II was produced a year later in the same quantity.

Another special printing was made for the U.S. 5th Army in 1945 by Vannini of Florence. The kings and jacks show servicemen, while the queens and backs show pin-up girls, with the insignia of the 5th Army also on the backs. The pack was produced at the instigation of the Public Relations Officer of the U.S. 5th Army!

As well as world leaders, most of Italy's political parties have at some time or another featured on playing cards. As early as 1928 Pietro Brevi of Bergamo issued a 52-card Fascist pack designed by Francesco Offredi. Two years later E. Pignalosa & Son of Naples produced a pack to coincide with the new Fascist regime, where the suits are: propellers, steel helmets, fasces and anchors. The 40-card pack has courts showing 'Italia' figures, the Armed Forces and Blackshirts. In 1951 a special printing was made for the Rome Electoral Committee of the Communist Party of Italy ridiculing the opposition. The backs show a flag and the initials PCI. In the same year A.G. Fanetto & Petrelli issued a similar pack for the local electorate in Rome with political caricatures on the courts. The cards were designed by Jaccovitti and the backs show books and political caricatures.

T.C. & S. issued the 'Politicards' which have courts designed by Massimo Vallese showing political caricatures. The diamonds show a hammer and sickle and represent the Communists; the hearts show shields representing the Christian Democrats; the clubs show leaves and the flag of Italy for the Fascists, and the last suit, spades, represents the Socialists.

Perhaps Italy's greatest contribution to playing cards in recent times is their many facsimile packs, which have brought rare and historically important packs of cards into the reach of the general public. In particular, the Milan based firm Stampati Arienti has produced a number of high quality reproductions, although they are usually printed in small limited numbers. In 1978 the firm produced a glossy 'Art Catalogue' showing illustrations of the packs made from 1969–78. Among the many famous packs are: Brianville's heraldry cards and another heraldry pack by Mariette; P. Du Val's geographical cards; Pasquin's Windkaart; Mitelli's tarot cards. They also reproduced various 18th and 19th century standard patterns of Italy, Spain and France.

Among the modern packs they have sponsored are a number of tarots, including ones by Domenico Balbi, Andrea Picini, and Osvaldo Menegazzi. There are also two Zodiac packs by Sandro Bellenghi and Giorgio Tavaglione.

# STANDARD PATTERNS

## *ITALY*

Today, Italian packs are made with 40 or 52 cards. Each suit comprises the three court cards of king, knight and jack (Ital. *re, cavallo, fante*), an ace and 7–2 or 10–2 in numerical cards. The kings are always shown seated, the knights ride horses and the cards no longer feature the turn-over edges which in earlier packs formed a raised protective border around the fronts of the cards.

Three different types of suit signs are used in Italy: traditional, Spanish-suited, and French-suited. The traditional Italian suits of *spade* (swords), *bastoni* (batons), *coppe* (cups or chalices) and *denari* (coins) are now mainly used in the north and north east of Italy.

The southern two thirds of Italy (south of the River Po) uses a suit system termed 'Italo-Spanish'. Although so called, it is in fact the same as the Spanish suit designs but, having been initially introduced into this area of Italy by the Spanish, it was subsequently manufactured in Italy. This much is known because, when, in the 18th century, the Spanish adopted breaks in the border of their cards, and dropped the Italian fashion of having turn-over edges, Italo-Spanish cards continued to be produced within the old Italian tradition.

The exact date when the Spanish introduced their suit signs to Italy is not known. However, it is interesting to note that the Spanish King Alfonso V 'The Magnanimous' (1416–1458) reconquered much of Corsica in 1420 and all of Naples in 1442. Naples became the centre and capital of the Aragonese empire until Alfonso's death. The King was very conscious of culture and literature and supported various Renaissance artists. Since Naples and the surrounding areas do use Italo/Spanish suits, it could well have been that they first appeared at this time and under his guidance.

The third suit system used in Italy is that of the French. This was probably introduced during the 18th century and is mainly used in the north west of Italy.

Some eighteen different standard patterns are currently in use in Italy. They originated at a time when Italy was split up into states which were ruled by their own princes or dukes with their own laws and cultures. As in other countries with a constantly changing geography, the patterns have a number of details which make them individual, but through continuous warfare and trading they also have many features which are common to all.

An interesting modern variation of the Italian standard pattern are the 'Duplex' cards. These feature two different standard patterns on the same card. For instance Masenghini of Bergamo made a pack in 1968 showing the Lombard pattern on one end of the double-ended cards and the Piacentine pattern on the other end. The next year he issued two more packs with the Venetian and Neapolitan patterns together and the Lombard and Neapolitan patterns together.

*Left to right*: 'Florentine Football' pack by A.G.A.B. of Florence, *c*. 1978; early film stars appear on the coins suit and the court cards of all suits in this 'Cinematografica' pack by J.M. Arnau, Barcelona, *c*. 1920; this 40-card pack has suits of propellors, helmets, fasces and anchors – an Italian fascist pack by R. Pignaosa, Naples, *c*. 1930.

## ITALIAN SUITED

**Venetian Pattern** (*Venete, Trevigiane* or *Trevisane telate*)

The Venetian pattern is the most widely used and thought to be the oldest of the Italian-suited patterns. The packs were made originally with 52 cards (king, knight, jack, ace, 10–2), but they are now also made with 40 cards (king, knight, jack, ace, 7–2). The cards are of the traditional Italian long, narrow shape and the double-ended design was introduced in the early 19th century.

### Kings

The crowned kings are all similarly arranged. They look to their left, hold their respective suit signs in their right hand and a spear in their left hand. On some packs the king of batons has a shield motif in the centre of the card showing the arms of the town Treviso with its Latin name Tarvisium.

### Knights

All the knights ride horses, with the knights of swords and cups riding to the left-hand side of the card's face, while those of batons and coins ride to the right-hand side of the card's face. The knights look the same way as they are riding, with the knights of swords and coins being in profile. The knight of swords holds a curved sword behind his head in his raised right hand. The knights of batons and coins also hold a suit sign in their right hand, while the knight of cups holds his in his left hand.

### Jacks

The jacks of coins and cups hold their respective suit signs upright in their right hand. The jack of batons holds his suit sign in both hands and that of swords a downward pointing sword in his right hand. The jacks of coins and swords look to their right and the latter has a decapitated head where his left hand should be. The jack of cups' head can be seen in right profile and he has a crescent moon containing a man's face where his left hand should be. The jack of batons looks to his left.

### Aces

The mottoes on the aces read: Swords – *Non ti fidar de me se il cuor ti manca* ('Don't put your trust in me if you have no heart to'); Cups – *Per un punto Martin perse la capa* ('For a point, Martin lost his cloak'); Coins – *Non val saper a chi ha fortuna contra* ('It's not worth knowing some one whose luck is always out'); Batons – *Se ti perdi tuo dano* ('If you lose, you're damned').

### Other Cards

Some' of the other distinguishing cards in this pattern are the 6 of swords which shows a woman carrying a basket of flowers; the 4 of swords which

19

*Left to right*: **Venetian Pattern, ace of cups and jack of swords; Triestine Pattern, ace and knight of batons.**

features a woman carrying a garland of flowers; and the 2 of swords which pictures a winged Mercury holding a caduceus. The Italian tax stamp is shown on the ace of coins and the maker's name on the 4 of coins.

## Triestine Pattern (*Triestine telate*)

This pack comes with either 52 or 40 cards (king, knight, jack, ace 10–2 or 7–2) and has the narrow Italian shape. Apart from different artistic interpretation and the different mottoes on the aces, it is similar to the Venetian pattern, of which it is probably an offshoot.

The main difference between the two patterns is that the Triestine cards are all numbered and the court cards are named. The Arabic numerals appear on the upper left-hand side of the card and the name is written on a panel at the centre of the card.

Other differences between this pattern and the Venetian are that the knight of batons has a sprig of leaves in his hat; the knight of cups looks to his left, not right. The jacks of swords and cups no longer have their extra heads and crescent moons. The jack of batons looks to his right, not left. Lastly, the king of batons loses his shield and looks to his right, not left.

The mottoes on the aces of the Triestine pattern (numbered 1) read: swords – *Il giuoco della spade a molti*

*non aggrade* (Swordplay is not to everybody's liking); cups – *Una coppa di buon vin fa coraggio mor bin* ('A goblet of good wine gives you the courage to die well'); coins – *Non val saper chi ha fortuna contra* ('It's not worth knowing some one whose luck is always out' – as on Venetian pattern); OR *Son gli amici molto rari quando non si ha danari* ('Friends are rare when one has no money'); batons – *Molte volte le giucocate van finire a bastonate* ('Games will often end in blows').

The pack currently made by the German card manufacturers ASS has stylized court figures with geometric designs on their clothes and red and yellow hair.

## Trentine Pattern (*Trentine telate*)

This pattern contains 52 or 40 single-ended cards (king, knight, jack, ace, 10–2 or 7–2) and has the narrow Italian shape. The number cards have Arabic numerals while the court figures (which in the ASS pack have red, yellow and blue hair) are all positioned on platforms. They wear short tunics and tights and, except for the kings, are bareheaded.

### Kings

All the kings are seated, wear crowns and hold their respective suit signs in their right hand. As in the Venetian pack the king of batons holds his suit sign in both hands. The king of coins faces straight ahead, the kings of cups and swords look to their right and that of batons to his left. The maker's name and a circle where the tax stamp normally goes is found on the king of coins.

### Knights

The knights of swords and batons ride prancing horses to the right-hand side of the card's face. They carry their suit sign in their right hand and the knight of swords has a curved sword. The knights of cups and coins ride trotting horses to the left hand side of the card's face, and again carry their suit signs in their right hand.

### Jacks

The jacks are all standing and except for the jack of swords look to their right. The jacks of swords and batons hold their suit signs in their right hand, together with an extra downward pointing sword or baton in their left hand. Behind the jack of swords is a small tree and the jack of batons has a flower behind him. The jack of cups holds his suit sign on his right side but in his left hand, which is necessarily extended to the other side of his body. There is a dog jumping up his right leg. The jack of coins holds his suit sign in his right hand and there is an extra 'coin' on the floor at his right.

### Other Cards

The aces in this pattern are decorative, with the ace of cups featuring a cupid standing on the suit sign and the ace of coins showing a medallion bust portrait of a woman. The maker's name is found on 2 of swords and on the 4 of coins can be seen a vignette, which in the ASS pack has a sailing ship.

## Bresciane Pattern (*Bresciane telate*)

This pattern is clearly a variant of the Trentine pattern. It contains 40 or 52 cards (king, knight, jack, ace, 7–2, 10–2) and is slightly smaller than the Trentine pack. The cards are single-ended and unnumbered.

The main differences between this pattern and the Trentine is that the jacks of swords, batons and coins have lost their extra suit sign and background tree or flower motifs. The jack of cups now holds his suit sign in both hands. Also the knight of swords has a straight, as opposed to curved, sword, the knight of coins looks to the left-hand side of the card's face and all the knights and jacks appear to be on rough ground. The maker's name is shown on the king of batons and the knight of coins.

With regard to the number cards, the ace of coins has lost its·portraiture, simply having the maker's name (and tax stamp if any). The 4 of swords shows a

woman in a field and the 4 of coins a lion and the maker's name. The maker's name is also on the 2 of swords.

## Bergamasche Pattern (*Bergamasche telate*)

This double-ended pack contains 40 unnumbered cards (king, knight, jack, ace, 7–2). The pattern is interesting as it is again an offshoot of the Trentine pattern and I suspect first appeared after the Bresciane pattern. Subsequently the Bergamasche pattern contains cards which are similar to ones in both packs. I shall however compare it only to the present-day Trentine pattern.

The most changed card in the Bergamasche pattern is the knight of coins. He still holds his suit sign in his right hand but now rides his horse to the right-hand side of the card's face. The knight looks the same way in which he is riding, whereas the horse's head is turned and looks to its right.

Naturally as a double-ended pattern, all the lower features of the Trentine pattern, such as the dog, tree, flower and extra 'coin', have disappeared in the Bergamasche pattern. Apart from that, some of the other differences are that: the king of cups now looks to the left and his left arm is across his chest; the king of batons holds his suit sign in his right hand only; and the king of coins now looks to his left, not full-faced, and this card no longer features the maker's name. Also, the knight of swords carries a straight, not curved, sword and the horse he rides wears blinkers. The knight of cups is now full-faced and that of batons looks to his right. With regard to the jack of swords, only the hilt of the sword held in his left hand is visible and he now looks to his left. You can no longer see the extra baton on the jack of batons.

This pattern has several distinctive number cards. The 2 of swords shows crossed bugles; the 3 a crown; and the 4 a woman. The 4 of coins shows a pair of scales and the 5 of coins has a sun motif around the middle coin. The ace of cups shows the familiar blindfold Cupid and the ace of batons a banner with the words 'Vincerai'. The maker's name and address is on the ace of coins.

## Bolognese Pattern (*Bolognese telate*)

The Bolognese pattern is basically the same as the Bolognese tarot pack, minus the trumps and queen court cards. Packs usually contain 40 cards (king, knight, jack, ace, 7–2) and are double-ended. At one time packs were made single-ended with the jacks portrayed as maids. The courts are clean shaven, except for the king of coins and knight of cups. One interesting feature of the Bolognese pattern is that the king of cups looks more like the tarot version of the queen of cups rather than the king of cups.

*Kings*

The kings of cups, swords and batons hold their suit sign in their right hand. The king of cups looks to his right and has an additional suit sign at the right-hand side of the card's face. The other two kings look to their left. The king of coins is full-faced and has a suit sign where his right hand should be and two more extra suit signs, one at each side of his head.

*Knights*

The knights hold their suit signs in their right hand. The knights of swords (who has a curved sword) and cups ride horses to the left-hand side of the card's face. The other two knights ride in the opposite direction.

*Jacks*

The jacks all hold their suit signs in their right hand. In his left hand the jack of swords holds a shield, the jack of coins an additional suit sign and the jack of cups a circular object. The jacks of swords and coins look to their left while the jacks of batons and cups look to their right.

The main differences between the ordinary Bolognese and the tarot Bolognese patterns is that in the tarot pack: the king of coins looks to his right; the knight of cups does not have a moustache and looks in the same direction in which he is travelling (as opposed to his left); the knight of coins has a moustache and the jack of coins has a moustache and beard.

There are in fact a number of standard tarot patterns in Italy and other European countries which are still used to play ordinary card games. Descriptions of these can be found in the chapter dealing with tarot cards.

## ITALO/SPANISH SUITED

### Piacentine Pattern (*Piacentine telate*)

This pattern contains 40 unnumbered cards (king, knight, jack, ace, 7–2) and both double-ended and single-ended versions are available. Italian-made packs retain their narrow Italian shape but French and Spanish-produced cards are broader in format. This pattern is used in a wide area of western Italy from Piacenza to Rome. Packs made for use in France and Spain are sometimes made with 48 cards.

The designs employed are complicated, each figure being different. They are finely executed and retain a medieval appearance. The knights still ride horses as in Italian suited packs, but the kings now all stand as in traditional Spanish packs. The kings are all crowned and the other court figures wear feathered caps.

*Kings*

The king of swords looks to his left and holds his upright sword on the right side of his body, but in his left hand, which is necessarily extended across his chest. The king of cups looks and is slightly turned to the right-hand side of the card's face. He holds his cup in his left hand and a sceptre in his right hand. The king of batons looks to his right and holds his suit sign in his right hand. The king of coins is seen from a right side view and holds a halberd in his left hand. His suit sign is in the top right-hand corner of the card.

*Knights*

The knight of cups suit sign is in the top right-hand corner of the card and that of coins holds his in his right hand. The other two knights hold their suit signs in their left hand. The knight of swords rides to the left-hand side of the card's face and looks to his left. The knight of cups looks and rides to the right-hand side of the card's face. The other two knights are unusual as they ride into the card's face on the right-hand side – giving a back view. The knight of batons looks to his left so we can only see part of his face, while that of coins leans awkwardly and looks to his right so that we can see his chest and face.

*Jacks*

The jacks of swords, cups and coins look to their left, while the jack of batons looks to his right. Both the jacks of swords and coins hold their suit signs in their right hand; and that of batons holds a crowned baton in his left hand. The jack of cups suit sign is in the top right hand corner of the card and he holds a spear in his right hand and a sword hilt in his left. As opposed to the other jacks who appear stationary, the jack of coins seems to have been frozen in motion.

*Other Cards*

The ace of coins features a crowned single-headed eagle, the maker's name and traditionally the tax stamp. The ace of swords shows a winged cupid holding on to the sword which also has a garland entwined around it. The maker's name is also found on the 4 of coins. Makers portray the coins of the coin suit differently; sometimes they show faces at the centre of the suit mark, and at other times a sun motif.

### Romagnole Pattern (*Romagnole telate*)

This pattern comprises 40 single-ended and unnumbered cards (king, knight, jack, ace, 7–2) and is used in an area between Ravenna and Rome, the territory of the old Papal states. The pattern seems to be newer than the Piacentine (*c*.18th century) and simpler, although there are some similarities such as the cherub on the ace of swords, which in this pattern stands.

The kings wear crowns and the other court figures hats, and all the court figures stand on a stony or grass-like surface.

*Kings*

The differences between the crowned kings are quite distinctive and interesting to observe. Basically they can be split up into two pairs, that of swords and batons, and cups and coins.

The kings of swords and batons hold their suit signs in their right hand, but whereas the king of swords looks to his right, that of batons looks to his left. The other two kings are in complete symmetry with each other: the king of cups looks to his left, holds an axe in his right hand and his suit sign is in the top right-hand corner of the card. The king of coins looks to his right, holds an axe in his left hand and has his suit sign in the left-hand corner of the card. All the kings wear long cloaks over their tunics.

*Knights*

The knight of cups rides to the left-hand side of the card's face and has his suit sign in the top left-hand corner of the card. The rest of the knights ride to the right-hand side of the card's face and hold their suit signs in their right hand. The knights of swords and cups look the same way in which they are riding, while the other two knights look to their right.

*Jacks*

The jacks of batons and coins look to their left; the jack of batons holds his suit sign in both hands and that of coins in his left hand. The face of the jack of swords is in left profile and he holds his suit sign in his right hand. The last jack, of cups, looks down to his right and holds a spear in his left hand. His suit sign is in the top left-hand corner of the card.

## Sarde or Sardinian Pattern *(Carte Sarde)*

This single-ended pattern, which is now used on the island of Sardinia, has a rather interesting history. Although today it is regarded as a regional Italian pack it does in fact still retain strong links with Spain. Evelyn Goshawk states that it is based on a Spanish non-standard pack made by Martinez de Castro at the Royal Factory of Madrid in 1810. This pack was one of the most beautiful of the Spanish non-standard 19th century packs and was copied in varying degrees of accuracy and artistic skill by many other card makers. Bertschinger y Codina produced such a copy c.1840 where the cards are slightly narrower, the background details omitted and the aces simplified. Another cruder copy was made by Sebastian Comas of Barcelona. An excellent reproduction, however, was recently made by Fournier of Spain and entitled the 'Neoclasica' pack.

Unlike its Spanish counterpart the Sarde pattern (made for Sardinia by Dal Negro in the 1960s and 1970s) does not have breaks in the border to denote the suits. It does have the Spanish numbering of 1–12 and the standing kings. The pack comprises 40 cards (king, knight, jack, ace, 7–2) and has a broad Spanish format. The pattern is very decorative and elaborate with all the court figures pictured against a scenic background. In fact the present Sarde pattern has some additional background details not present in the original Spanish version. The swords suit shows battlefield scenes with tents, castles and men fighting in the background, while the rest of the court cards appear in a rural setting or, as in the case of the kings of cups and coins, indoors. All the kings wear crowns and the other court figures wear feathered hats. The jack and knight of the swords suit wear armour and helmets while the rest of the court figures wear 16th century costumes.

*Kings*

The kings of swords and batons look to their right and each holds his suit sign upright in his right hand. The king of swords has his helmet and shield by his feet on the grass. The king of batons holds his cloak with his free hand. The other two kings are pictured by tables upon which are placed their suit signs. The king of cups' table is on his left side and he is seen full-faced, holding his cloak with his right hand, while his left hand rests on his suit sign. The king of coins' table is on his right side. He looks and rests his right hand upon his suit sign while his left hand is behind his back.

*Knights*

All the knights hold their suit signs in their right hand. The knights of swords and cups ride horses to the right-hand side of the card's face, but whereas the knight of swords looks in the same direction as he is travelling, the knight of cups looks down to his right. Both of their horses have their heads turned to their right. The knights of batons and coins ride horses to the right-hand side of the card's face and look down to their left. Their horses look the same way as they are riding.

*Jacks*

All the jacks hold their suit signs in their right hands. The jack of swords is full-faced and walks to the left-hand side of the card's face with a shield in his left hand. The jack of cups looks, and is, slightly turned to the left and holds the major domo's staff in his left hand. The other two jacks look to their left and the jack of coins also holds the major domo's staff in his left hand.

*Left to right*: Trentine Pattern, king of batons; Bresciane, jack of cups; Bergamasche, knight of coins; Bolognese, king of coins.

*Other Cards*

To add even more interest to this pack, there are vignettes on the fours of each suit. The 4 of coins shows a Roman man and woman sitting on some grass; the 4 of cups shows a woman and cherub lying on some grass; the 4 of batons shows a woman with a baton sitting outside a castle; and the 4 of swords shows a Roman soldier ready to strike a man lying on some grass. The ace of swords shows a cherub holding a large sword with tents and shields, helmets, etc., in the background. The ace of batons again shows a cupid holding a leafy baton and the ace of coins shows the maker's name and traditionally the tax stamp.

**Neapolitan Pattern** (*Napoletane* or *Baresi telate*)

This pack and the next one to be discussed, the Sicilian, form a section of their own within the group of Italo/Spanish suited patterns. They are smaller and squatter than other Italian cards and their designs are more finely executed. Both patterns are single-ended.

A novel feature of these two patterns is the different coloured bases on which the court figures stand and from which, in the Neapolitan pattern, one can determine the suit. In the coin suit the bases are yellow; cups red; batons green; and swords blue, i.e. the king of coins stands on a yellow base and that of swords is

on a blue base. The pattern contains 40 unnumbered cards (king, knight, jack, ace, 7–2) and they have no framed borders as have the other Italian packs so far described. All the kings stand and wear crowns and the knights ride horses. The other court figures wear hats.

*Kings*

The kings of swords and batons are in symmetry with each other. The king of swords looks to his right and holds his suit sign in his right hand while that of batons looks to his left and holds his suit sign in his left hand. Both the kings of cups and coins look to their right. The king of cups holds a mace in his left hand and his suit sign is in the top left-hand corner of the card; that of coins holds a sword in his left hand and has his suit sign in the top right-hand corner of the card.

*Knights*

The knights of swords and cups ride their horses to the right-hand side of the card's face and those of batons and coins to the left-hand side of the card's face. The knight of swords looks to his right and that of coins to his left, while the other knights look in the same direction in which they are travelling. The knights of swords, cups and coins hold their suit signs

*Left to right*: **Piacentine Pattern, king of coins; Romagnole, jack of cups; Sarde, jack of swords; Neapolitan, jack of spades.**

in their right hand and that of batons in his left hand. The sword held by the knight of swords is curved.

*Jacks*

The jack of cups is full-faced, that of coins looks to his right and both hold their suit signs in their right hand. The jack of cups also holds a dagger in his left hand. The jack of swords looks to his left and holds a downward pointing sword in his left hand and an upright leafy branch in his right hand. The jack of batons has his back to us, looks to his left and holds an upright baton in his left hand.

*Other Cards*

The ace of coins shows a double-headed eagle, maker's name and traditionally the tax stamp. The maker's name also appears on the 4 of cups. In packs produced by some manufacturers the 4 of coins pictures an Italian flag and shield; the 3 of batons, a mask-like face; and the 5 of swords, a vignette of silhouetted figures.

**Sicilian Pattern** (*Siciliane telate*)

This pack again contains 40 single-ended cards (king, knight, jack, ace, 7–2) which are unnumbered and unframed. In this pattern the different coloured bases refer to the values of the cards. The kings stand on a green base, knights on yellow bases and jacks on red bases. Regarding the actual suit signs, the cups

seem more like Grecian vases and the swords are thin and similar in execution to the Sicilian tarot.

*Kings*

The kings of swords and batons wear crowns, while those of cups and coins wear cloth hats. The kings of swords and coins are almost identical. Both look to their right (with that of coins being in profile) and hold their suit signs upright in their left hand. Their right hands are raised to their chests. The kings of cups and batons look to their right; the king of cups holds his suit sign in his right hand and that of batons in his left hand. Their free hands are on their belts.

*Knights*

Only the knight of coins holds a suit sign in his right hand. The other knights have their suit sign in the top left-hand corner of the card. The knights wear cloth caps, except for the knight of coins who is bareheaded. The knights of swords and cups are in right profile and ride to the left-hand side of the card's face, with that of cups riding into the card showing a back view. The other two knights ride to the left-hand side of the card's face and look to their left. Again one of the knights, that of batons, rides into the card.

*Jacks*

The jack of cups wears a feathered cap, the jack of

coins a turban and the other jacks are bareheaded. The jacks of swords and batons hold their suit signs in their right hand and look to their left (with the jack of swords being in profile). The jack of cups looks to his right and has his suit sign in the upper left-hand corner of the card. The jack of coins has his back to us with the left-hand side of his face showing. He holds his suit sign in his left hand.

## Other Cards

The majority of the other cards show small vignettes, making this one of the most delightful and imaginative of the packs used in Italy, other than the tarot. On the 2 of swords can be seen a dog carrying a parcel; and on the 4 of swords is a dog begging and a dice; on the 4 of batons are two men fencing. On the coins suit can be seen: on the 3, a man, and the motif inside the suit sign is three legs joined together, similar to the Isle of Man symbol; on the 4, the maker's name; on the 5 a charioteer and on the ace a single-headed eagle, with the maker's name and space for the tax stamp.

## FRENCH SUITED

### Florentine Pattern (Carte Fiorentine Grandi) and Tuscan Pattern (Carte Toscane)

Today the Florentine and Tuscan patterns are identical except that the Florentine cards are larger than the Tuscan ones and there are other minor differences between manufacturers as regards artistic style, etc. It has been suggested that the different names denote only the selling areas. However, at one time there was a different Tuscan pattern in which the queens wore no crowns, the jack of spades carried a short spear and that of hearts an arrow. The kings all held short batons. This pattern is no longer produced.

The modern pack contains 40 single-ended cards (king, queen, jack, ace, 7–2) which are unnumbered. It is thought the pattern originated in the 19th century. All the kings and queens wear crowns, the jack of spades wears a feathered cap while the other jacks are bareheaded. All the court figures stand on a floor and cast shadows. The maker's name can be found on the ace and four of hearts. Packs made in France feature the maker's name on the ace of hearts only.

### Kings

The kings of spades, clubs and hearts look to their right, while that of diamonds looks to his left. The king of spades holds a thin sceptre in his right hand while the king of clubs is empty-handed. The king of hearts holds a sceptre in his left hand and his right hand rests on a scroll on a table which has the maker's name on it. The king of diamonds reads a scroll held in both

hands, which again has the maker's name on it.

### Queens

The queen of spades looks to her left and holds a letter in her right hand. The queen of clubs is slightly turned and looks to the left-hand side of the card's face and holds a garland in her right hand. Similarly positioned, the queen of hearts is shown from a left side view holding a page of a letter in her right hand. The queen of diamonds is shown from a right side view holding a flower in her left hand.

### Jacks

The jack of clubs is slightly turned and looks to the right-hand side of the card's face; the jack of spades looks to his left while the other two jacks look to their right. The jack of spades holds a shield in his right hand and the hilt of his sword in his left hand. The jack of clubs holds a book in both hands upon which is the maker's name. The jack of hearts holds an old fashioned downward-pointing bow in his right hand and the hilt of his sword with his left hand. The jack of diamonds holds a downward-pointing sword in his right hand.

### Lombard or Milanese Pattern (Milanesi telate)

This French-suited pattern contains 40 or 52 numbered or unnumbered cards (king, queen, jack, ace, 10–2 or 7–2) and is used in Lombardy and Milan. It is also used in Italian-speaking areas of Switzerland, where it is called Ticinese. The cards have the narrow Italian shape and most examples are double-ended.

The kings and queens wear crowns, except for the queen of diamonds who wears a veil. The jacks all wear feathered caps. The maker's name is on the 7 of hearts.

### Kings

The king of spades is seen in left profile with his back to us carrying a sceptre over his right shoulder in his right hand. The other kings look to their right. The king of clubs holds a spear in his right hand and a sword hilt in his left hand. The king of hearts is similarly positioned although his left hand is obscured. The king of diamonds holds a mace in his right hand and a bird is perched on his left arm.

### Queens

The queen of spades looks to her right and that of hearts to her left; the queen of spades carries a mace in her left hand and the queen of hearts carries the same in her right hand. The queen of clubs looks to her right and is empty handed. The queen of diamonds is seen in complete left profile and holds a letter in her right hand.

### Jacks

The jack of spades is facing the left-hand side of the

card's face, looks to his left and has both hands resting on a halberd. The jack of clubs looks to his right, carries a spear in his left hand and has the badge of Milan embroidered on his robes. The jack of hearts looks to his left and holds a halberd with both hands. Again there is a coat of arms embroidered on his robes. The last jack, of diamonds, shows his back and the right side of his face and holds a halberd in his right hand.

## Genoese and Piedmont Pattern (*Genovesi telate* and *Piemontese telate*)

These two double-ended patterns are practically identical to the Paris pattern except that they use green, red, blue and black colouring, and the court cards are unnamed.

The main difference between the two 52-card packs (king, queen, jack, ace, 10–2) is that the Genoese court cards are divided by a diagonal line, while the Piedmont pattern court cards are divided by a horizontal line. The cards are unnumbered.

# SPAIN

## SPANISH SUITED

The Spanish suits are intrinsically the same as the Italian ones [Span. *espadas* (swords), *bastos* (batons), *copas* (cups) and *oros* (coins)], but their designs are simpler and smaller. The Spanish swords are straight and short, while the batons look like menacing wooden cudgels, and both of these are uncrossed.

Early Spanish-suited packs had 52 cards with each suit containing a king, knight, jack, ace and 10–2 in numerical cards. Now, however, most Spanish packs comprise 40 cards, suitable for the Spanish national game of Hombre. In this pack the eights and nines are suppressed. The cards are now numbered, with the court cards corresponding to 12, 11 and 10.

Another main difference between Spanish and Italian packs is that the kings are always shown standing. Also, during the 18th century, the Spanish adopted a system of breaks in the card's border as an extra aid to identifying the suit: the coins suit has no break, the cups one break, swords two and batons three.

During the Spanish conquests, Spanish playing card designs spread to many countries. Today Spanish-suited cards are still used in Latin America and former Spanish colonies.

## Castilian Pattern

This pattern was introduced in 1889 by Heraclio Fournier.

The pack comprises 48 or 40 cards (king, knight, jack, ace, 9–2 or 7–2) which have breaks in their borders. It is well executed with an 'illustrated' look and very colourful. All the kings are crowned, bearded and wear or hold swords. They are dressed in long robes with only their feet showing. The knights all ride horses. With the exception of the jack of swords, the knights and jacks wear feathered head gear. The cups suit signs in this pack are very rounded (like an egg cup). Both single- and double-ended packs are made.

*Kings*

The king of swords looks, and that of cups is also slightly turned, to the left-hand side of the card's face. The king of swords holds his suit sign in his right hand, while the king of cups is empty-handed with his suit sign in the top left-hand corner of the card. The king of batons is slightly turned to the right-hand side of the card's face and holds his suit sign in his right hand (his face is in profile). The last king, of coins, is again slightly turned to the left-hand side of the card's face but he looks to his left. His right hand rests on his sword hilt and the suit sign is in the upper left-hand corner.

*Knights*

The knights of swords and batons ride horses to the right-hand side of the card's face (with that of swords looking to his right) and hold their suit signs upright in their right hand. The knights of cups and coins ride horses to the left-hand side of the card's face but look to their left. The knight of cups holds his suit sign in his right hand while on the knight of coins the suit sign is in the upper left-hand corner.

*Jacks*

The jacks of swords and cups look to their left, hold their suit signs in their right hands and each has his free hand on his hip. The other two jacks look to their left. The jack of batons holds his suit sign in his right hand, while the jack of coins points to his – which is in the upper left-hand corner – with his left hand. The jack of coins often has his cloak wrapped around his right arm.

*Other Cards*

The tax stamp and maker's name are found on the 5 of swords. The maker's name is also found on the 4 of coins and other information regarding the cards or the manufacturer are on the 4 of batons and cups and the 2 of batons and swords. The aces are elaborate and stylized, with the ace of coins featuring the maker's name, a medallion portrait and flags.

## Modern Spanish Catalan Pattern

This design is quite simple and emerged around

*Left to right*: Sicilian Pattern; knight of swords; Florentine, jack of spades; Tuscan, jack of spades; Lombard, jack of diamonds.

1850. The courts are usually clean shaven. The kings wear crowns, tunics, stockings and long over-robes. The knights and jacks sometimes wear feathered head gear. The court figures in the sword and baton suits hold their suit sign in their right hand, while the suit sign in the cups and coins suits is in the top left-hand corner of the card's face. The cups' suit sign is very rounded in shape and resembles a goblet or egg-cup.

### Kings

The king of cups looks to his left while the other three kings look to their right. All the kings have their left hand on their hips. The king of cups holds a sceptre in his right hand.

### Knights

All the knights look in the same direction as they are riding, and all the horses are shown rearing. The knights of swords and batons ride to the right-hand side of the card's face and hold their suit signs in their right hands. The other two knights ride to the left-hand side of the card's face. The knight of coins points in the air with his right hand.

### Jacks

All the jacks look to their left and the jacks of cups, coins and swords have their left hand on their hip. The jacks of coins and cups point to their suit signs with their right hand. Sometimes the jack of cups is found looking to his right.

### Other Cards

The tax stamp and maker's name are found on the 5 of swords. The 4 of cups also features the maker's name and a stag running in a field. The ace of coins shows a medallion portrait, Spanish flag, anchor and a horn of plenty.

### National Pattern

This single-ended pattern by Fournier is rather interesting although not particularly attractive. It is a 20th-century design and in Fournier's Museum Catalogue there is an example dated 1936 termed 'National' (Cat. No. 705). However, it should not be confused with the Spanish National Pattern to be described next.

Packs contain 48 cards (king, knight, jack, ace, 9–2) and in many respects the pattern is similar to the Modern Spanish Catalan pattern, especially the cups and swords suits, although the clothes and general appearance are very different.

A peculiarity of this pattern is the presence of the coat of arms of León and Castile; in fact the court figures were supposedly inspired by the reconquest of Spain during the Renaissance period.

It is interesting to note that in the Schreiber Collection, housed in the British Museum, there are several Spanish packs dating back to the 18th century where the coat of arms of León, Castile and Aragon are featured.

In the Fournier pattern the courts of batons and swords all hold their suit sign, while on the cups and coins court cards the suit sign is positioned in the top left-hand corner. The kings all wear crowns and, with the exception of the jack of cups, the knights and jacks wear head gear. The courts of the swords suit wear some armour. Most of the court figures in the same suit share common characteristics.

*Kings*

The king of coins looks to his left, has his left hand on his hip and points to his suit sign with his right hand. He wears a long open robe, stockings and a tunic. The king of cups looks to his right and is beginning to draw his sword. He wears a long robe, a short tunic, and socks which reveal his bare knees. The king of swords looks to his left, holds a shield in his left hand and an upright sword in his right hand. He wears some armour underneath a long robe and tunic. The Moor king of batons looks to his right and holds his baton in his right hand. He points in the air with his left hand.

*Knights*

All the knights are shown riding horses from a side view. The Moor knight of batons and the knight of cups ride to the left-hand side of the card's face, and the knights of swords and coins ride to the right-hand side of the cards. The knight of coins is shown in a back view. The knight of swords wears a helmet, holds a shield and sword. The Moor knight of batons carries his club on his back.

*Jacks*

The jack of coins looks to his left, has his right hand on his hip and points to his suit-sign with his left hand. The jack of cups looks to his right and holds his hat in his left hand. The jack of swords wears some armour, looks to his left, carries a shield in his left hand and a sword in his right hand. The Moor jack of batons looks to his right, leans on a staff with his left hand and holds a baton in his right arm.

*Other Cards*

The tax stamp and maker's name are found on the 5 of swords. A single-headed eagle and the coat of arms of León and Castile are featured on the ace of coins and 4 of swords. The aces are stylized and cherubim are shown on the aces of batons and swords. The year of manufacture is sometimes shown on the 2 and 4 of coins.

## Spanish National Pattern

The exact date of origin of this pattern is unknown, although it is thought to have been in use in Spain before 1600. After the early 19th century it was no longer used in Spain in its original form, but it has continued to be produced by the French, for use in North Africa, and some South American countries. As such, it is the only early Spanish design to have survived to the present day.

Packs contain 48 or 40 cards, although around the 1800s packs were also made with 52 cards (king, knight, jack, ace, 10–2, 9–2, 7–2). Some distinguishing features of this pattern are that the kings are clean shaven and wear long robes which hide their feet. In the batons suit the king's club is forked, the knight's club is twisted into an S-shape and the jack's club is more funnel-shaped. Another feature is that from the mid-18th century the word 'AHI VA' or 'AHIVA' or 'AIVA' is invariably found on the knight of coins card. The ace of coins usually shows a central coin with ribbons above and below. The cups suit sign is straight-sided.

## Parisian Spanish Pattern

This pack was made by the Real Fabrica de Madrid in the beginning of the 19th century as a variant of the Spanish National Pattern. Its main distinguishing feature is the use of female knights, although in later versions by other makers male knights were also used.

Packs contain 48 or 40 cards (king, knight, jack, ace, 9–2 or 7–2) and variations of this design are still widely used in South American countries. Packs are often found with a tethered hound in the background of the jack of coins card. The kings wear short tunics, stockings and long over-robes. Sometimes the ace of batons shows a club being held by a hand; the 4 of swords shows hands holding palm branches; and the ace, 2 and 3 of batons can feature small arrows.

## Cadiz Pattern

This pattern is also a variant of the Spanish National Pattern and was originally made in Cadiz for export to such countries as Mexico. From the early 20th century it was produced in Barcelona.

Today, it is no longer used in Spain, but is exported to, and made in, Mexico. It is also used in Central America and the Philippines.

Packs contain 48 or 40 cards (king, knight, jack, ace, 9–2 or 7–2). The kings and knights usually have moustaches and all the kings' feet are visible underneath their robes. The knights and jacks wear knee-breeches and waist-length tunics, most of which have balloon-shaped upper sleeves. 'AHIVA' 'AHI VA' or 'AIVA' often appears on the knight of cups. The ace of coins shows a central coin with a ribboned crown above the olive and palm branches below.

*Left to right*: Genoese Pattern, jack of clubs; Piedmont, jack of clubs; Castilian, jack of cups; modern Spanish Catalan, king of swords.

The suit signs are similar to the Spanish National Pattern, with the cups suit sign being straight-sided.

**Macia Pattern**

Several variants of this pattern have been made in both Spain and Italy. The earliest known dated example was made by Rotxotxo of Barcelona in 1816.

Packs usually contain 48 or 40 cards (king, knight, jack, ace, 9–2 or 7–2). The main distinguishing features are that the kings wear capes over their long, open robes and have stockinged legs. The kings of swords and cups wear laurel wreaths instead of crowns. The ace of coins often shows a central coin framed in drapes and surmounted by a crown. The cups suit sign is shaped like an urn and has a lid.

**García Pattern**

This pattern was used in the 19th century and was first produced by Raimundo García of Madrid. The cards often bear his name, sometimes together with the name of a manufacturer employed on his behalf. Later, unrelated card-makers produced this pattern.

Packs contain 48 or 40 cards (king, knight, jack, ace, 9–2 or 7–2). The kings have their ankles and feet showing under their long robes and the king of cups has no sceptre, but holds his suit mark. The jack of batons occasionally wears trousers instead of knee-breeches, and the jacks of cups and coins wear sashes around their waists. The ace of coins shows a central wreath containing a shield, with a ribbon above and below. The cups suit sign is very rounded in shape.

## PORTUGAL

The Portuguese probably received their first Italian-suited cards at approximately the same time as the Spanish. Like the Spanish they adopted the Italian suits but with certain modifications in the design. Termed as Italo-Portuguese suits, the swords are straight and cross each other in a trellis design and in most packs female jacks called *sota* appear in all of the suits. But the most original feature of the old Portuguese standard pack is the ace, which featured a dragon holding a suit sign in its mouth. Although 'Portuguese Dragon' packs are no longer produced, in their day they influenced a great many countries of the world, especially during the time of the Portuguese and Spanish conquests. For instance, the Italo-Portuguese suit designs are used on some Italian tarots including the Minchiate and the present-day Sicilian tarot.

*Left to right*: National Pattern, king of batons; Spanish National, knight of cups; version of Parisian Spanish jack of coins, as used in Uruguay; Cadiz, knight of coins.

Today Portuguese packs are French-suited and contain 52, 40 or 32 cards.

## PORTUGUESE SUITED

### Portuguese Dragon Pack

Unfortunately this pack ceased to be produced in Portugal during the 19th century. It is thought to date back to the 16th century, one of the earliest existing examples having been made in 1597 by Pietro Ciliberto.

Comprising 48 cards, this pack differs from Spanish packs in a number of fundamental ways, with two of the most obvious differences being the female jacks called *sota* and the dragons on the aces. The names of the suits and courts are: *copas* (cups) *espadas* (swords) *ouro* (coins) and *bastoes* or *paus* (batons); *rei* (king) *cavalo* (knight) and *sota* (female jack). The design of the sword suit sign is also interesting, the swords being portrayed as long and slim rapiers. This type of sword is found only in Portugal, Sicily and Florence and there is speculation that the Portuguese Dragon pack actually evolved as a shortened version of the Florentine Minchiate tarot pack.

By the 17th century, after the period of great exploration by the Portuguese, the Dragon pack spread to Brazil, Japan, India, Java and the Celebes. In Japan the pack still exists today, although in an almost unrecognizable form.

The pack described here was made in the 19th-century and is fairly typical of the pattern at this time. At various times, however, the designs have changed slightly, and even as late as the 19th-century differences between packs occur which make it rather hard to identify some examples. The kings and sotas all wear crowns with the sota of swords also wearing a veil. Three of the knights wear plumed helmets while the knight of cups wears a feathered hat. All the court figures hold their suit sign upright in their right hand.

### Kings

The king of cups is full-faced and holds a sceptre in his left hand and has a shield by his right side. The kings of swords and coins look to their left with that of coins supporting a shield with his left hand. The king of batons is shown in right profile. All the kings wear swords positioned behind them.

### Knights

The knights of swords and coins ride to the right-hand side of the card's face with that of coins looking to the front of the card. The other two knights ride to the left-hand side of the card's face and that of batons

*Left to right*: **Macia Pattern, king of coins; Portuguese Dragon, ace of cups; Standard Portuguese, French suited, ace of diamonds.**

looks to his left and holds the hilt of his sword with his left hand.

*Sotas*

All the sotas look to their left. The sota of cups holds a small bunch of flowers in her left hand and that of coins holds a casket in her left hand. The sota of batons is pictured with a dog on the floor to her left. Originally this card showed the sota ready to strike a serpent with her baton. Packs have been made omitting both the casket and dog.

*Other Cards*

There are various other interesting cards in this pack. All the aces show dragons holding their suit signs in their mouths and a few cards feature shields with various devices on them. The 2 of batons often shows a boy or man entwined around the batons.

## FRENCH SUITED

A number of French-suited designs are used in Portugal, most of which are imported. The most common standard pattern, however, is the Portuguese French-suited version of the Paris pattern which is similar in style to the German Berliner and Rhineland cards. The pack usually comprises 52 cards (king, queen, jack, ace, 10–2). The kings and queens all wear

crowns with the queen of hearts also wearing a veil. The jacks wear hats.

*Kings*

The king of spades is full-faced and holds a sword in his left hand and an orb in his right hand. The king of hearts looks to his left and again holds an orb in his right hand but a sceptre in his left hand. The other two kings look to their right. The king of diamonds holds a shield in his right hand and a sword in his left hand. This arrangement is reversed for the king of clubs.

*Queens*

The red queens look to their right and each holds a flower in her left hand, with the queen of diamonds also holding an open fan in her right hand. The queen of spades is full-faced and holds a closed fan in her left hand. The queen of clubs looks to her left and holds a flower in her right hand.

*Jacks*

The jacks of hearts and spades look to their right and hold halberds in their left hand. In his right hand the jack of hearts carries a bird and the jack of spades carries a shield. The jack of clubs is full-faced and carries a shield in his left hand and the jack of diamonds looks to his left and holds his sword hilt with his left hand. In their right hands both jacks carry spears.

32

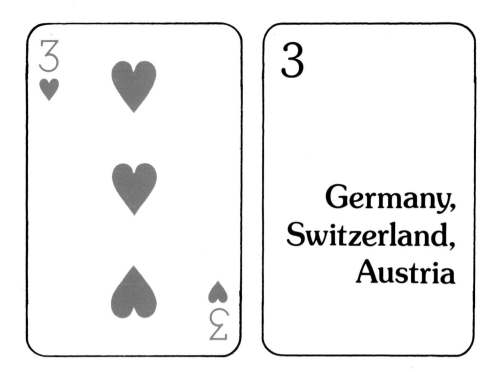

# Germany, Switzerland, Austria

THE FIRST mention of playing cards outside of Italy was in a manuscript dated 1377, written by a monk named Johannes from Basle in Switzerland.

Johannes wrote about the introduction of playing cards into the city and although he claimed no knowledge of where, when and by whom they were initially invented, he does compare them to the game of chess, in that both contain kings, queens, rulers and commoners. The monk goes on to say that the pack consists of 52 cards of four suits within which are seated kings, two 'marschalli', and ten numerical cards. Unfortunately, Johannes does not give a sufficiently detailed description for us to identify the cards, although it is presumed that they were of Italian stock.

Concerning the meaning and symbols of the suit signs, Johannes observes that two suits are evil and two suit signs are good. If it were the Italian suits to which he was referring, his comments are understandable. Batons and swords naturally evoke war and hostility, while cups and coins denote commerce, prosperity and merry-making. A copy of this manuscript is in the British Museum.

It seems that from Italy playing cards opened out in three main directions almost simultaneously: to France, Spain and Portugal; to Switzerland, Germany and Austria; and then to the East European countries. In 1378 references to playing cards are found in Regensburg; in 1379 St. Gallen and Brabant; in 1380 Nuremberg; in 1382 Flanders and Burgundy; in 1388 Constance; in 1389 Zurich; in 1390 Holland; in 1391 Augsburg; in 1392 Frankfurt-on-Main; and in 1399 Ulm. Typically, many of these early mentions came in the forms of decrees against their use.

Of all the European countries, Germany was the first to make a complete break from Italian playing card designs by introducing the four novel suit signs of: *Herzen* (hearts), *Schellen* (bells), *Grun* or *Laub* (leaves) and *Eicheln* (acorns). Many people have interpreted the German suits as: the hearts representing the church; bells the nobility; leaves for the citizens or the middle classes; and acorns for the peasantry. An alternative suggestion is that they simply represent the four seasons, or the contrast between town and country.

Within each suit was a king (*König*), upper valet (*Obermann* – now shortened to *Ober*), an under valet (*Untermann* – now shortened to *Unter*), a deuce – in German *Daus* (card No.2) – and 3 to 10 in numerical cards. Aces were only used on 'fanciful' packs. In some early packs a queen is found among the court cards.

A characteristic of the early German-suited cards was that during the 15th and 16th centuries card No. 10 was shown with a banner and a Roman numeral. Today, this 'banner card' is only used in traditional Swiss packs.

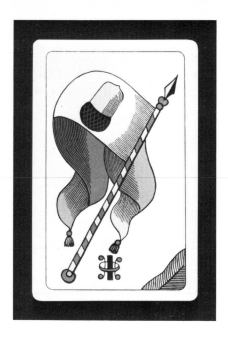

Single-ended Swiss Jass Pattern: the banner card.

Facsimile of the 15th-century circular cards of Cologne – the original edition by 'Meister PW'.

During the 15th century Germany became an important card producing country, exporting cards all over Europe. One of the major reasons for this was that Germany was the first European country to develop wood-block printing techniques, enabling cards to be produced cheaply and so become accessible to every section of the community.

In time the composition and suit signs of the German packs spread to Switzerland, Austria, Poland, Russia, Czechoslovakia, Yugoslavia and other East European countries. Switzerland was the only country to modify the German suits. They adopted bells, acorns, shields and flowers, and dropped the German hearts and leaves suit signs.

The standardization of the German and Swiss suit signs, however, did not stabilize until the 16th century. Indeed early German cards are noted for their variety, versatility and imagination.

German playing cards were made in varying degrees of quality, with wood blocks used only for the cheaper end of the market. At the top end of the quality scale we find *objets d'art*, pure fantasies which are a test of anyone's imagination. These cards, which were made from engraved copper plates and were hand-painted, were destined for museums or to be put on display in the houses of the wealthy – rarely to be played with. Most of these fine packs employed both whimsical suit signs and elaborate, charming and sometimes vulgar portrayals on the court and number cards. The scenes varied from everyday life to mythology. On the number cards it is not uncommon to find men fighting, giants devouring children, children playing with each other, and lovers meeting or parting. Animals were also a popular theme and there are packs where the court cards portray a chase. One such pack made in Stuttgart in 1440 has the suits of hounds, falcons, stags and ducks.

One of the most celebrated early packs with non-standard suits are the 'Circular Cards of Cologne', *c*.1500. The suits are hares, parrots, pinks, columbines and roses; although it has been suggested that the fifth suit of roses is either not part of this pack or was intended as a replacement suit. Each suit comprises a king, queen, two jacks and 1–9 in numerical cards. The title cards of this pack show three crowns in a trefoil and the inscription *Salve Felix Colonia*. An extra card shows Death clutching at a nude woman. Two later versions of this pack were made. The first by Telman von Wesel has only the first four suits and the initials TW at the bottom of each card. The second was an adaptation by Johann Bussemacher in which the cards are rectangular and have coarse two-line sayings.

Another famous 16th century German pack is that by Virgil Solis (d.1562), a famous book illustrator for the Nuremberg publisher Sigmund Feyerabend. Comprising 52 cards, the courts are king, queen and jack while the suits are lions, monkeys, peacocks and parrots. The maker's monogram is found on the aces. The numerical cards have their values indicated in Roman numerals, while the court cards bear no marks of value at all. As with many of these packs, the respective number of animals appear on each of the number cards, e.g. three monkeys on the 3 of monkeys. The kings and queens are mounted, while the jacks are foot soldiers.

In 1588 Jost Amman designed a pack called 'The Book of Trades' where the suits are: printer's ink balls, books, wine cups, and goblets. The court cards are king, upper and under valet. The main part of each card is occupied by an illustration with a Latin and German verse above and below respectively. Jost Amman played an important role in the development of German playing cards. He was born in Zurich in 1539 and moved to Germany in 1560 where he also worked for the publisher Sigmund Feyerabend in Nuremberg. Although playing-card collectors are generally familiar with Jost Amman through his 'Book of Trades', he was principally a famous and gifted book illustrator and many of his figures and designs used in books have found their way on to the faces of playing cards.

Among the other non-standard suit signs used on playing cards are parakeets, frogs, dragons, bears, dogs, various birds, unicorns, rabbits, and helmets.

When considering the history and development of German playing cards one is continually coming across innovations. An idea with the most far-reaching consequences was the educational card, first conceived by Thomas Murner, a Franciscan monk, at the turn of the 16th century.

Thomas Murner was born in Oberehnheim in Alsace on 24 December 1475 and was ordained at the age of nineteen. He was an opponent of the Reformation and his fame rests on a number of satirical poems attacking the corruptions of the age. In 1506 Emperor Maximilian I made him Poet Laureate.

During his time as a teacher, Murner was constantly aware of the difficulty with which some of his students grasped certain lessons. With this in mind he proceeded to devise two card games using the principles of mnemonic pictures. The first of these games to be published (although the second to be designed) was *Chartiludium Logicae*, issued in book form in 1507. So successful was this new teaching method that the monk was suspected of using witchcraft. In order to

clear his name he had to produce the cards to the doctors of the University of Cracow. The book pictured 52 cards divided into the suits of bells, lobsters, fish, acorns, scorpions, caps, hearts, grasshoppers, suns, stars, birds, moons, cats, shields, crowns and serpents. The higher authorities were obviously very impressed with his cards as, in a second edition published in 1508, there is an epilogue by Master Johannes de Glogovia of the University of Cracow and Canon of St. Florian at Clepardia expounding the virtues of such a method of teaching. This game was revised in 1569 in Paris by Jean Balesdens.

Thomas Murner's other game *Chartiludium Institute Summarie* was not published until 1528 at Strasbourg. Again in book form, this time there are 120 cards in the pack, split equally into the twelve suits of falcons, combs, acorns, hearts, crowns, buckets, church bells, bellows, beads, shields, fish and knives. The first card in each suit depicts a German ruler.

Educational cards began to be designed all over Europe. In 1603 Andreas Strobl of Sulzbach in Bavaria published *Das Geistliche Deutsche Carten Spiel*. This time the lesson was in religion with the cards showing illustrations and an explanatory text from the Bible. Issued in book form, the suits are hearts, bells, leaves and acorns.

Another educational pack with geography as a subject, called *Typus Orbis Terrarum*, was published in c.1678 by Johann Hoffman of Nuremberg and shows countries and cities of Europe. The ace of spades gives the designer's and engraver's names as I.H. Seyfrid and Wilhelm Pfann. The cards were invented by Johann Pretorius. By the same makers is a pack showing maps and charts from various countries and seaboards of the whole world. In an upper margin is the name of the place represented, the denomination and French suit signs. Spades and hearts feature regions of Germany, Austria and Prussia; diamonds show maps of Switzerland, Belgium, Holland, Flanders, Spain; while the clubs show England, Scotland, Hibernia, Norway, Poland and Italy.

In c.1693 an interesting pack of heraldry cards was produced in Germany which shows the arms of the ruling families of Europe. A coat of arms occupies the centre of each card, with the title above and descriptive text below. The value is indicated by a numbered French suitmark in the upper left corner. Among the families represented are the Grand Duke of Florence on the 4 of spades, Prince of Waldeck on the 2 of hearts; the Duke of Mantua on the 3 of hearts.

Closely linked with heraldry are playing cards which feature war and military instructions.

A pack which was issued in pamphlet form in c.1630

*Left to right*: German musical pack with court cards depicting musicians in comical postures and music scores for the waltz and polka, the number cards show a music score, *c*. 1840; The 'Greeks & Turks' pack, *c*. 1750; the 'New Oval Salon Playing Cards' made by Friedrich Gunthel of Leipzig, *c*. 1880.

by the Hapsburgs is concerned with the events which led to the Thirty Years War. The cards ridicule and attack Protestant Bohemia, its King Frederick V of the Palatinate, Bethlem Gabor, Prince of Transylvania, and George William, Duke of Brandenburg. The suit signs are acorns, bells, hearts and grapes. The Thirty Years War involved most European countries. At the end of the war the German losses were tremendous, with half the original 18 million population killed. For instance, before the war there were some one million people in the Palatinate and after about 50,000.

On a happier note there is another pack commemorating the Pyrenean Peace, the Peace of Oliva and the Peace of Westphalia (of the mid-17th century). The designers of the cards hoped these treaties might result in a united front against the Turks, Muscovites and Tartars. The kings are the Kings of England, Spain, France and the German Emperor, while the enemy is shown on the deuce cards.

The Crimean War became subject matter for cards throughout the world. Such a pack was produced in Frankfurt in 1854. The cards are double-ended and French-suited. On the aces are two battle scenes. One card shows, at one end, the Battle of Alma, which took place on September 20, 1854, where the Russian troops under Alexander Menshikov stopped the British and French troops from marching on the Sebastopol naval base, and at the other end, the Battle of Inkerman of November 5, 1854, which was Russia's attempt to break the British and French siege at Sebastopol. The court cards show royalty and generals, with Nicholas I, Tzar of Russia, as the king of clubs.

A similar pack of the same period shows the victories of Napoleon. Among the battles depicted on the aces are Jena, held on October 14, 1806, where the Prussians and Saxons under King Frederick William III joined forces; and also the Battle of Lutzen in 1809 with the Prussians and Russians against Napoleon.

From Switzerland comes a 52-card pack depicting soldiers in the uniforms of England, Germany, Highlands and Pandures. The pack was published by Hauser of Geneva in 1744 and is called *Jeu d'Officiers*. At the bottom of each card is a caption written in French, German and Italian while the value is indicated by a suit sign, Roman numeral and the word Roi, Dame or Valet in the top left hand corner. A similar pack was issued a little later by the same manufacturer showing a few different figures and called *Nouveau Jeu d'Officiers*.

Apart from the subjects already mentioned, a vari-

*Left to right*: A pip and court card from the 'Joan of Arc' pack, Cotta's first transformation pack, 1805; court card from Cotta's 1806 pack, showing classical figures.

ety of other themes were used on German cards. For instance, J. Glanz of Vienna made a double-ended pack where the court cards show historic personalities such as Attila, Scanderbergo and Corvinus. On the deuces are: hearts, an Austrian crown; bells, a river god; acorns, the Austrian eagle; and leaves, the arms of Hungary.

An attractive and interesting pack was also made by Friedrich Gunthel of Leipzig under the name 'New Oval Salon Playing Cards' of 1880. Packs were made with either German or French suits and as the name suggests they are oval in shape. Each of the suits represented different estates of life including: trade, agriculture, defence and the clergy. The cards were printed by A. Twietmeyer of Leipzig.

Another pack made in Leipzig called *Bergmanns-Karte* illustrates the silver and cobalt mining industry in Saxony. The court cards show various officials and workmen, while on the number cards are vignettes showing the details of the work. The same makers, Industrie Comptoir, made a similar pack called *Jagd-Karte* which shows hunting and shooting.

Van der Heyden is accredited with having issued a pack in Strasbourg *c*.1640 which had court cards representing the twelve months of the year, while the deuces show the four seasons. The remainder of the number cards show various domestic and humorous incidents. At the top of each card is a four line verse in German referring to the subject. In 1719 J.P. Andrea of Nuremberg issued a 52–card astronomical pack. Each card has in the centre a constellation, with a suit sign above and description below. There is an additional card and frontispiece which shows two boys standing by a celestial globe with one looking up at the zodiac through a telescope.

During the early 1800s a completely different type of playing card came on to the market – the transformation pack. This is so-called because the 'pips' (suit signs) form an integral part of the card's design, being transformed into all manner of ingenious things such as hats, waistcoats, angels' wings, bags and windows. It is thought that this type of card originated from a game of artistic skill. A person would draw the face of a playing card with all the pips in the correct position, and then proceed to draw a picture around it, such as a man rowing, being careful to absorb the pip in the design. In certain books, specifically made for amusement purposes, and in pocket almanacs which were given as New Year presents in Germany, the odd card transformed in such a way is sometimes found.

Transformation pack showing hand-coloured cards in classical designs, by H.F. Müller, Vienna, *c.* 1818.

---

One of the earliest 52-card transformation packs was made by the German publisher J.G. Cotta of Tübingen. Cotta produced six different transformation packs. With each pack only the number cards are transformed while the court cards show figures from a set theme.

The first Cotta pack of 1805 has the court figures depicting characters from Schiller's play *Die Jungfrau von Orleans*, with Joan of Arc featured as the ace of Spades. The designs for the pack are attributed to Countess Jennison-Walworth. Cotta's second pack was issued in 1806 and has courts showing classical figures including Ulysses on the king of hearts; Pirrhus on the king of clubs; Agripine on the queen of diamonds; and Burrhus on the jack of spades.

The third of Cotta's issues *c.*1807, has Schiller's Wallenstein as a subject matter for the court cards. In 1808 the court figures are dressed in Arabic costumes; the 1810 pack features mythological figures and caricatures on the court cards, and the 1811 issue has court figures representing various orders of chivalry and knighthood. For some reason there was no issue in 1809.

Transformation packs quickly became very popular all over Europe. However, more often than not, lazy manufacturers would pirate either Cotta's or some other famous designs.

The artist C.F. Osiander designed a pack of transformation cards in 1815. The four kings show: Wellington, Blücher, Schwartzenburg and Kutusoff, who were the generals of the allied armies of England, Prussia, Austria and Russia. The queens are symbolic figures of these countries and the jacks are soldiers. Osiander is also credited with designing Cotta's 1810 pack.

The Austrian maker, Müller, was quick to produce the novel transformation cards, the most famous of which was made *c.*1818 and called the *Fracas* or *Beatrice* pack. The designs are exotic, showing classical Romans, Greeks and Turks. Müller was apt to cheat a little, and if he could not fit the pips into the design he would leave them untouched. This design was nevertheless very popular and widely copied. Later Müller issued two more packs, but neither is of such high quality or imagination.

Two famous and prolific German card makers of the 19th century were B. Dondorf and C.L. Wüst, both based in Frankfurt.

The firm of B. Dondorf was founded in April 1833 by the lithographer Bernhard Dondorf. The cards produced bore the imprint of B. Dondorf, Frankfurt, until 1906 when the firm became a limited company, although in fact it had been run by Dondorf's sons Carl and Paul since 1872. Packs made after 1906 carry the mark B. Dondorf GmbH Frankfurt.

As well as playing cards, the firm made various games, greeting and postcards and at one time, in co-operation with the printing firm of C. Naumann, banknotes for the Italian National Bank and Imperial Japanese Government. A lot of the firm's business also concentrated on exports to such countries as Denmark, Norway, Sweden and Indonesia.

The firm had a high reputation for quality and colour printing and it is said that they eventually ran into trouble because of the expense incurred through using so many different colour separations on their cards. In 1929 the firm was forced into liquidation. The playing card section was bought by Flemming & Wiskott of Glogau who continued to use the traditional imprint until 1933 when they in turn sold out to ASS.

One of Dondorf's most celebrated packs is 'The Four Corners of the World' published in the 1890s. Beautifully produced and coloured, the four suits represent different continents, while the number cards show scenes relating to the history of a particular continent. The spades suit shows Africa, with the courts bearing pictures of a Sultan, Sultana and a Janizany. The hearts typify Asia and the court cards show the Great

*Left to right*: the 'Four Corners of the World', by B. Dondorf, Frankfurt, *c*.1880; non-standard pack in which the suits represent: hearts France, spades Germany, diamonds Turkey and clubs Venice, by B. Dondorf, Frankfurt, *c*. 1870; a pack commemorating the first shooting festival at Frankfurt, C.L. Wust, *c*. 1862.

Moghul, a Hindu Princess and a Hindu warrior. Diamonds stand for Europe and feature an Emperor, Empress and lance bearer. The clubs represent America and show Ferdinand and Isabella, King and Queen of Spain, and a Spanish ambassador. The number cards in this suit show Columbus's early experiences in America. In this pack the aces and court cards are coloured whilst the number cards are in cameo.

Dondorf made several other packs where each of the suits represent continents, such as one designed by Hausmann in *c*.1895 and another, which is sometimes called the 'Frankfurt Jewish' pattern, showing views of world capitals on the aces. This pack was made in several editions, including one where the indices were specially enlarged for use by handicapped players.

Among C.L. Wüst's many famous packs is a set of war cards produced in the early 19th century. The cards are French-suited and double-ended. On each ace can be seen two battle scenes. The ace of hearts shows an attack on Frankfurt and the battle of Hanau; that of diamonds shows the battle of Leipzig; that of spades the engagement at Brienne and Katzback; and that of clubs the attack on Montmartre and the entry into Paris. Among the court cards are the busts of the Duke of Wellington as the jack of diamonds and Marshal Blücher as the jack of clubs.

In 1862 Wüst commemorated the first shooting festival at Frankfurt with a pack where the kings are riflemen; the queens are symbolic figures of Germany; and the jacks humorously depict various famous personalities. The aces show scenes from the celebrations under the captions: *Gabentempel*, *Ueberreichung der Bundesfahne*, *Rossmarkt*, *Festhalle* and *Bornheimer Haide*. Several versions of this pack exist, including one where the king of hearts holds a banner inscribed *Ueb Aug & Hand für's Vaterland* and the aces show *Gabentempel*, *Fest-Halle*, *Eingangs Pforte* and *Vogelperspective des Schützen-Festes in Frankfurt a'M Juli 1862*. In yet another version the knave of clubs (representing Napoleon) holds the inscribed banner.

Most of the Swiss non-standard playing cards come under the category of costume packs. One attractive example shows the regional dress of Fribourg, Undervald, Berne, Grison, Appenzell, Soleure, Lucerne. The court cards portray various personalities, such as woodcutters, boat-women and cobblers as well as members of the clergy and aristocracy. Another favourite subject of the Swiss was hunting. A 'Huntsman's' pack of *c*.1850 has double-ended engraved and stencilled courts showing different weapons associated with various forms of hunting. The queens portray Diana 'goddess of the chase' and the king of clubs shows David, holding a club in one hand and the head of Goliath in the other. Each of the four aces shows two different highly detailed hunting scenes. The ace of spades shows a deer hunt, the ace of clubs wild fowling, and the ace of hearts whaling. But the most unusual card is the ace of diamonds which shows a man holding a spear and riding a black horse through Hell. Accompanying him are evil-looking monsters, prehistoric animals and a fire-breathing snake.

# MODERN CARDS

Some of the rarest and most eagerly sought 20th-century non-standard playing cards are the ones produced by Germany to spread political propaganda during the First and Second World Wars. These cards were produced either to boost the confidence of Germany's allies or to ridicule and demoralize the enemy.

United Stralsund P.C. Co. were among the first German manufacturers to produce such packs when in c.1915 they made the 'Germany United Pack' and the 'Heroes' pack. The 'Germany United Pack' has German suits and either 32 or 36 cards, with the seven and eight in each suit showing German warships. The rest of the cards picture named German princes, military leaders and ministers – with the king of acorns depicting von Bayern. The backs show the Iron Cross and the legend 'German Unity Cards'. The second pack, 'Heroes', is again German-suited and contains the same amount of cards with double-ended courts showing two different German kings and military leaders. This time Kaiser Wilhelm II and von Freussen are featured on the king of acorns. The number cards in this pack show scenes from various campaigns from the first two years of the war, such as *Auf Gallipoli* on the 10 of bells. The backs show branches, oakleaf garlands, the Iron Cross and Imperial Eagle.

A similar series of cards was made by the Altenburg Playing Card Co. and sold to raise money for the Air Force Welfare Fund. Their first pack, called 'German War Cards I', features Kaiser Wilhelm as the king of acorns. Two other packs, both called 'German War Cards II', were produced in 1916. They have the same court cards as the 1915 pack with just some minor variations on the number cards. The difference between the two 1916 versions is that on the 10 of bells one card shows four money bags, and the other shows five money bags. Yet another version of this pack was issued in 1917 under the name 'German War Cards III'. There are some changes on both court and number cards including seven money bags on the 10 of bells and Prince Leopold von Bayern on the king of acorns.

In 1918 the Altenburg P.C. Co. obviously thought it was time to both change their designs and the destination of the proceeds from the sales. On this occasion the courts are German princes, soldiers and aviation pioneers and although Prince Leopold von Bayern is still featured on the king of acorns the 10 of bells now shows the Iron Cross. Two other interesting court cards are the Ober of hearts which shows Otto Lilienthal who built the first glider in 1887, and the Unter of acorns on which is Rittmeister Manfred Frh. v. Richthofen, who brought down 80 planes between 1916 and 1918. The money raised from the sale of these cards went to the Air Pilots Welfare Fund. This and the other three packs mentioned above were designed by Fritz von Lindenau.

A French-suited pack called 'Empire Cards' was made in 1915 by the same maker. The kings show German princes, the jacks military and political leaders and the queens symbolize such things as welfare, engineering, science and agriculture. The popular Kaiser Wilhelm is featured on the king of clubs and the aces show various coats of arms. Predictably the backs show the Imperial Eagle and the Iron Cross. Another

---

French-suited 'World War One' pack by ASS, c. 1917.

French-suited pack was made by Stralsunder entitled *Kaiserkartes*. The kings show the heads of Prussia, Bavaria, Saxony and Wurtemberg. The military forces of sea, air and land are represented on the jacks by Hindenburg, Tirpitz and Zeppelin, together with the Reich Chancellor. The queens show Gewerbe, Handel, Landwirtschaft and Wissenschaft. The aces in this pack are also interesting. The ace of clubs shows a plane and a Zeppelin; the ace of hearts pictures a 42cm howitzer; the flags of the Central Powers of Germany, Turkey, Austria and Bulgaria are on the ace of diamonds; and the ace of spades shows Kommandant Weddigen and the U–9 and U–29 boats.

The 'Fatherland' pack was issued in 1915 by F.A. Lattman, Goslar, and designed by Ferdinand Herwig. The cards are German-suited and single-ended, with the kings showing the current German rulers such as the king of Württemberg on the king of acorns together with his coat of arms. On the jacks are soldiers 'in the field', while various battle scenes and weapons are shown on the number cards and the Iron Cross and Imperial Eagle are on the backs.

One of the few German war packs where the suit signs actually are changed is the *Frankfurter Kriegskarte*. The hearts and diamonds are the same and

joined with the Iron Cross and artillery shells. The court cards show allegorical figures symbolizing Honour, Glory, Industry, Bravery and Love of Country.

A non-standard suited pack which was not sold but given away to the German troops was made by Richard Burrow & Co. of Hamburg for Steinway & Sons – the piano manufacturers. The suits are hearts, diamonds, cannon balls and Iron Crosses.

Moving on to the Second World War, Linden designed the 'Soldiers' pack of c.1942 which has courts showing officers, non-commissioned officers and women auxilliary members of the German Armed Forces. The aces show various Russian cities. Lastly a war pack made in 1943 called the 'Propaganda' pack features caricatures of monarchs and political leaders of the Allied countries, etc, and was supposedly dropped on England from German aircraft during the war.

Happily, not all German card manufacturers were caught up in the 'war effort' and continued to produce beautiful whimsical designs, with no secondary purpose except to be enjoyed. Such is the case with B. Dondorf who, following his old tradition of high quality and colourful designs, produced a number of modern packs which, through countless reprints, are still available today.

Most of Dondorf's modern cards concentrate either on historical or costume courts. At the turn of this century he produced the 'Hohenzollern' pack showing historical personalities and soldiers from Prussian history, with various coats of arms on the backs. Another attractive pack of 1905 features figures in medieval costumes – a theme he later developed in a pack showing various professions of medieval life on the Obers and Unters. In 1910, Dondorf produced a pack called 'Mecklenburg Royalty' which features royal personages and prominent personalities from Mecklenburg. Again the aces are scenic and the backs show coats of arms. It was, however, with the 'Centennial' pack of 1933, made to commemorate 100 years of the playing card firm, that the firm of Dondorf excelled itself. The courts show figures from medieval history against a pale background scene of jesters, courtiers and ladies-in-waiting. The cards are in pastel shades with the crowns and borders in gold. The backs show coats of arms, pages, and the Wartburg castle.

Like many manufacturers, Dondorf's playing card firm experimented with the suit mark designs. In 1928 they produced the 'Bedo' pack where the hearts are red, spades black, diamonds orange and clubs green. In c.1930 they used the same suit colours for a specially printed pack for the New York firm of Saks & Co., combined with special *jugendstil* court designs.

In 1965 F.X. Schmid of Munich issued two packs in an attempt to introduce new modified designs for the diamond and heart suit signs. The Bielefelder Spielkarten GmbH in 1964 designed a pack where the diamonds were yellow with a red border and the spades dark green with a black border. The design finally adopted by both firms from 1965 onwards was a red diamond with a black border. ASS Spielkartenfabric, Leinfelden, in the same year adopted a diamond design with another smaller diamond inside it and again they have used this design since.

Experimental new designs were not restricted only to the suit signs. C.L. Wüst of Frankfurt issued the 'Congress' pack in 1900 where the cards are divided diagonally and show at one end a German court design or 'pip' and at the other end a French court design or pip. A similar 'Congress' pack was made in 1928 by the Altenburg Playing Card Co. Again they used French and German suit signs and designs and the cards are divided by a horizontal line. These *Kongress Karte* made by the Altenburg Playing Card Co. were in fact designed for use in the International Skat Tournament held in Germany in 1928. These tournaments were first devised in 1886 and held in Altenburg. However, as the tournament attracted players from all over Europe there was a lot of controversy as to the type of cards to use – German- or French-suited? After ceaseless quarrels they eventually adopted cards with both French and German suits (an idea which goes back to the 19th century). These cards were used only a few times and now German-suited cards are used for Skat competitions.

F.X. Schmid in 1965 issued a pack which employed both French suits and the additional sports suits of pennants, loving cups, trophies and balls. An unusual pack by Ferdinand Piatnik & Son of Vienna, called the 'Brocades' advertising pack of 1970, has conventional double-ended suit signs combined with single-ended court figures. Each suit is also printed in a different colour combination with: hearts, red on white; diamonds, white on red; spades, black on gold; and clubs, black on blue. Piatnik also made two packs with ultra-modern court figures in 1962. They were both designed by Josef Schuller and have court figures formed from geometric lines and shapes. The first pack was just printed in blue while the second has the four colours of blue, red, yellow and black.

Some other Austrian card makers were more concerned with the materials from which playing cards were made rather than experimenting with what was drawn on them. In 1925 Häusermann of Vienna made an aluminium-coated pack of playing cards. A year later, Franz Adametz of Vienna made the 'Perpetual'

The 'Nazi' pack which features the standard Rhineland pattern, but the suit of clubs is replaced by the suit of Swastikas and the eagle badge of the Nazis appears on all aces, by H. Behrmann, Flensburg, *c*. 1935.

playing cards out of celluloid. However, the cards were found to be inflammable and were confiscated by the police. This did not deter the Reorez Playing Card Co. of Vienna, who made a similar pack with costume courts in 1928.

Back in Germany, a bizarre but interesting pack was made by Werkstatt Rixdorfer Drucke of Berlin in 1968 under the name of *Rixdorfer-Spiel*. The courts were designed by four separate artists: spades by Uwe Bremer; hearts by Arno Waldschmidt; clubs by Ali Schindehütte; and diamonds by Josy Vannekamp. The backs are suitably adorned with two question marks!

The firm ASS is one of the biggest present-day German card producers, making both standard regional designs and non-standard designs. The history of ASS started in 1832 in Altenburg when the brothers Otto and Bernhard Bechstein founded the playing card factory under the imprint of Gebrüder Bechstein. In 1892 the name was changed into Schneider & Co., Altenburg. In 1898 the company merged with Vereinigte Stralsunder Spielkarten-Fabrik A.G. from Stralsund and the name for the Altenburg branch was changed to 'Vereinigte Stralsunder Spielkartenfabriken, Abt. Altenburg, vormals Schneider & Co.' In

*Left to right*: **Three modern packs by F. Piatnik & Sons of Vienna: a 'Baroque' pack; 'Folk Costume' bridge pack, showing costumes of the Austrian provinces, *c*. 1965; a 'Roccoco' pack.**

1923 the first playing card museum was founded in Altenburg by director Carl Schneider and in 1931 the Stralsund branch stopped manufacturing. The whole production was then taken to Altenburg under the new name, (which the company has kept until today), Vereinigte Altenburger und Stralsunder Spielkartenfabriken A.G. Altenburg or just ASS. Before and after 1931 many smaller factories had been taken over by ASS, for instance in 1933 the well-known and reputable firm Dondorf which had its seat in Frankfurt a.M.

After the Second World War Germany was separated into Eastern and Western Germany. As Altenburg was situated in Eastern Germany, the factory and the museum collection were confiscated by the Soviet Union. Unfortunately during the process of dismantling the factory, the museum's collection was lost. However, thanks to director Reisig of ASS, most of the factory's documents, records, sample books and printing patterns had been taken to West Germany before the Altenburg factory was confiscated.

In 1947 they were given permission to start up production again in West Germany under the name of Ariston in Detmold and Casino in Stuttgart. In 1950 the company was given permission to use their old name in Western Germany of Vereinigte Altenburger

und Stralsunder Spielkartenfabriken A.G., Stuttgart, or in shorter form, ASS. This is the old name, but its use is now limited to that part of the firm in the German Federal Republic. In 1957 a new factory was built in Leinfelden (near Stuttgart) and the company celebrated its 125th anniversary in the same year.

In the German Democratic Republic production was also started up, but now under the name VEB Altenburger Spielkartenfabrik (the VEB signifies Volkseigener Betrieb, or nationalized and publicly owned).

Among ASS's many packs are: 'Rococo' and 'Imperial' which show costumed courts from the Rococo period; *Fussball Skat* (Skat being a card game) with satirical courts and aces showing footballers in comical dress and poses; *Wickuler Skat* – an advertising pack for beer; 'Frolic' – a limited edition of 5,000 showing different dogs on the court cards – also on the animal theme are 'Birds' and 'Little Hare'; 'Casanova' with cartoons of pin-up girls; 'Icelander' which shows views of Iceland on the aces; and 'Skat Express' which is a 32-card pack, combining English and Berliner style courts. ASS have also made several reproduction packs. Their *Kaiserkarte* pack has courts dressed in costumes of various periods and was originally made in 1910 exclusively for the use of the Imperial family.

*Left to right*: 'Historic Berlin' pack by ASS; 'Jugendstil' or 'Art Nouveau' pack, ASS; *Alte Bergman Karte* **Mining pack; Modern reproduction of the Dondorf Centennial Pack originally made in 1933.**

ASS also re-issued the Dondorf 'Centennial' cards of 1933.

One of the most artistic packs made by ASS is the 'Historic Berlin' pack. The courts show famous rulers and military figures such as Bismarck on the jack of diamonds, Frederick Wilhelm II as the king of hearts and Kaiserin Auguste Victoria on the queen of diamonds. The number cards show scenes and famous buildings while the aces show coats of arms.

Ferdinand Piatnik is to Austria what Dondorf and ASS are to Germany. Ferdinand Piatnik was born in Buda (Ofen) in 1819 and started his apprenticeship as a playing card maker in Pressburg in 1839. He took over his relative A. Moser's factory (f.1824) in 1843 and his sons Adolf and Ferdinand joined him in 1882 under the new company name of Ferd. Piatnik & Söhne Wien.

Piatnik died in 1885 and his sons carried on the business. Expansion became a key policy. In 1891 they founded a new factory in Hütteldorferstr. 227; in 1896 they established a subsidiary in Budapest under the name of Piatnik Nándor és Fiai; in 1903 another new factory was erected in Budapest in Rottenbiller Str.; in 1907 a paper mill was bought in Ratschach, Austria, called Gebrüder Piatnik, Ratschach; in 1923 a factory

was established in Prague called Ferd. Piatnik Synové, Ritter a Spol; and in 1926 a new factory was opened in Cracow, Poland. In 1912 the firm took over the firm of Josef Glanz and began making their subsidiaries limited companies; and in 1939 they changed the firm's name to Wiener Spielkartenfabrik Ferd. Piatnik & Söhne. Unfortunately during the Second World War they lost control of all their factories outside of Austria. Business, however, continued to thrive. In 1951 they introduced four-colour offset printing, and added board games and puzzles to their range in 1968. They celebrated their 150th anniversary in 1974. Piatnik have for a long time been conscious of the playing card collectors' market and the suitability of playing cards as an artistic canvas. Many of their packs concentrate on the costume courts, such as the 'Baroque' pack which shows 17th- and 18th-century costumes and the 'Folklore' pack which shows regional costumes. The latter was first issued in 1935 and the queens are portraits of four members of the Piatnik family.

Piatnik made several historical packs. In 1924 he issued the 'Francesi Pichetto' pack where authors, named statesmen, monarchs and symbolic figures appear on the court cards, with King Lear on the king of clubs. Polish history is related on the 'Wistowe' pack with the courts featuring famous personages and the aces showing two different Polish buildings. European history is the subject of the 'Rococo' pack, first issued in 1953. Several editions of this pack have been made which have on the backs either a horseman, a castle, Beethoven, Mozart or a simple filigree pattern. Concentrating on Austria, Piatnik made the 'Kaiser' pack where the beautiful court cards showed members of the old Austrian royal family with their names and dates.

On the subject of biblical history, Piatnik made a pack specially for El Al airways showing scenes from the Old Testament. These 'Jacob's Bible Cards' come in a modernistic and classic version and both show Jacob and other related characters from the Bible on the courts. The firm has also recently issued an Arab pack showing Bedouins on the heart suit; Berbers on the diamond suit; Turks on the spades suit and Touregs on the club suit.

Most of the Swiss modern non-standard packs of playing cards are the souvenir, costume and historical persons variety, such as those by Müller and Hächler Söhne of Zurich.

The Wagner pack by Müller was first designed in 1920 but was not issued until 1968 when Dr. E. Brum-Antonioli (a Swiss apothecary and playing card collector) commissioned a print run of 500 double-ended packs. The backs show a portrait of Wagner and the court cards show characters from Wagner's operas. Müller & Co. made another pack for Dr. E. Brum-Antonioli in 1967 which shows medieval distilling furnaces on the backs of the playing cards and medieval scenes relating to the subject on the court cards.

Another special printing by Müller & Co. in c.1963 for the French chemical firm of Morinol has modernistic-type courts showing figures from mythology, such as Triton and Amphitrite.

# STANDARD PATTERNS

## GERMANY

Most of the German-suited standard patterns in current use in Germany have their roots in the 17th and 18th centuries, although in some cases it was not until the 19th century that patterns as we now know them finally stabilized.

Several features from the early German cards have survived to this day, but the standard pattern with the oldest ancestry, the Ansbach pattern, died out during the Second World War. Of the other German patterns it seems that the Bavarian and Franconian are the oldest, after which comes the Saxon pattern, the Württemberg-Palatine, then the Prussian pattern, which probably evolved around the 1800s. During the 18th century the Germans adopted the French-suited pack called the Berliner pattern and later a similar French-suited Rhinelander or Frankfurt pattern.

The very early German packs contained 48 cards (king, Ober, Unter, deuce, 10–3). For a time the ten was called a 'banner card' as it showed a banner. Today the German pack has dwindled down to 36 or 32 cards. With the 36-card pack the 3, 4 and 5 of each suit have been omitted and for the 32-card pack the 6 of each suit has also been missed out. Most German cards are long and slim, measuring about 100mm × 55mm and all double-ended packs are divided by a horizontal line. The traditional German suit signs are hearts, leaves, acorns and bells.

Originally the leaves and acorns suit motifs were coloured green while hearts and bells were red. Only the hearts and leaves have remained the same, while the acorns and bells are now coloured in red, yellow and green. It is customary in German-suited packs to place the suit sign for the Ober card at the top left-hand side of the card's face, while for the Unter card the suit sign is at the bottom of the card. The king's suit sign is placed at the top left-hand corner of the card, although in some packs the king card has two suit signs, one at each side of his head.

### GERMAN SUITED

**Ansbach Pattern** (*Ansbach Bild*)

The Ansbach pattern is probably one of the oldest standard German patterns and was used in the Nuremberg area of Germany. Its production ceased earlier this century. Packs contain 36 single-ended cards (king, Ober, Unter, deuce, 10–7) and the designs are simplistic and sometimes quite crude with no vignettes on the number cards. Several of the court figures hold their suit signs, with the suit motifs of acorns and leaves having particularly long stems.

*Kings*

The kings are all seated, although sometimes they appear to be standing. The king of hearts is full-faced and the other kings look to their right. The kings of hearts and leaves hold their suit signs in their right hand and a sceptre in their left hand. The king of acorns just holds his suit sign in his right hand and the king of bells holds a sceptre in his right hand.

*Obers*

The Ober of acorns is depicted walking to the left-

*Left to right*: Ansbach Pattern, Unter of leaves; Bavarian, Ober of leaves; Franconian, Ober of acorns.

hand side of the card's face and holding his suit sign. The Ober of leaves looks to his left and holds his suit sign in his right hand. The Ober of hearts also holds his suit sign in his right hand but looks to his right. The Ober of bells looks to his left and points with his left index finger. Usually all the Obers wear moustaches.

*Unters*

The Unter of bells is depicted walking to the right-hand side of the card's face and pointing with his index fingers. The Unter of acorns is oppositely positioned. The other two Unters look to their right and in his right hand the Unter of leaves holds his suit sign – which has a particularly large stem forming an S shape. Packs are sometimes found where the Obers and Unters are facing in opposite directions to the descriptions above.

*Deuces*

The deuce of acorns shows a lion and a shield. The deuce of leaves shows a scribe writing, above which is a coat of arms, or just two birds. The deuce of hearts carries the tax stamp and the deuce of bells shows a ribbon.

**Bavarian Pattern** (*Bayrisches Bild*)

The modern Bavarian pattern is produced with both double-ended and single-ended cards. In the double-ended pattern all the details normally shown at the bottom of the single-ended card pack are omitted.

This pack contains 36 cards (king, Ober, Unter, deuce, 10–6). The cards bear indices with the court cards corresponding to K O U while the deuce is usually lettered A. All the kings wear crowns and sit in stately chairs. These are seen from a side view positioned at the right-hand side of the card's face. All the Obers and Unters are standing on ground.

*Kings*

The kings of leaves and acorns are seen in left profile and carry sceptres in their right hands. The king of acorns has his left hand on his sword hilt, although on the double-ended design this is no longer visible. The king of leaves is the only king to have his legs crossed (right over left). The kings of hearts and bells also carry sceptres in their right hands, but while the king of hearts is full faced, that of bells looks to his left. The maker's name is found on the king of hearts.

*Obers*

The Obers of hearts and bells look to their right with the Ober of bells' face being in profile. The Ober of hearts holds a downward pointing sword in his right

47

*Left to right:* Saxon Patterns, Unter of leaves; Prussian, 7 of acorns and Ober of leaves.

hand. The Ober of bells is seen beginning to draw his sword, with his right hand, from its hilt which he holds in his left hand. The Obers of leaves and acorns look to their left and again one of the Obers, that of acorns, has his face in profile. The Ober of leaves plays a drum while that of acorns holds a sword in his right hand and a shield in his left.

### Unters

The Unters of leaves and acorns look to their left. The Unter of leaves plays a flute while the Unter of acorns holds a sword in his right hand. The Unter of hearts is seen from a left-side view and holds a spear with both hands on the far side of his body. The Unter of bells is shown from a right-side view and holds a curved sword above his head.

### Deuces

The deuce of hearts features the maker's name and a cherub while the deuce of bells shows a dog attacking a wild boar. The deuce of leaves simply shows a vase of flowers and the deuce of acorns shows Bacchus sitting on a barrel.

### Other Cards

The rest of the number cards all feature a picture at the bottom of the card's face. Included are, on hearts: 7, a shield and the maker's name; 9, a man shooting birds. On bells: 7, a woman pushing a man in a wheel barrow; 8, a woman by a grave. On acorns: 6, a windmill; 7, a boy with a bird basket; and on leaves; 7, a man fishing.

### Franconian Pattern *(Frankisches Bild)*

Although the Franconian state no longer exists a double-ended version of its pattern is still being produced. The pack comprises 36 or 32 cards (king, Ober, Unter, deuce, 10–6 or 10–7) and was probably originally based on the Bavarian pattern as there are a number of similarities. The court figures on the Franconian pack are, however, less flamboyantly dressed and their actions do not inspire the same sense of urgency or reality as those on the Bavarian pattern.

Below are the main differences between the corresponding court cards of the Franconian and Bavarian patterns. Apart from style of dress and other minor variations, details not mentioned should be taken as the same as for the double-ended Bavarian pattern.

### Kings

The king of hearts now looks to his left and holds the hilt of his sword in his left hand as well as a sceptre in his right. The king of bells now looks to his right and the king of acorns holds his sceptre in his left hand. Both the kings of leaves and acorns are shown in a more frontal position and look to their right, as opposed to being in profile. The king of acorns also now holds his sceptre in his left hand.

### Obers

The Obers of hearts and acorns are totally different from those of the Bavarian pattern. A left-side view of

48

the Ober of hearts is shown, although his head is turned to the front of the card's face. He carries a spear in his right hand, the top of which extends beyond the card's frame line. The Ober of acorns looks to his right and is shown in a fencing position holding his rapier in his left hand. Apart from artistic details and style of dress the other two Obers are the same as in the Bavarian pattern.

*Unters*

The Unter of hearts holds an axe, not a spear. The Unter of bells holds a straight sword in his raised left hand (as opposed to a curved sword held in the right hand) and the Unter of leaves now looks to his right, not left. The Unter of acorns is different from the one in the Bavarian pattern and is shown with his face in left profile holding a spear in his left hand.

*Deuces*

The deuces are all totally different from those of the Bavarian pattern. The deuce of hearts shows cornucopias of flowers; that of bells a laurel wreath; that of leaves an eagle with his left foot on an orb; and the deuce of acorns shows a heraldic lion.

**Saxon Pattern** (*Sächsisches Bild, Thüringisches Bild* or *Chemnitzer Bild*)

Before World War Two the Altenburg playing card firm produced this pattern under the name 'The Altenburg Pattern'. The main difference between this and the Saxon pattern is that in the Altenburg pack a lion is featured on the deuce of acorns whereas the Saxon pattern shows a bear on that card. In 1832 Glanz of Vienna also made a variation of the Saxon pattern under the name of the 'Brunner Pattern'.

The Saxon pattern contains 36 or 32 cards (king, Ober, Unter, deuce, 10–6 or 10–7). The cards are double-ended and bear no indices. The kings are all crowned and have two suitmarks, one on each side of their head. The suit signs on the Ober and Unter cards are placed in their usual position, although the suit signs of leaves and acorns are shown with stems.

*Kings*

All the kings carry a sceptre; the kings of hearts, leaves and acorns hold theirs in their left hand while that of bells holds his sceptre in his right hand. The kings of acorns and hearts look to their right and those of bells and leaves to their left. The kings are all shown with beards and moustaches.

*Obers*

The Obers of hearts and leaves are shown from a left-side view. The Ober of acorns looks to his right and that of bells looks to his left. The Ober of acorns holds his suit sign by the stem in his right hand and

that of leaves in his left hand. The remaining Obers of hearts and bells point into the air with their right index fingers.

*Unters*

The Unter of hearts looks to his left and carries his hat under his left arm. All the other Unters wear their hats. The Unter of acorns looks and is slightly turned to the right-hand side of the card's face and the Unter of bells is similarly positioned but facing in the opposite direction. The Unter of leaves is shown from a left-side view, holding a walking stick in his right hand.

*Deuces*

The maker's name, the words *Schwerdter-Karte* and a bear appear on the deuce of acorns. On the deuce of bells can be seen a courting couple watched by a third party. The deuce of leaves shows the coat of arms of Saxony and the deuce of hearts shows a basket of flowers and the maker's name. The maker's name also appears on the 7 of hearts.

**Prussian-Silesian Pattern** (*Preussisch-Schlesisches Bild*)

The Prussian-Silesian pattern contains 32 cards (king, Unter, Ober, deuce, 10–7). In older packs the cards were all single-ended but in modern packs only the number cards are single-ended, while the court cards and deuces are double-ended. The number cards bear Arabic numerals although packs are made with and without indices on the court cards and deuces. The kings have two suitmarks, one placed at each side of their head. The rest of the suit signs are traditionally positioned. However, as in the Saxon pattern, the suit signs of leaves and acorns are shown with stems.

This pattern is easily recognizable, having a number of distinguishing features including the number cards which show pictures of German towns and buildings with their names underneath. It is interesting to see that although Prussia now no longer exists this pattern still retains many of the old places, such as Danzig and Breslau, which once belonged to the region. Also, new buildings have been added, for instance the packs made by ASS show a picture of their factory on the seven of bells.

The kings all wear crowns and are traditionally portrayed while the rest of the court cards are dressed in 19th century costumes and represent different town and country characters.

*Kings*

The kings of hearts and bells are full-faced, while those of acorns and leaves look to their left. The king of hearts holds a sceptre in his right hand and the hilt of his sword with his left hand. The king of bells is

Turkish and the sceptre he holds in his left hand is surmounted by a crescent moon. The king of acorns also holds his sword hilt with his left hand and just the top half of a sceptre is visible at his right side. The king of leaves holds a sceptre in his right hand.

*Obers*

The Ober of hearts looks to his left and holds a rifle under his left arm. The Ober of leaves is seen from a left-side view, has a rifle on his back and holds a pipe in his left hand. The other two Obers, of acorns and leaves, are slightly turned and look to the left-hand side of the card's face; that of acorns holds an axe in his right hand; while the Ober of bells is shown as a city gent, with a cigar in his right hand and a walking stick in his left hand. All the Obers wear head gear.

*Unters*

The most distinctive Unter is that of hearts. He looks and is slightly turned to the left-hand side of the card's face and carries a bottle of hock in his right hand and a napkin in the other. The Unters of leaves and bells look and are slightly turned to the right-hand side of the card's face. In his left hand the Unter of leaves carries a dead bird while that of bells holds a slate often with a number written on it. The Unter of acorns is the least interesting court card, simply looking to his right with his hands in his pockets.

*Deuces*

The deuces are particularly decorative in this pack. On the deuce of leaves can be seen a representation of the goddess Diana with her dog, bow and arrow. On the deuce of hearts is a female Roman warrior; on that of bells a German fraulein holding a banner with the words *Deutsche Karte* on it; and that of acorns the god Bacchus sitting on a barrel. The maker's name is found on the deuce of hearts and 7 of bells.

After Silesia became part of Poland, the Polish playing card enterprise (KZWP) still continued to produce a variation of the Prussian-Silesian pattern. The number cards feature modern Polish cities, and where some of the old Prussian cities appear they are shown with their new Polish names, such as Wraclaw (Breslau) on the nine of bells.

There are also a number of differences on the court cards which are as follows: the king of leaves holds a scroll as well as a sceptre; the Unter of leaves has a bunch of grapes; the Ober of hearts holds a crossbow; the Unter of hearts a jug and beaker. The court figures on the bell suit have an oriental appearance with the Ober holding a bow and arrow and the Unter a hawk by a chain. The acorns suit shows the Ober as a Spanish soldier and the Unter as a minstrel.

## Württemberg-Palatine Pattern
*(Württembergisch-Pfalzisches Bild)*

The Württemberg-Palatine pattern contains 36 double-ended cards (king, Ober, Unter, deuce, 10–6). The cards bear indices and in most packs the word 'Ober' is also printed at each end of the Ober cards. The kings all wear crowns and the Obers ride horses. Two distinctive features of this pack are that the Ober of leaves is a Moor and the Unters are dressed in 19th century clothes. The other court cards are dressed in medieval costumes.

*Kings*

The kings are reminiscent of those in the Berliner pattern (*see* page 51); they all look to their left with the king of hearts almost full-faced and holding a sceptre in his right hand and an orb in his left. The king of bells just holds a sceptre in his left hand. The king of leaves holds his sceptre in his right hand and has a harp in his left hand. Lastly the king of acorns holds a sceptre in his left hand and his right hand is on his shield.

*Obers*

All the Obers ride their horses to the left-hand side of the card's face. The Obers of hearts, bells and leaves look to their left while that of acorns looks in the same direction in which he is travelling. The Ober of leaves wears a turban, while the other Obers wear feathered head gear. The Obers of bells and acorns hold swords in their obscured right hand while the Ober of leaves carries a whip.

*Unters*

The Unter of bells is slightly turned and looks to the right-hand side of the card's face. The other Unters are slightly turned to the left-hand side of the card's face but look to their left. The Unter of hearts holds a pipe in his left hand; that of bells has a satchel on his back and rests both his arms on a walking stick. The Unter of leaves holds a spear in his left hand and the Unter of acorns holds the butt of his rifle with his right hand and a walking stick in his left hand.

*Deuces*

In this particular pattern the maker's name is found on the deuce and seven of bells and the seven of hearts. The deuces show: hearts, bottles and glasses; bells, a vase surrounded by flowers and fruit; leaves, a goblet and two bottles; acorns, a boiling punch bowl and fruit.

## Bohemian or Prague Pattern *(Böhmisch-Deutsches Bild, or Präger Bild)*

The Bohemian pattern is basically a Czech version of the German Franconian pattern and is produced by the Czechoslovakian playing card enterprise Obchodni Tiskarny np Kolín (OTK).

The pack consists of 32 single-ended cards (king, Ober, Unter, deuce, 10–7) and card No. 10 in each suit bears a Roman numeral, while the rest of the cards are without indices. Unlike the Franconian pattern, the kings have two suit signs, one on each side of their head.

Although there are many common characteristics between the Bohemian and Franconian pattern their appearance is totally different. The court figures of the Bohemian pattern are simply dressed and appear very stoical, as though carved from stone, and very reminiscent of Gothic art.

*Kings*

The chairs on which the kings sit are all shown from a side view. The kings of hearts and leaves sit facing the left-hand side of the card's face and hold sceptres in their right hand. The kings of acorns and bells sit facing the right-hand side of the card's face; and while the king of acorns also holds his sceptre in his right hand, that of bells holds a sceptre in his left hand.

*Obers*

The Obers of hearts, bells and leaves are effectively the same as those in the Franconian pattern. The Ober of acorns carries two swords instead of one.

*Unters*

The Unters of leaves and bells are also basically the same as those of the Franconian pattern; except that the pipe-playing Unter of leaves now looks to his left and the Unter of bells holds his sword with both hands at the hilt. The Unters of hearts and acorns are the same as their counterparts in the Franconian pattern but with their respective designs reversed.

*Deuces*

The deuces all show coats of arms with the deuce of acorns also showing a bear and the maker's name. Most of the number cards carry illustrations, including, on the 10 of hearts, Cupid shooting an arrow into the heart of a pyramid; on bells: 10, two musicians and a performing bear; 9, a prancing horse tethered to a stake; 8, a dog and the maker's name; on acorns: 9 a transfixed bird; on leaves: 9, a goat.

## FRENCH SUITED

Today Germany uses two types of French-suited cards, both being variations of the Paris pattern. The first, oldest and most widespread pattern is the Berliner. The second pattern, called Rhineland or Frankfurt, is rather less ornate than the Berliner. Although used throughout Germany it is less popular.

Packs are found containing either 32, 36, or 52 cards

(king, queen, jack, ace, 10–7, 10–6 or 10–2). Occasionally packs are also found with two duplicate packs of 24 cards for the game of Gaigel and Binokel. Most packs are double-ended, being divided by a horizontal line. Generally, the German indices of K D B are used, although packs are also found with English indices of K Q J. In Germany both patterns are usually referred to as Französisches Bild or French pattern.

The Rhinelander pattern was originally designed by B. Dondorf and is used in Poland with either the English indices or the Polish ones of K D W. Variations of both patterns are also found in many other countries, including Scandinavia.

### Berliner Pattern *(Berliner Bild)*

All the kings wear crowns, the queens wear veils and the jacks wear feathered caps. The court cards are richly decorated and flamboyantly dressed. The maker's name is found on the jack of clubs and the ace of hearts and other details are on the 7 and 10 of diamonds.

*Kings*

The kings of spades and hearts look to their right while the kings of clubs and diamonds look to their left. The face of the king of diamonds is in profile. In their left hand the kings of spades, clubs and diamonds hold sceptres, and that of hearts an upward-pointing sword. The king of spades holds a harp in his right hand while the king of clubs holds a shield and that of hearts an orb.

*Queens*

The queens of spades and diamonds look to their left with the face of the queen of spades being in profile. The other two queens look to their right. The black queens each hold a flower in their right hand and the red queens hold the same in their left hand.

*Jacks*

All the jacks carry halberds in their left hand. The jacks of spades and clubs look to their right and hold the hilt of their sword in their right hand. The red jacks look to their left and the face of the jack of diamonds is in profile.

### Rhineland or Frankfurt Pattern *(Rheinisches bild* or *Frankfurter bild)*

In this pattern all the kings and queens wear crowns and the jacks wear hats. The pattern is fairly simple with all the court figures of a particular suit looking the same way. The court figures of clubs are full-faced while on hearts and diamonds all the court figures look to the left-hand side of the card's face, with the king and queen of diamonds being shown in profile. Those of spades look to the right-hand side of the

*Left to right*: Württemburg Pattern, Ober of leaves; Bohemian, Ober of acorns; Berliner, queen of hearts.

card's face.

*Kings*

The kings of clubs and diamonds carry a sceptre in their left hand and an orb in their right hand. The king of hearts also holds an orb in his right hand but a sword in his left. The king of spades merely carries a sceptre in his left hand.

*Deuces*

The queens of hearts, diamonds and spades carry a flower in their right hands while the queen of clubs holds a closed fan in her left hand.

*Jacks*

The jacks of clubs and diamonds hold a halberd in their left hands, with that of diamonds also holding the hilt of his sword in his right hand. The jack of hearts carries an upward-pointing sword in his left hand and the jack of spades holds the hilt of his obscured sword in his left hand.

## AUSTRIA AND HUNGARY

### GERMAN SUITED

**Salzburg Pattern** (*Salzburger Bild*)

This is an Austrian version of the Bavarian pattern and contains 36 or 32 cards (king, Ober, Unter, deuce, 10–6 or 10–7). The Salzburg pattern is always single-ended and bears no indices. Card No. 10 in each suit is numbered with a Roman numeral, whereas the rest of the cards are unnumbered.

The kings are all seated as in the Bavarian pattern, but, except for the king of leaves, they also have a shield beside them. The shield of the king of hearts shows an anchor; that of bells, the arms of Salzburg; and that of acorns, a cupid. In the Salzburg pattern the king of leaves now holds an orb in his left hand as well as a sceptre in his right hand.

There are three other main differences between the Salzburg and Bavarian patterns. In the Salzburg pattern all the swords are curved and the Ober of hearts is shown just beginning to draw his sword from his scabbard, as opposed to fully drawn. The Ober of leaves' drum is on his left side, while in the Bavarian pattern the drum is positioned on the Ober's right side.

The deuces of hearts, bells and acorns are the same for both patterns. The deuce of leaves shows a unicorn, deer and griffin or sometimes a unicorn, hart and owl.

The number cards show illustrations such as on hearts 9, a woman carrying a tub on her head and a

*Left to right*; **Rhineland Pattern, king of hearts; Salzburg, king of bells; Tyrol, Ober of acorns.**

man with a stick over his shoulder; 8, an elephant; 7, a snake and maker's initials. On bells: the 10 shows a shepherd with his sheep; 7, a peasant girl with a goat; 6, the 'Welli' card traditional in Austrian packs. It shows the bells, acorns and hearts suit signs. On acorns: 10, a man smoking a cigarette; 8, a man running with his dog and holding a hawk on a lead. On leaves: 10, a man holding a rifle with his hounds; 7, a couple fishing.

In the 36-card pack by ASS the five of each suit shows a snake and the maker's initials.

### Tyrol Pattern *(Tiroler Bild)*

The Tyrol pattern is very similar to the Salzburg pattern with the leaves' suit and the Ober and Unter of bells practically identical. Packs contain 36 single-ended cards (king, Ober, Unter, deuce, 10–6) with the traditional 'Welli' card on the 6 of bells. The Tyrol pattern was made in Bolzano and Innsbruck and was used in both north and south Tyrol but is now superseded by the Salzburg pattern.

#### Kings

All the kings sit on chairs facing the left-hand side of the card's face. The king of hearts is the only king to look over his shoulder to his left. The king of bells is usually shown in complete profile. All the kings carry

sceptres in their right hand. The kings of hearts and leaves wear long robes, while the other two kings show their legs. As in the Salzburg pattern there are shields by the side of the chairs.

#### Obers

The Ober of leaves looks down to his left and plays a drum. The Ober of bells is shown in left profile and prepares to draw his sword. The Ober of acorns looks to his right and holds a sickle in his left hand. The Ober of hearts is shown from a back view looking to his left and holding a staff in both hands.

#### Unters

The Unters of acorns and leaves look to their left. The Unter of leaves plays a flute while the Unter of acorns holds a downward-pointing sword in his left hand and a rose in his right hand. The other two Unters are shown from a right-side view. The Unter of bells holds a raised sword in his left hand and the Unter of hearts holds a staff in both hands.

#### Deuces

The deuce of acorns shows two men and a horse. The deuce of bells depicts a man, woman and cow while the deuce of leaves has a man, woman and cart. The deuce of hearts shows a shield and roses. Early versions sometimes use the Salzburg designs for the

Linz Pattern, Unter of bells.

deuces of acorns, bells, hearts and leaves.

*Other Cards*

Other interesting cards include, on hearts: 10, a lion; 7, a scroll with the maker's name; 6, an eagle on a rock. On leaves: 8, a man shooting. On acorns: 7, a man smoking a pipe and pulling a cart. On bells: 8, the tax stamp and the maker's name; 7, a man waving a banner; 6, the Welli card.

## Linz Pattern (*Linzer Bild*)

This pattern is very simple in design and was used in Austria during the mid-19th century. Packs comprise 36 or 32 single-ended cards (king, Ober, Unter, deuce, 10–7 or 10–6). The king cards have two suit signs, one at each side of the king's head. The deuces and number cards show charming vignettes. The kings wear regal medieval dress while the other court figures are dressed in 18th-century costumes.

*Kings*

The kings are all seated. The king of bells is shown in right profile, holds a sceptre in his right hand and a suit sign in his left hand. The other kings all look to their left. The kings of hearts and leaves hold sceptres in their left hand. The king of leaves also holds his suit sign in his right hand. The king of acorns holds a suit sign in his left hand.

*Obers*

The Ober of leaves shows a hunter looking to his right and holding the butt of his rifle in his left hand. The Ober of bells is a soldier wearing a sword and looking to his right. The Ober of hearts looks to his right and holds a stick in his left hand. The Ober of acorns looks to his left and prepares to draw his sword with his right hand. The two latter Obers have a Spanish appearance.

*Unters*

The Unters of acorns and bells look and are slightly turned to the left-hand side of the card's face and hold their hats in their left hand. The Unter of leaves looks to his left and holds his hat in his right hand.

*Deuces*

One of the most distinctive cards in this pack is the deuce of hearts which shows a man pushing a wheel, and this is sometimes referred to as the 'wheelpusher'. The deuce of acorns shows a pig and a flower while the deuce of bells depicts two men at a table. The deuce of leaves shows a hunter with his dog drinking at a table.

*Other Cards*

Interesting vignettes on other cards include, on hearts: 10, a jester with a bottle and a sausage; 9, a woodcutter; 8, a man playing tennis; 7, a snake and the maker's name. On acorns: 10, a lion; 9, a woman walking with an animal dressed in human clothes behind her; 6, two birds and a dog fiddling. On bells: 10, a Chinaman; 8, a rooster; 6, the Welli card and an owl.

## Imperial Trappola Pattern

As mentioned in the Italian section, trappola cards originated in Italy and spread to Germany, the Austro-Hungarian Empire, Bohemia and Silesia. The game died out of use earlier this century, with the last pack probably made in Prague in 1944. Packs comprise 36 cards (king, knight, jack, ace, 2 and 10–7) and were made with either single-ended or double-ended courts. The pack is Italian-suited and the courts are very flamboyant and colourful, with the knights and jacks of cups and swords having Russian influence in their dress. Packs can be distinguished from other Italian patterns by the Roman figure indices on the number cards and the eagle on the ace of cups. The tax stamp usually appears on the ace of swords or the 10 of coins and the maker's name is found on the 10 of coins, ace of batons, the 2 of swords or the ace of coins. The coin suitmark often resembles flowers.

*Kings*

The kings all look to their right and hold their suit sign in their right hand. The king of coins carries two suit signs, one in each hand.

*Knights*

The knight of coins rides a horse to the left-hand

side of the card's face and holds a suit sign in both hands. The other three knights ride horses to the right-hand side of the card's face. The knight of cups, who looks to his right, is the only knight who does not look in the same direction as the one in which he is travelling. The knights of swords, batons and cups carry their suit signs in their right hand. All the knights have moustaches.

*Jacks*

The jack of batons looks to his left and holds his suit sign in both hands on his right side. The other jacks look to their right and hold their suit signs in their right hands, with the jack of coins again carrying an additional suit sign in his left hand. Both the knight and jack of coins' hands are obscured by their suit signs.

*Aces*

The ace of swords is depicted with a man's hand holding the sword. The ace of cups shows an eagle. The ace of batons has the maker's name and the ace of coins shows a face of a woman wearing a bonnet and ruff.

## German Trappola Pattern

The trappola cards used in Germany are slightly different from the Austro-Hungarian pattern. The artistic execution is more restricted and traditional and all the court figures are Western and more simple in appearance. The only card which is the same is the knight of swords. In the single-ended version the kings sit on chairs. The main differences between the two patterns are that the jack of swords' sword is straight, not curved, and all the kings carry sceptres. Most of the cards have their designs reversed from the Imperial pattern, either in the direction they look or in which hand they hold their suit sign. Characteristics of the pattern are given below.

*Kings*

The kings sit on thrones and hold their suit signs: that of swords in his right hand and the other kings in their left hand. In their free hand all the kings hold sceptres. The king of coins looks to his left and the other kings look to their right. The king of coins has an extra suit sign positioned by his right hand.

*Knights*

The knights of cups and batons ride horses to the left-hand side of the card's face. Both knights hold their suit sign in their left hand and the knight of batons looks to his left. The other two knights ride horses to the right-hand side of the card's face. The knight of swords holds his suit sign in his right hand

55

*Left to right*: Four Seasons Pattern Type A, deuce of acorns; Four seasons Type B, deuce of acorns; Oedenburg /Sopron, king of bells.

and there are two 'coins' on the knight of coins' card.

*Jacks*

The jacks all look to their right, with that of coins being in profile. The jacks of cups and batons hold their suit sign in their left hand with that of batons also holding a dagger in his right hand. The jack of swords holds his suit sign in his right hand. The jack of coins has a suit sign in both hands.

### Hungarian Pattern (*Ungarisches Bild*) or Seasons Pattern

The Hungarian pattern, or Seasons, or Tell pattern, as it is commonly called, is one of the most charming of all the German-suited cards. The designs are detailed, imaginative and usually well executed. The pattern has its roots in the Austro-Hungarian empire and today is still produced in Austria, Hungary and Czechoslovakia. In Austria this pattern is often referred to as the *Kaffeehaus doppel-deutsche*, as they are used in Austrian coffee houses where they are served at a special price with coffee. Full packs comprise 36 double-ended cards (king, Ober, Unter, deuce, 10–6), although packs are also made with 32 or 24 cards (king, Ober, Unter, deuce, 10–7 or 10–9).

The reason this pack has been christened the Seasons pattern is because each deuce is devoted to one of the four seasons, the names of which are written on the deuces in either English, German, Hungarian or Czech.

Another distinctive feature of this pack is that the Unters and Obers are all named characters from Schiller's play *Wilhelm Tell*; with William Tell himself featured on the Ober of acorns. Schiller's play was first performed in Hungary in 1833 and it seems that this pack evolved very shortly after. One of the earliest known examples was made by Josef Schneider of Pest in *c*.1835, although the deuce designs may come from far older German card patterns.

Two basic varieties of the Seasons pattern exist called patterns A and B. In both patterns the kings are conventionally depicted – they are unnamed, wear crowns and ride horses. The main difference between the two patterns is the designs on the deuce cards. However, there are also a few differences between the names and designs of the jacks in the two patterns. In pattern A the Unter of hearts is shown as a rich merchant, while in pattern B he is a simple shepherd with his horn, walking stick and skull cap. The Ober of hearts in pattern A looks to his left and in pattern B to his right. The Ober of bells has his left hand raised in pattern A but in pattern B he has his hand in his bag and has a bow on his back. In pattern A the Ober of acorns (William Tell) holds his crossbow in his left hand and in pattern B in his right hand.

## Pattern A. Hungarian Proper

All the kings ride horses to the left-hand side of the card's face and carry a sceptre in their left hand. The kings of bells, acorns and hearts look in the same direction as the one in which they are riding, but that of leaves looks to his left. The court cards and deuces do not bear indices although the rest of the cards are numbered.

The names on the Obers are: Ober of hearts, Hermann Gessler; Ober of bells, Stüssi Vadász or Arnold v Melchthal; Ober of leaves, Ulrich Rudenz; Ober of acorns, Wilhelm Tell.

The names on the Unters are: Unter of hearts, Kuoni pásztor or Werner Stauffacher; Unter of bells, Itell Reding; Unter of leaves, Walter Fürst; Unter of acorns, Rudolf Harras.

The scenes on the deuces are (the names in the brackets are in the order of German, Hungarian, Czech and Slovak): on hearts, Spring (Frühling, Tavasz, Léto, Leto) showing a peasant girl picking flowers; on bells, Summer (Sommer, Nyár, Jaro, Jar) showing a peasant sitting and holding a scythe; on leaves, Autumn (Herbst, Ósz, Podzin, Jesen) showing a peasant sitting drinking by a tub; on acorns, Winter (Winter, Tél, Zima, Zima) showing a peasant warming himself by a fire.

Most of the number cards show small illustrations which include: on hearts, 8, a man rowing; 7, a mounted nobleman with an arrow in his heart; on bells: 7, William Tell's famous crossbow and apple (sometimes only the maker's name).

## Pattern B. Austro-Czech

The kings in this pattern are the same as for pattern A, except that the king of acorns now looks to his left.

In this pattern the Unter of hearts is called Kuoni d. Hirt and the Ober of bells is called Stüssi d. Flurschütz.

The designs on the deuces are: on hearts (Spring) a peasant girl holding a basket of flowers; on bells (Summer) a peasant girl holding a scythe and a sheaf of corn; on leaves (Autumn) two peasant boys pressing grapes; on acorns (Winter) an old woman carrying sticks of firewood on her back and holding a walking stick.

The designs on the number cards are the same but they have two more designs: on the 8 of leaves can now be seen a stone fortress and on the 8 of acorns a lake, mountain and tower.

Packs made in Czechoslovakia no longer carry titles on the deuces and sometimes not even on the Ober and Unter cards. In packs made for use in Austria there is an extra card, the 6 of bells (the Welli card) which shows a heart, acorn and bell suitmark.

## Oedenburg/Sopron Pattern

This pattern has a number of outstanding characteristics. The kings ride horses and there are vignettes on the deuces and most of the number cards. Packs comprise 32 single-ended cards (king, Ober, Unter, deuce, 10–7) and they were used in several parts of Hungary.

The kings wear crowns although they are not easily apparent. The other court figures wear hats and some of the courts have Russian-type features.

### Kings

The kings all ride horses to the left-hand side of the card's face. They all look the same way in which they are travelling and hold sceptres in their right hand. The king of hearts has a moustache and turban-type head gear.

### Obers

The Obers are dressed in various local costumes. The Obers of leaves, hearts and bells look to their right. In his right hand, the Ober of leaves holds a slim downward pointing sword, that of hearts a pickaxe and that of bells his suit sign. The Ober of acorns looks down to his left, holds a stick in his right hand and wears a sword.

### Unters

The Unter of bells is full-faced, while the other Unters look to their right. The Unter of leaves plays a drum while the Unter of bells plays a flute and wears a sword. The Unter of acorns holds a bird in his left hand and a staff over his right shoulder. There is a flower growing in the background of the Unter of hearts' card.

### Deuces

The deuce of acorns shows a lion holding two shields. Above him is a ribbon carrying the maker's name and a crown surmounted by an orb. The deuce of bells shows Bacchus astride a barrel holding a wine goblet in his right hand and three sausages on a stick in his left hand. The deuce of hearts shows a lion rampant holding a shield. The deuce of leaves simply shows a very elaborate sword.

### Other Cards

Among the vignettes featured on other cards are: bells: 10, two lions sword-fighting; 9, a donkey; 8, a bird with a worm in its mouth; 7, a lion's face. On leaves: 10, a dog chasing a deer. On hearts: 10, a fox pushing a pig in a wheelbarrow; 9, a man; 8, two birds. On acorns: 8, two dogs.

## Lemberger Pattern

This is undoubtedly the most distinctive and origi-

*Left to right*: **Lemberger Pattern, Ober of acorns; Austrian Large Crown, king of spades; Austrian Small Crown, jack of clubs.**

nal of all the German-suited standard patterns and because it is so easily recognizable it needs little explanation. Packs contain 32 single-ended cards (king, Ober, Unter, deuce, 10–7) and were used in the eastern areas of the Austro-Hungarian Empire and later Poland. The example I have seen is by Piatnik, who at one time recorded them as 'Moorish' cards. This is a fitting title as the characters portrayed on the court and number cards show Moors, Russians, Negroes and Chinese, and only a few Western-type figures. A distinctive feature of the pack is that the kings ride horses (to the left-hand side of the card's face) and carry sceptres; that of leaves in this left hand and the other kings in their right hands. The sceptres carried by the kings of leaves and hearts are surmounted by crescent moons.

The deuces are also particularly striking in this pack. The deuce of bells shows a young peasant girl with a basket of flowers balanced on her head kneeling to pick up another basket of flowers from the ground. The deuce of hearts shows a table-like platform on which a loving couple are on a sleigh which is being pulled by two small birds. The deuce of acorns shows a Negro and a large monumental cup. The deuce of leaves also shows a Negro who is holding a torch-like object from which sprout the leaves, suit signs. Most

of the other number cards are preoccupied with showing Chinese and Negroes in their natural habitat. The 7 of hearts, however, shows two men (16th-century Spaniards?) by a barrel drinking and the 9 of hearts shows a Western fisherman standing on the beach by his boat with an oar in his hand.

In the Piatnik pack the maker's name appears on the deuce of hearts, the seven of bells and, together with the tax stamp, on the eight of bells. The maker's address is found on the deuce of acorns.

## FRENCH SUITED

Today there are two types of French-suited cards in use in Austria, the large-crown pattern (pattern A) and the small-crown pattern (pattern B). The names arise because the crowns and hats worn in pattern A either touch or go beyond the card's frame line. In both packs all the court figures wear head gear and ornate costumes. Packs are made with either 52 or 32 double-ended cards (king, queen, jack, ace, 10–2 or 10–7). As with all the other double-ended cards used in Germany and Austria the cards are divided by a horizontal line.

### Austrian Large-Crown Pattern (Pattern A)

Packs bear either no indices or the German ones of K

*Left to right*: single-ended Swiss Jass Pattern, king of shields; double-ended Swiss Jass Pattern, Under of shields; Swiss Piquet, jack of spades.

D B. This pattern is currently made in Austria, Italy and Czechoslovakia.

*Kings*

The kings of spades and diamonds look to their right and carry a sceptre in their left hand. The kings of clubs and hearts look to their left and in their left hand hold a sceptre and scroll respectively.

*Queens*

All the queens look to their right, with the faces of the queens of clubs and diamonds being in profile. The queen of spades holds a flower in her left hand, while the other queens hold a flower in their right hand.

*Jacks*

The jacks of spades and diamonds look to their left and hold halberds in their left hand. The jack of hearts also looks to his left but holds a baton in his left hand which in some packs carries a pennant. His right hand is on his sword hilt. The jack of clubs' face is shown in left profile and he holds a sceptre in his left hand.

The maker's name and tax stamp are found on the ace of hearts.

### Austrian Small-Crown Pattern (Pattern B)

*Kings*

All the kings carry sceptres in their left hand. The kings of spades and clubs look to their right while those of hearts and diamonds look to their left. The king of spades wears a sash inscribed with the maker's name.

*Queens*

All the queens are slightly turned and look to the left-hand side of the card's face, with the faces of the queens of clubs, diamonds and hearts seen in profile. In their right hand the queens of hearts and diamonds hold a flower; the queen of clubs a mirror; and the queen of spades a basket of flowers.

*Jacks*

The jacks of spades and clubs look to their right (with the jack of clubs' face being in profile) and carry halberds in their left hand. The jack of diamonds also carries a halberd in his left hand but looks to his left. The jack of hearts looks to his left and carries a baton with a pennant on it which is either blank or bears the name of the manufacturer's town.

## SWITZERLAND

### SWISS SUITED

Although Swiss cards originally bore Germanic suits, by the 15th century the Swiss adopted the two new suits of flowers and shields and other new characteristics which make them easily distinguishable.

Known as Jass cards, patterns produced today retain the 'banner card' which was dropped by Germany in the 16th century and the overall designs are medieval in appearance. The court cards, which are named, are the king, Ober and Under (rather than Unter as in German packs) and as in German packs the suit signs on the king and Ober cards are in the top half of the card and for the Under card in the bottom half of the card.

## Single-ended Jass cards

Unfortunately single-ended Jass cards stopped being produced earlier this century. The pack comprises 48 or 36 cards (king, Ober, Under, deuce, 10–3 or 10–6). The cards are without indices and the flower and acorn suit designs have stems on them. The maker's name is found on the deuce of bells and shields.

### Kings

The kings of acorns, shields and bells are shown in a left-side view sitting on chairs. The kings of acorns and bells hold their suit sign in their right hand. The king of shields holds a goblet in his right hand and has his suit sign in the top left hand corner of the card and a canopy over his chair. The king of flowers stands, looks to his right and holds his suit sign in his right hand. All the kings wear crowns, and the king of acorns has a beard.

### Obers

All the Obers are shown in a side view facing the right-hand side of the card's face. The Obers of flowers and shields hold their suit sign in their left hand; the Ober of bells holds his suit sign in his right hand and smokes a pipe. The Ober of acorns also smokes a pipe held in his left hand and his suit sign is in the top left hand corner of the card's face.

### Unders

The Unders of acorns and flowers hold their suit signs in their right hand and look to their right, with the Under of flowers' face being in profile. He smokes a pipe. The Under of shields is shown in a side view walking to the left-hand side of the card's face with a feather in his mouth and a letter in his right hand. His suit sign is at the bottom of the card. The Under of bells is one of the most distinctive cards in this pattern, being dressed as a jester. He holds his suit sign at his right side but in his left hand, which is therefore extended over his body. His right hand holds a pyramid-shaped object.

## Double-Ended Jass Cards

The kings and Unders are the same in the double-ended pack as in the single-ended pack, except that all the details normally shown at the bottom half of the card in the single-ended version are omitted in the double-ended pattern. Two differences are that the feather in the mouth of the Under of shields is now placed between his ears in the double-ended pack and he holds his suit sign as well. The king of bells has a beard. The Obers in the double-ended pack have changed direction and now all face the left-hand side of the card's face and the Ober of shields smokes a cigarette.

Müller has made a modern patience-size, double-ended pack where the court figures are more modernistic and geometric in style. Most double-ended packs bear indices.

## FRENCH SUITED

### Ticinese Pattern

This is identical to the Milanese or Lombard pattern of Northern Italy.

### Piquet Pattern

The French-suited piquet pack used in Switzerland is virtually the same as the French-suited German Berliner pattern, although the cards do not bear indices and are far less ornate in appearance. The main differences between the two patterns are that the king of clubs does not hold a shield in his right hand, while the jack of spades holds a shield on his right arm instead of holding the hilt of his sword. The queen of diamonds looks to her left instead of her right and the queen of clubs looks to her right instead of left.

The maker's name is found on the queen of spades and the cards are double-ended.

# France and other countries

WITH France's long-standing reputation as a country where beauty, art and culture are part of the national heritage, it is not surprising that their playing cards are among the most beautiful in the world. Whereas today many fashion designers copy and modify the 'Paris' originals, so it was that at one time most of Europe was influenced by the different playing card designs France produced.

The first written mention of playing cards in France is an entry in the records of Laurent Aycardi, a notary of Marseilles, written on 30 August 1381. The very next year an ordinance issued in Lille prohibited gaming with dice, draughts and playing cards.

It can be supposed from these dates and events that playing cards had been only recently introduced into France, possibly by way of the Belgians who in turn might have received their first cards from Germany. So, although the long-standing myth that playing cards are of French origin has been discredited, it is still to the credit of the resourceful French artists that they lost no time in capitalizing on the new invention; and card manufacturing centres were quickly established.

By 1393 the game of cards was known to the bourgeoisie, while by c.1397 cards had infected every sector of the community; with a Paris decree prohibiting their use on working days. Playing cards were also banned by the Bishop of Langres in 1404.

Probably the cards then used in France were of the German-suited variety, with the French suits of *coeurs* (hearts), *piques* (spades), *trèfles* (clubs) and *carreaux* (diamonds) appearing in the first quarter of the 15th century.

The design of the suit signs played an important rôle in the future of the French playing card industry. In contrast to the suit designs of Italy and Germany, the French suits are clear, simple and compact. Added to this is the innovation of using only two colours – red and black. The result is an easy, quick and cheap design that eventually enabled the French to produce more cards per day than their competitors. In the long term this enabled France to cater for larger export markets. This led to the eventual adoption of the French suit signs by countries such as Britain, America, the Low Countries and Russia.

France also produced a large number of non-standard playing cards which were adopted in other countries, including one of the most famous series of educational cards of all time. So beautiful and original were their designs that they were continually republished in sheet, book and pack form in France, Germany, the Low Countries and Italy for more than fifty years after their first publication in 1644. The idea to produce the cards is said to have come from Cardinal Mazarin, French Minister of State, under whose charge was the young Louis XIV. Mazarin had been

Left to right: *Le Jeu des Reynes Renommées* by Jean Desmarests, 1644; *Jeu de Géographie* by Desmarests, *c*. 1644; French heraldry pack by Claude Oronce Fine, M. de Brianville, *c*. 1676–89.

worried about the young King's lack of interest in academic study, so he asked Jean Desmarests to prepare a series of games which had some educational qualities. Desmarests designed the cards and employed Stefano Della Bella, a famous Florentine artist and engraver, to finish the illustrations and engravings. Four different packs were produced.

The first pack to be issued was *Le Jeu des Fables ou de la Metamorphose*. These were intended to instruct the king in ancient mythology and fable, and are arrayed with an assortment of gods, demigods, goddesses and heroes of antiquity. Each of the 52 cards has a picture subject occupying the top half of the card, below which is the title and a descriptive text. The suit marks and values are shown in the bottom right-hand corner. In this pack the hearts represent Jupiter, Juno and Mars; diamonds, Saturn, Venus and Apollo;

spades, Pluto, Diane and Bacchus; clubs, Neptune, Pallas and Mercury.

The next pack was *Le Jeu des Rois de France* or *Le Jeu de l'Histoire de France* and shows various kings from Pharamond to Louis XIV. Again each card features a portrait of the person named and described underneath. In the top left hand corner is the particular king's number in the pack's sequence and in the right-hand corner the number of years in his reign.

The third pack published was *Le Jeu des Reynes Renommées*, in which famous female figures from Dido to Queen Elizabeth are displayed. The personalities are classified as: Saints and Holy women, Good women, Wise women, Clever women, Celebrated women, Brave women, Happy women, Cruel women, Licentious women, Capricious women, Unfortunate women. There are 52 cards which have

*Opposite above:* *Das Festung Bause Spiel* by Peter Schencken, Amsterdam, *c*. 1700 which is a copy of the French pack *Jeu des Fortifications*.

*Opposite belo w:* *Das Krieg Spiel* by Peter Schencken, Amsterdam, *c*. 1700 which is a copy of the French pack *Jeu de la Guerre*.

the same format as the other game packs.

The last of the games was *Le Jeu de la Géographie* showing figures in national costumes as personifications of different parts of the world. Again underneath is an account of the countries represented.

All of the games were issued with a title card and in some of the packs the court values are indicated by R D VA, i.e. the jack and ace are together on one card. They were originally sold by Henry Le Gras of Paris.

This series of cards started a whole new avalanche of playing card designs, with the card's face being employed to instruct in many useful areas of everyday life. But the French, not content to be the originators of just one new idea for cards, also produced in 1658 the first pack of cards devoted to heraldry.

The man responsible for this heraldry pack was Claude Oronce Fine, M de Brianville of Lyons. The designs met with a warm reception, and were produced in many editions in such places as France, Italy, Holland, England, Scotland, Germany and Spain. The format of the cards is similar to the Desmarests cards, with a drawing and instructive text, and the suit mark in the upper left-hand corner.

The cards show the armorial bearings of the kingdoms and provinces of France, Italy, Spain, England, Germany and Scandinavia. On the king of clubs or money (depending on the edition) was featured the coat of arms of the reigning Pope.

Another notable heraldry pack published in 1692 was *Le Jeu de Cartes du Blason contenant les Armes des Princes des Principales parties de l'Europe par Père C.F. Menestrier*. Issued by Thomas Almaury of Lyons the suits are: lions for Spain and Portugal, roses for Italy, fleur-de-lis for France and eagles for Germany and Flanders. The court cards show portraits of the European rulers including Louis XIV. The pip cards show their armorial bearings. The value of the cards is indicated by the number of shields featured on a card.

Continuing a military theme, France can also be credited with having produced some of the first packs to feature war as the subject matter. The two earliest war packs are *Jeu des Fortifications* and *Jeu de la Guerre*. Both were published by Daumont.

The *Jeu des Fortifications* was designed by Gilles de la Boissière of Paris in 1668, and was also issued in Amsterdam, Germany and Spain. The cards, which are in black and white, offer instructions on military engineering science. Diagrams in the lower half of the cards illustrate various fortresses, with a title and a descriptive text above. The pack was made by I. Mariette and formally dedicated to the 'illustrious youth of the Royal Military Academy'. The other pack, *Jeu de la Guerre*, was also issued in Paris in 1668 by Gilles de la Boissière, and engraved by Pierre le Pautre. Copies are known to have been issued in Amsterdam and Germany. Each of the 52 cards shows a military operation in the top half of the card with a title and text underneath. The suit signs and values are in the upper left-hand corner.

Geographical packs were also beginning to be produced in France at this time. Pierre Duval, the Royal Geographer, published a pack called *Les Tables de Géographie* in 1669 which not only classified countries but also cities, rivers and other important geographical phenomena. The denomination is shown in the middle of a border at the top of the card together with the suit sign. On the court cards can be seen medallion portraits of the respective countries' rulers. Pierre Duval also published the *Jeu des Nations* pack in *c*.1684.

Another geographical pack of this period has Africa on the spade suit, hearts devoted to Europe, diamonds to Asia and clubs to America. It also includes the longitudes and latitudes of every part of the world, and the number of kingdoms and provinces as specified by the geographer Nicholas Sanson.

Among the transformation packs produced in France is an interesting set of the first quarter of the 19th century which satirizes the dominant political party of the time by attacking the various reactionary newspapers in circulation. The king of clubs shows the editor of *Journal des Débats* carrying two large bags called Empire and Débats. Through his legs can be seen two donkeys caressing. The queen of clubs personifies the *Gazette* and shows an elderly lady seated at a table looking up at a caged magpie. The jack of clubs is particularly amusing and shows Talleyrand, under the title of *Clopineau*. This pack, and another transformation pack called *Cartes à Rire* are attributed to Baron

*Opposite above, left to right: Cartes à Rire*, one of the two transformation packs attributed to Baron Louis Atthalin, *c*. 1819, the courts in this pack have a theatre theme; the 'Joan of Arc' transformation pack, so called because Joan of Arc is featured on the Queen of Spades, by B.P. Grimaud, Paris, *c*. 1856.

*Opposite below, left to right*: French costume pack *Jeu Impérial*, showing the four empires: British, French, Austrian and Russian, by B.P. Grimaud, Paris, *c*. 1855; *Jeu des Cartes Historiques*, by B.P. Grimaud, Paris, *c*. 1880.

VAUDEVILLE.

Louis XIV

32-card French léger-de-main cards showing grotesque figures, *c*. 1800.

French 'translucent' court card: when held to the light a hidden pornographic scene is revealed, *c*. 1850.

Louis Atthalin.

A famous transformation pack, originally made in France by B.P. Grimaud in 1856, but copied in Leipzig and Darmstadt, is the 'Joan of Arc' transformation pack. It is so called because Joan of Arc is featured on the queen of spades. Also on the court cards can be seen: Cupid, an Indian chief, a medieval king, a ballet dancer, market women and various 'servants' on the jacks of each suit. On the number cards can be seen amusing scenes embracing all walks of life, with soldiers getting drunk, aristocrats fighting duels, Orientals smoking pipes and entertainers performing tricks.

During the early 19th century a variety of other types of non-standard packs were introduced by France, including music, costume, botany, natural history and léger-de-main cards. The latter show two figures, one at each end of the card, with their heads meeting in the centre to give the appearance of many faces pointing in various directions. But the most unusual breed of French playing card to make its début in the 19th century was the transparent or translucent card. Not much is known about the history of these cards, though one of the most comprehensive

books on the subject is *Translucent Playing-Cards* by Trevor Denning. It is thought that they originated in Paris in the early 1800s. Most known examples date from between 1830 and 1890.

Although there are different categories of transparent playing cards, their basic characteristic is that when held up to the light a hidden picture is revealed. This effect is achieved by making the card out of two pieces of paper, rather than the normal three. On the top piece of paper is printed the card's face design with an extra design printed on the back. This printed piece of paper is then glued on to a second plain piece of paper. The actual picture that is revealed can be completely innocent, mildly erotic or pornographic. Sometimes it is only the number cards which contain a hidden picture. When the court cards contain a hidden design, a common practice is for the figure in the hidden picture to be actively and sexually involved with the apparently ordinary, printed court figure. Another example is the one which shows a perfectly respectable king when first looking at the court card, but on holding it to the light one observes that he is in fact only half dressed.

Most of these cards are of cheap manufacture,

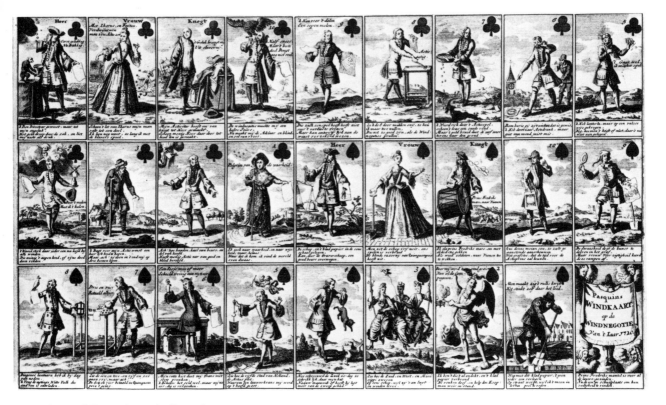

Uncut sheet of 'Pasquins Windkaart', *c*. 1720.

intended to be sold as novelties. Indeed, sometimes the number cards contain an assortment of suits. For example the six in the black suit may feature three clubs and three spades. It is therefore obvious that they were not intended for ordinary play.

Due to the high taxes placed on playing cards in France during the 16th century, many French card makers emigrated to other countries, there to start up their industry again. This, together with the large export orders the French developed, meant that the French playing card designs were the most widely circulated. So it is quite natural that other countries such as Russia, Holland, Belgium and Poland modelled their playing cards on those of France. Today these countries have standard patterns which are merely variations of the French Paris pattern, differing slightly in details and colouring. However, it is also possible to observe the strong Germanic influence in the actual artistic interpretations.

## LOW COUNTRIES

The first evidence of playing cards in the Low Coun-

tries is in a document in the Audit Office Register in the State Archives in Brussels, dated 14 May, 1379. The document describes the purchase of cards by the Duke Wenceslas of Luxemburg. The same year the Duke commissioned his court painter Ingel Van der Noet to paint a pack of cards at a price of '2 sheep' – the equivalent today of 20,000 Belgian francs.

As in France playing cards quickly became popular in the Low Countries and in 1391 a police ordinance in Lille (at that time a Flemish town) prohibited people from playing cards.

One of the first card industries to be set up in the Low Countries was in Tournai in the 15th century, where it is recorded that Michel Noel and Philippe du Bos made cards. In those days to produce cards one had to be a member of the Painters' Guild, for which one paid a fee of 40 sols Tournaisian and 10 sols Tournaisian for enrolment. Between 1427 and 1537 26 master cardmakers and 37 apprentices were listed.

During the 16th century, Antwerp became the focal point for playing cards. Cards from here were exported to London, Cologne, Frankfurt, Nuremberg, etc. Two of the most noted card makers of that time were Robert Péril and Jean Maillart. The latter exported cards under such pseudonyms as Pierre Haynault and Jean Charpentier.

As we approach the next century we find a new card-producing centre – Namur; although cards were also produced in Brussels, Ypres, Courtrai, Nieuport, Ostend, Louvain and Ghent.

Not many early cards from the Low Countries have survived. One interesting pack made in Antwerp c.1666 is called the 'Spiritual Card Game with Hearts Trumps' or 'Game of Love' by the Rev. Father Joseph of St. Barbara. The card game comes in book form and features only the hearts' suit. Full of religious knowledge and implications, the pack has a king card which shows saints kneeling before God. The queen shows two saints before Mary, while the jack shows people before the throne of Christ. The number cards show various scenes relating to Christian doctrine which correspond to the number of the card. For example, on card No. 10 are the Ten Commandments and card No. 3 shows the Holy Trinity.

The Low Countries' most notable contribution to the history of playing cards is the series of 18th-century political packs. One of the earliest examples of these is an 'Anti-Papal' pack of c.1719. Each card has an illustration relating to papal scandals with a caption at the bottom of the card. The value is indicated by a suit and number or name. Pope Joan is featured on the three of hearts, Luther and Calvin on the club suit, while the spades are devoted to Pasquier Quesnel and the Jansenist controversy.

In 1720 two packs featuring Bubble Companies were produced, one called April-Kaart or Kaart Spel van Momus naar de Nieuwste Mode and the other Pasquin's Windkaart op de Windnegotie van't Iaar, 1720. The two sets are identical in that they feature the same illustrations of a scandal surrounding bogus companies established in c.1720, but the captions at the bottom of the cards differ. Among the ventures featured are John Law and the Mississippi venture, the South Sea and West India company.

Other interesting early Dutch cards include Mortier's Le Jeu des Metamorphoses d'Ovide of c.1705 and Le Jeu Hommes et Femmes Illustres, c.1700, which shows busts of Greek and Roman personalities. Also by Mortier are Le Jeu de Boufon, c.1690, and Le Jeu de quatre partes du Monde c.1700.

By 1826 the main card-producing centre had moved to Turnhout, from where playing cards were later exported to, among other places, England, France, Germany, Holland, Spain, Portugal and East Asia. The standard cards at that time bore little originality and many card producers used the same designs, and did not put their names on their cards. This makes it very difficult to identify cards and makers.

P.J. Brepols was one of the first of the Turnhout playing card makers. He began his career as an apprentice in Pieter Corbels' printing shop in Louvain. In 1796 the firm moved to Turnhout, and in 1800, on Corbels' death, Brepols took over the modest business. Brepols managed to expand the business to cover all areas of the paper trade, including prayer books, administrative printed matter, book-bindings, banners, childrens' picture books and holy pictures. At this time he mainly bought his playing cards from suppliers but by 1827 his letterhead carried the inscription 'Manufacturer of Playing Cards'.

In 1887 the company produced the Cartes Union to commemorate the 50th anniversary of Belgian independence. The courts show kings and queens of the ruling house and their Austrian kindred. The aces show important events in Austrian history, while the backs feature the Belgian coats-of-arms and the motto L'Union Fait la Force. By 1880 he produced both single- and double-ended cards for the English market with the 'Great Mogul', 'The Valiant Highlander' and 'The Steamboat' trademarks.

Antoon van Genechten was another Turnhout card maker, formerly associated with J.E. Glenisson. Van Genechten specialized in exports and in the 1850s he was the sole owner of the Belgian patent to export cards with round corners and gold and silver edging. He also started printing cards with Chinese- and

---

*Opposite above, left to right:* **The 'Florentine' pack by Philibert of Paris, c. 1955; non-standard Russian jubilee pack made in 1967 to commemorate 150 years of Russian card making; non-standard Russian 'Souvenir' pack showing court figures in Slav costumes, GKM, Leningrad, c. 1930.**

*Opposite centre, left to right:* **Bulgarian non-standard 52–card pack, the courts showing Bulgarian kings and queens and the aces Bulgarian towns, c. 1880; a French prisoner-of-war card made from bone during the Napoleonic wars; Czechoslovakian pack showing Czech heroes, by Piatnik, c. 1939.**

*Opposite below, left to right: Union fait la Force* **pack depicting leaders and soldiers of the Allies with Hitler as the joker, by Maesmaekers, Turnhout, 1945;** *Cartes Moyen-Age,* **a 52-card non-standard pack with courts in medieval costume, by Daveluy, Bruges, c. 1880;** *Le Jeu des Allies* **pack by Maesmaekers, 1945.**

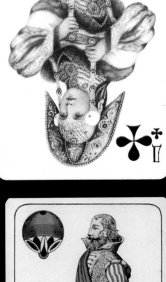

*Left to right:* **German-suited, 36-card Russian 'Circus' pack by the Russian Playing Card Monopoly, *c.* 1898; Bohemian pack with the suits of barrels, gems, corn and leaves, by M. Severy Nastupce, Prague, *c.* 1890; Polish pack showing courts as Polish heroes and scenic aces, by Piatnik, *c.* 1930.**

Japanese-type paintings in 1868.

The firm of the Mesmaekers brothers, 1859–1968, of Turnhout, introduced in 1886 cards with figures drawn from Hindu mythology, known as the 'Hindu Fables'. These were mainly exported to the British colonies until 1913. They also produced in 1870 a pack showing 'pin-up' girls. These had a miniature playing card in the right hand corner taken from the Hindu Fables pack. They first used a joker in 1882 christened 'The Little Joker'.

Today the S.A. Carta Mundi firm (1970) holds the playing card monopoly in Belgium. It is an amalgamation of all the playing card factories that managed to survive up until 1970. The most common pattern now found in Belgium and Holland is an adaptation of the Paris pattern.

## RUSSIA

Russian playing card history begins at the close of the 18th century. Originally the playing cards used in Russia were of the Germanic type, with German suit marks, but gradually French-suited cards gained the upper hand. Nineteenth-century Russian cards are often recognized as being the most beautiful and eleg-

ant ever produced, which makes it all the sadder that so few examples have survived. It is even very hard to obtain modern packs.

In 1842 Thomas De La Rue obtained the job of Superintendent of the Russian Playing Card Monopoly for his brother Paul. Supposedly the money raised from the profits of the company was to go towards the running costs of the Russian Foundling Hospital. The hospital's seal, a pelican in her piety, is featured on the ace of diamonds under the Russian eagle. There is a 36-card Russian pack in the British Museum, *c.*1820, with German suitmarks, where the pelican is featured on the ace of bells and the ace of acorns while the Imperial Eagle appears on the aces of hearts and leaves.

Russia's most famous pack of non-standard playing cards is a 19th century pack of geographical cards. Each card is divided into four sections showing: the arms of a Russian province, the suitmark, a list of the principal towns and villages, and a figure in the costume of a particular province. On the back of each card is a map of the province in question. The pack contains fifty-two cards plus six extra cards showing surrounding states. Catherine Hargrave in her book on playing cards (*see* Bibliography) gives a full description of this pack.

Left to right: Belgian *Quatre Partes du Monde*, 48-card Spanish-suited pack, the coins represent Asia, cups Africa, swords, Europe and batons America, by Daveluy, Bruges, *c*. 1870; miniature 52-card pack from the Netherlands showing historical figures *c*. 1720; Slovenian 'Patriotic' pack, the suits are sword handles, leaves, banner points and shields with axes, by Fran Cebolki & dr, Ljubljana, *c*. 1900.

## MODERN CARDS

One of the most acclaimed packs of the 20th century is *Le Florentin* pack made in 1955 by Philibert of Paris. The double-ended courts show two different pictures of people in rich Renaissance costume, in mildly erotic but very artistic and classic poses.

Philibert produced a number of now famous packs in the 1950s. These include *Les Mousquetaires* designed by A. Dubout in 1954, which shows humorous caricatures; and the can-can pack, designed by Monique Arietti in 1955. This pack shows amusing representations of can-can dancers and Lautrec-type figures of the turn of this century.

An amusing political pack was produced in France in 1976 showing caricatures of President Giscard d'Estaing which so displeased the President that he had it banned within months of its publication. The same makers produced another political pack in book form, where the four suits represent the four political parties: clubs, Gaullist; diamonds, Communist; spades, Giscardians; and hearts, Socialists. Each of the court cards bears a caricature of a prominent member from the particular party. The suit signs incorporate: clubs, the cross of Lorraine; diamonds, hammer and sickle; spades, Giscard's face; and hearts, a rose. In 1969, Dorchy issued the *Cartes de Siné* where caricatures of de Gaulle appear on the kings and queens, while the jacks feature his ministers.

The Belgians produced some memorable packs concerned with the First and Second World Wars. Brepols of Turnhout issued two packs in 1919, *Guerre Mondiale* Nos. 1 and 2. The first has the courts showing kings, queens, presidents and generals of the Allied countries including George V and Haig, with battle scenes on the aces. The second pack features some different personalities on the court cards such as Pétain and Kitchener and has scenes associated with the Armistice on the aces.

The winning of the Second World War was celebrated by Mesmaekers of Turnhout by the *Union Fait la Force* pack. The court cards show the heads of state of the allied countries together with their flags. In the same year, 1945, the company also issued *Le Jeu des Allies V*. Again the kings show the heads of state of the allied countries. The queens portray patriotic symbols and slogans. The jacks show soldiers. The flags of the allies are on the aces. The joker depicts Hitler!

An interesting political pack from Belgium is the *Cartes de la Démocratie Socialiste* by F. Buelens. On the

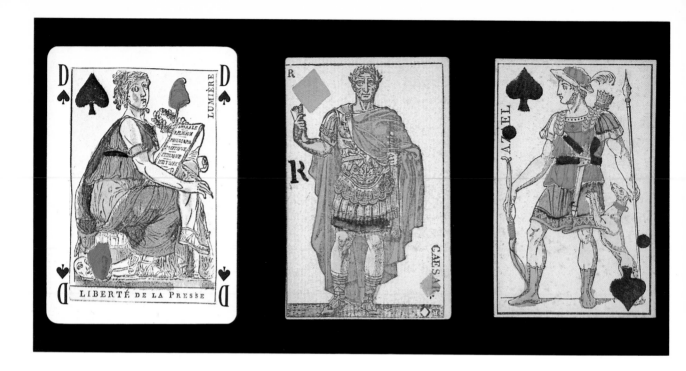

*Left to right*; three French Revolutionary packs; a pack dated *c*. 1793 where the courts are replaced by Génies, Libertés and Egalités; a pack commissioned by Napoleon from the designer David, 1810; pack made for export to Italy by Gatteaux, *c*. 1810.

---

jacks and kings are featured two named, well-known male workers or socialists. The queens show two famous socialist women and, with a touch of the macabre, the aces show bones. The back shows a freedom fighter.

Russia's best known modern pack is the 'Anti-Religions' deck of *c*.1930. The court cards satirize the world religions and depict such subjects as a nun praying to God but secretly having erotic fantasies. The hearts represent the Catholics; diamonds, Jews; clubs, Greek Orthodox; and the spades, the Eastern religions.

About the same time the Russians also issued a 'Literary' pack, where the courts of each suit are devoted to a literary work such as *1001 Nights*. The pack was issued with both English and Russian indices. But Russia's latest masterpiece is a pack of 1967 issued to commemorate 150 years of Russian card making. The cards are on a black background with the fanciful courts coloured in striking reds, blues, greens and yellows, as well as having generous sprinklings of gold. The backs are coloured similarly, producing a most original and beautiful effect.

Poland and Czechoslovakia have produced a

number of packs showing historical personalities and views of cities. An interesting 'Patriotic' pack of *c*.1890 has the four suits of garnets, wheat sheaves, barrels and leaves. The court cards show historical figures and the number cards show buildings. A patriotic Cego pack issued in Slovenia at the beginning of the century has the suit marks of sword handles, leaves, banner points and shields with axes. The court cards show historical and military scenes. Czechoslovakia issued an 'Animal Skat' pack in about 1925 in which animal caricatures are featured on the court cards.

Various non-standard costume packs have been made and used in the Russian satellite countries. One pack used in Poland, Latvia, and probably elsewhere, has all the kings carrying orbs, the queens flowers, and the jacks shields in their right hands. The court figures are dressed in elegant costumes of the region, with the king of spades looking very much like a Mongol. In this pack the indices are the traditional K Д B although they are also known with K Q J. The ace is lettered T and has a design at the top and bottom reminiscent of the embroidery produced in the Soviet states. The colours are well-executed, but have a slightly pale, washed-out effect.

Reproduction of the *Jeu Bonaparte* originally made in France *c*. 1858. The modern edition is by Boechat Frères, Bordeaux.

French *Jeu des Drapeaux* 32 cards plus title card pack, *c*. 1814.

# STANDARD PATTERNS

## *FRANCE*

### FRENCH SUITED

As more and more card manufacturing industries were set up in France, so individual patterns began to emerge, until by the 18th century there were at least twelve different designs in production. Although this may have pleased the majority of people, it was viewed with great disapproval by the tax collectors.

The French government, realizing that vast profits were made by playing card manufacturers, placed a tax on playing cards in the 16th century. However, many of the playing cards produced did not necessarily feature the maker's name or address, and because there were no allocated patterns, the tax collector had difficulty keeping track of the amount a card producer was supposed to pay. In 1613 Louis XIII made it a law that the maker's name had to be featured on the jack of clubs, which was an attempt to resolve the situation for the tax collector. But unfortunately by this time

many French card makers, not wanting the government to have such a large percentage of their profits, had started to emigrate to others countries such as Switzerland, Germany and the Low Countries.

The tax was abolished later in the 17th century and the playing card industry flourished once again. This did not last. In 1701 a tax, at the rate of 18 deniers a pack, was re-introduced. To make life easier for the tax collectors, the Controller-General of France established nine card-tax regions. These regions were: Paris, Lyons, Burgundy, Auvergne, Limousin, Dauphiné, Provence, Languedoc and Guyenne. Each region was allocated a certain pattern, which the card makers could not modify or diverge from by law.

The tax that brought about the use of standard regional designs was abolished in 1719, re-introduced in 1751 and again disappeared in 1791 to be replaced by an import duty.

The standard regional patterns devised were not new as such, but based on designs already in use in France for some 200 years. In fact, although they differed from each other in certain details by which they can be identified, they all had a common ancestor and contained many of the same basic 'ingredients' simply re-arranged in varying orders or in different suits. For example, as Sylvia Mann points out in her book on playing cards, a king carrying a hawk is personified as the king of clubs in Auvergne, the king of diamonds in Dauphiné, and the king of hearts in Lyons and Provence. Similarly the king carrying an axe is featured as the king of clubs in Provence, the king of spades in Languedoc, the king of coins in Brittany and hearts in Britain. Most of the early French regional patterns contain 52 single-ended cards (king, queen, jack, ace, 10–2), although sometimes 32 card packs are found. The French suit signs are hearts, spades, diamonds and clubs. From *c*.1827 the Paris pattern was made double-ended and some Auvergne patterns are also known to have been made double-ended.

The regional designs continued to be produced until about 1780 when the Paris pattern was adopted as the national design. The only standard patterns that have survived today in France are the Aluette, Catalan and Paris patterns.

Another upheaval which affected the French card making industry was the French Revolution. With the great change in French society, it is not surprising that the court cards were a target for re-modelling. At first, the same playing card blocks were used, but with certain modifications, such as the removal of the crowns on the kings and queens.

Later new designs were introduced, one of the earliest being a pack designed by Saint-Simon, who, in keeping with current ideals, changed the kings to genii, the queens to freedoms, and the jacks to equalities. The aces represent law. The kings represent the genius of war, peace, the arts and trade. The queens represent the freedoms of marriage, religion, profession and the press. The male cards portray soldiers in costume.

Another famous Revolutionary pack, also made in 1793 (year II), was designed by Gayant. This time the kings are replaced by the philosophers Voltaire, La Fontaine, Molière and Rousseau. The queens are the Virtues of temperance, wisdom, and strength and the poor jacks are merely soldiers of the Revolution. The jacks get something of a better deal in another Revolutionary pack where they are featured as Hannibal, Decius Mus, Horace and Mucius Scaevola. The kings this time are Solon the Wise, J.J. Rousseau, Cato and Brutus. The queens are the Virtues of Justice, Unity, Prudence and Courage.

After the Revolution, once Napoleon had assumed power, he wanted to re-design the now outmoded Revolutionary cards. For this task he commissioned the artist Jacques Louis David, whom he had appointed as official painter of the Revolution in 1804.

Lacking imagination, David employed the traditional names for the kings, namely Charlemagne, Caesar, Alexandre and David; with their wives as queens and generals as jacks. Although David gave Napoleon the honour of posing as Caesar for the king of diamonds, Napoleon was not altogether happy with the designs. He then commissioned Gatteaux to come up with a new standard pattern.

Gatteaux's designs were finished in 1811 and his court cards are named: kings – Charles, David, Caesar and Alexandre; queens – Abigail, Hildegarde, Calpurnie and Statira; jacks – Azael, Ogier, Curion and Parmenion.

Unfortunately these cards were not popular and in 1813 Gatteaux re-drew the familiar Paris pattern, with the tried and tested court names of hearts: Charles, Judith and Lahire; clubs: Alexandre, Argine, and Lancelot; diamonds: Caesar, Rachel, and Hector; spades: David, Pallas and Hogier.

The first publication of the design in 1813 has the jack of clubs holding a shield with the inscription *Administ des droit réunis* 1813 and the name Gatteaux. Other dates to appear on this shield are 1816, 1827 (when the courts became double-ended) and finally 1853. The 1853 date was used for a number of years, after which the date on the shield finally disappeared.

Although Napoleon's attempts at introducing a new card design failed, as a subject for the court cards he himself was not forgotten.

A famous pack issued under the Restoration in honour of Napoleon's victories is the *Jeu de Drapeaux*. Containing 32 cards the suits represent: hearts, France; clubs, Russia; diamonds, Germany; and spades, Britain. Each of the cards shows a picture of a soldier firing a cannon, marching, or, as on the aces, doing sentry duty. The kings show the generals planning, while the jacks show the flag or mascot carrier. On all the cards a flag is featured which shows the 'pips' or court cards, therefore serving the purpose of a miniature playing card index. The title card shows a flag bearer and beside him is a pillar naming all Napoleon's victories from Ulm to Moscow. This delightful pack is hand-coloured and well executed. Many reproductions of this pack have been made.

## Paris Pattern

The Paris pattern was the most widespread and famous of the regional patterns. It was used in Paris and within a 150 mile radius. Its most distinguishing feature is the names on the court cards. Again this practice of giving the court cards titles or names was not new, but dated back to the mid-15th century. However, the present day names were not firmly

**Paris Pattern,** *c.* **1760.**

established until the mid-17th century. Card makers in other areas of France also occasionally named their courts, but their choice of names was far less consistent. Some of the names used were: Hélène, Roxane, Rachel, Fausta, Dido, Juno, Paris, Pucelle (Joan of Arc), Bathsheba, Pentesiba (Queen of the Amazons), Lucretia, Semiramis, Solomon, August, Clovis, Constantine and Clothilde.

The names finally adopted for the Paris pattern were: kings – Charles, Alexandre, Caesar, David; queens – Judith, Argine, Rachel, Pallas; jacks – La Hire, Lancelot, Hector and Hogier.

The reason for naming the court cards, or for the choice of names is not known. It has been suggested that they were a manifestation of the pre-occupation with chivalry of that time; and that they were intended to represent great rulers and heroes of antiquity. It is, of course, just as probable that they originated as a whim of a card designer, with no fixed purpose or meaning.

The king of hearts, Charles, is thought to personify Charlemagne, the King of France. The main features of this card are the sword the king carries in his right hand and the orb bearing the cross of Lorraine in his left hand. On modern cards the orb can no longer be seen, being obscured by the division of the court card to form the double-ended design. The king looks to his left.

The queen of hearts, Judith, formerly Judic, is often assumed to be the biblical Judith. She is shown looking to her right and holding a flower in her right hand.

The jack of hearts is La Hire. The actual name La Hire first appeared in the middle of the 17th century. Before this time the jack of hearts was portrayed as a thoughtful youth, with a feather in his cap and holding a big candle or torch in his hand symbolizing Love. Today the jack of hearts looks to his right and holds a halberd in his left hand.

The spades suit is often associated with the military or fighting classes, so it is appropriate that the king of spades should personify the biblical David who slew Goliath. The name David appeared as early as 1490 and shows the king holding a large sword and a harp. In recent packs the sword has been replaced by a sceptre.

The queen of spades is named Pallas after the Greek

goddess. She is shown bearing a shield on her robes and holds a flower in her right hand and her face is in left front profile. Pallas first appeared on a court card c.1493 and among her rivals were Bathsheba and Joan of Arc, who occasionally appeared as the queen of spades.

The jack of spades was called Hogier, or Ogier, from a very early date. It is said that he was one of Charlemagne's paladins. In early French packs he is seen with a dog at his heels – this being lost in the double-ended design. He can now be recognized by the feather in his cap. He holds a halberd in his left hand and looks to his left.

The king of diamonds, named Caesar, dates from around 1490. The king of diamonds is shown in right profile holding a sceptre in his left hand and a shield below his belt. In the double-ended design the sceptre has disappeared and only the top part of the shield can be seen.

The queen of diamonds named Rachel was a late addition, dating from around 1650. It is assumed that she is also the biblical Rachel. In early packs she is carrying a flower in her left hand, but in modern packs only the flower is seen, her hand being obscured by the card division. She looks to her left.

The jack of diamonds is entitled Hector and there are a number of suppositions as to his identity. Some claim him to be Hector de Galard captain of the French guard under Charles VII and Louis XI. Others say he is Hector of Troy. Yet another popular theory is that he is Hector de Main, half brother of Lancelot of the Lake and one of the Knights of the Round Table. On modern packs he is pictured in right profile and only an empty right hand is seen. Originally his now obscured left hand held a halberd.

The king of clubs is called Alexandre, after Alexander the Great, the Greek monarch and conqueror of Asia. In early packs he is pictured with a lion-like animal which has again disappeared in the double-ended design. Now he is seen holding a sceptre in his right hand, under which is a shield. He looks to his left.

The queen of clubs has the most unusual name in the pack – Argine – an anagram of Regina. Unlike all the other queens she used to hold a fan in her left hand rather than a flower. Again this is not seen in the double-ended version. She also looks to her left.

The last court card, the jack of clubs, is called Lancelot. Originally he held a halberd in his left hand, which is omitted from the double-ended design. In his right hand he holds a shield on a ribbon. Popular belief has it that this jack is the romantic Sir Lancelot of the Round Table and lover of Queen Guinevere.

For a long time this card went unnamed as the jack of clubs was used as the duty card in France which obliged the card makers to print their name on this card.

A more detailed account of the Paris pattern court card figures can be found in Gurney Benhan's book on playing cards.

The Paris pattern is now the only regular French-suited standard pattern in use in France. Various other European countries adopted patterns which are simply variations of the Paris pattern but without the names on the court cards.

## Lyons Pattern (*Portrait de Lyon*)

It is thought that Lyons was among the first of the French card-producing towns and quickly built up large export orders. Up until the 17th century the Lyons card makers produced a number of different designs with a stable pattern finally emerging in the 18th century. Early packs are extremely rare, most examples being in museums. One pack by François Clerc, who worked in Lyons between 1485–1496, which is in the Bibliothèque Nationale in Paris, has the king and queen of clubs in 'wild-men' costumes. The king's sceptre is replaced by a big club and the queen's by a stick. Another rare pack by Jean Personne, who worked in Lyons between 1493–1497, has courts which bear inscriptions such as: Le Duc de Langre, Le Duc de Ramis, La Belle Clème, La Sebule, Venus, Juno and La Pucelle. The queens of clubs and diamonds are still found with the inscription *Mais Bien Vous* until the early 18th century.

Early Lyons cards were normally slim in format and were exported to various German states, and Switzerland, Italy and Spain.

The characteristics of the established standard pattern are given below.

*Opposite above*: **Lyons Pattern**

*Opposite belo w*: **Rouen Pattern No. 1**

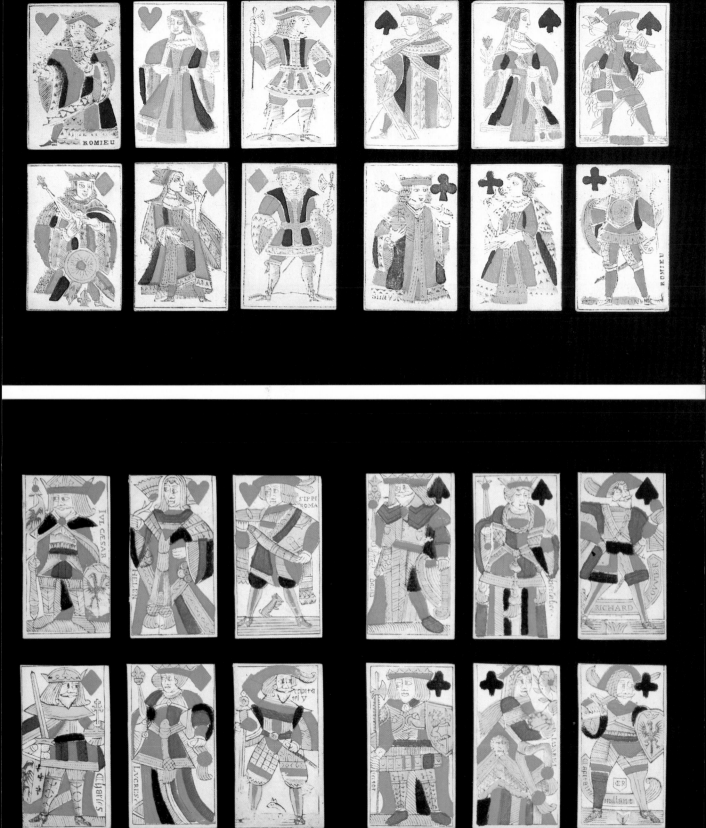

### Kings

The kings of hearts and spades look to their right, the king of spades being in profile. The other two kings look to their left. The king of hearts holds a sceptre in his left hand and a bird in his right. The kings of spades and diamonds simply hold sceptres in their right hand, while the king of clubs holds his sceptre in his left hand and an orb in his right.

### Queens

The queens of hearts and clubs look to their right, the queen of clubs being in profile. The other two queens are shown in right profile. The queens all carry a flower in one hand and a fan in the other. The queens of hearts and diamonds hold a flower in their left hand, and those of clubs and spades in their right.

### Jacks

The jacks of hearts and spades are in right profile. The jack of hearts holds an axe in his right hand while the jack of spades holds an axe over his left shoulder and smokes a pipe. The jacks of diamonds and clubs look to their right and hold halberds in their left hand. The jack of clubs also has a shield on his right arm.

D'Allemagne, in his book on playing cards (*see* Bibliography), illustrates the pattern just described under the title of the Lyons Export pack. He also illustrates some slightly different packs which he identifies as Lyons patterns of the early 17th century. His examples are taken from the Bibliothèque Nationale (Estampes) and have the following characteristics:

### Kings

All the kings look to their left, with the king of spades being shown from a side view. The king of clubs holds a sceptre over his left shoulder and the other kings hold their sceptres over their right shoulders. The king of hearts has an additional bird on his left wrist.

### Queens

The queen of diamonds looks to her right and holds a flower in her right hand. The other queens look to their left with the queen of clubs being in profile. The queens of hearts and spades carry sceptres in their right hand and the queen of clubs a letter page in her right hand.

### Jacks

The jacks of hearts and spades have their backs to the viewer and show the right sides of their faces. The jack of hearts holds a halberd in his right hand and that of spades an axe over his right shoulder. The jack of clubs looks to his right and holds a halberd in his left hand. He wears a curved sword and his right hand is on his hip. The jack of diamonds is in right profile and holds a halberd in his right hand.

## Rouen Pattern No. 1 (*Portrait de Rouen*)

The Rouen pattern is not one of the official designs as laid out by the 1701 tax law. However, since it is an important design for historical reasons and is now very rare some of the varieties of the Rouen pattern are described. The Rouen No. 1 pattern dates back to the first half of the 16th century and disappeared some hundred years later.

One of the earliest surviving recorded Rouen packs was made by Charles Dubois. All the court figures are named: on hearts the king is named Jullius Cézar, the queen, Héleine, and the jack, Siprien Roman; on diamonds the king is Charles, the queen, Thérèse, and the jack is Capita Fily; on spades the king is David, the queen, Bersabée, and the jack carries no name but a scroll bearing the maker's name Charles Dubois; on clubs the king is Hector, the queen, Pentaxlée and the jack, Capitaine Taillant.

In the British Museum are two sheets of early Rouen pattern cards, one made by Nicolas Besnière and the other by Robert Besnière. The designs are based on those by Charles Dubois but feature different names on a few of the court cards. In the Besnière packs the jack of diamonds is called Capitaine Metely, the jack of clubs is named Capitaine Vallante and also features the maker's initials, and the queen of diamonds is called Lucrelle (Lucresse). The maker's name and address are again found on the jack of spades.

Yet another variety, by Richard Bouvier has the court names of: hearts – Caesar, Helen, Sippi Roma; spades – David, Bersabée and the maker's name on the jack; diamonds – Charles, Lucresse, Capitaine Tely; and clubs – Hector, Isabel and Capitaine Millant.

Although the old Rouen packs are crude in appearance they do have an irresistible charm, with many of the court figures having individual expressions on their faces. The jack of hearts is clean shaven, the king of clubs has a beard and the other kings and jacks have beards and moustaches. The individual characteristics of the pattern are as follows:

### Kings

The kings of hearts, spades and clubs look to their right while the king of diamonds looks to his left. The king of hearts carries a shield in his left hand and a standard in his right hand. The king of spades has a sceptre in his right hand and a harp in his left hand. The king of diamonds has a sword and a shield in his right hand and an orb in his left. The king of clubs has a halberd in his right hand and a shield in his left.

### Queens

The queen of hearts looks to her right and holds a flower in her right hand. This design is reversed for

**Burgundy Pattern**

the queen of clubs. The queen of spades looks to her left and holds a sceptre in her right hand. The queen of diamonds also holds a sceptre in her right hand but looks to her right.

*Jacks*

The jack of hearts looks to his right and holds a sash in both hands. There is a dog in the background of this card. The other three jacks look to their left. The jack of clubs holds a shield in his left hand and has a sword held over his shoulder in his right hand. The jack of diamonds holds a sword in his right hand and his other hand is on his sword hilt. This card also has a dog in the background. The jack of spades has his right hand on his hip and holds a shield in his left hand, only part of which can be seen.

## Rouen Pattern No. 2

Later, another Rouen pattern emerged, which the Rouen card makers exported to Switzerland, Spain, Flanders, Portugal and England.

It is this second pattern on which the standard English pack is based.

*Kings*

The kings of hearts and clubs look to their right. The king of hearts wields an axe in his left hand (sometimes a sword in the English pattern) and the king of clubs holds an upright sword in his left hand and an orb in his right. The king of spades looks to his left and holds an upright sword in his left hand. The king of diamonds is shown from a left side view and holds an axe in his right hand.

*Queens*

All the queens hold long stemmed flowers in their left hands and the queen of spades has an additional sceptre in her right hand. All the queens stand at an angle with the queens of hearts and spades looking to their right and the other two queens looking to their left.

*Jacks*

The jack of spades has his back to the viewer and looks to his right and holds a halberd in his right hand. The jack of clubs looks to his right and holds a spear in his right hand. The jack of hearts is shown in right profile, holds a halberd in his left hand and a sword in his right hand. The jack of diamonds looks to his left

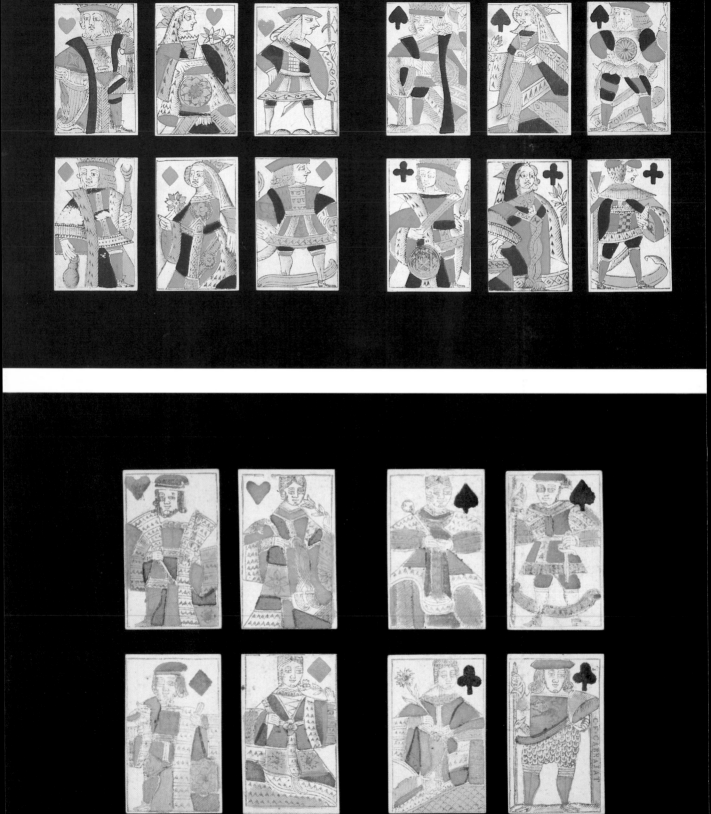

and holds a halberd in his left hand.

## Burgundy and Lorraine

This tax area embraced the towns of Dijon, Bescançon and Salins. Originally the pattern was made by Lyons card makers for export to Burgundy, Flanders and Lorraine. Later, makers in Burgundy and Lorraine manufactured the pattern themselves. It was replaced in 1751 by the Paris pattern.

The kings in this pattern wear large crowns and the queens have veils and crowns.

### Burgundy Pattern (*Portrait de Bourgogne*)
*Kings*

The kings of hearts, spades and diamonds look to their right, with the king of hearts holding a sceptre over his right shoulder and the king of diamonds one in his left hand. The king of clubs looks to his left and holds his sceptre in his right hand.

*Queens*

The queens of hearts and spades look to their right and hold a flower in their right hands. The queen of spades also holds a sceptre in her left hand. The queen of clubs looks to her left and holds a flower in her left hand. The last queen, of diamonds, is shown in left profile and is empty-handed.

*Jacks*

The jack of clubs is shown in left profile and wears a helmet. He holds a halberd in his left hand and carries a shield by a ribbon on his right arm. The jack of spades is similarly positioned but holds a sword in his right hand. The jack of hearts looks to his right, holds a halberd in his left hand and a shield by a ribbon on his right arm. The jack of diamonds is shown in left profile, holds a halberd in his right hand and carries the familiar shield by a ribbon on his left arm.

### Lorraine Pattern (*Portrait de Lorraine*)

The main difference between the Lorraine and the Bourgogne pattern is that in the Lorraine pattern the king of diamonds is empty-handed and the king of spades holds a scroll in his left hand.

## Guyenne and Languedoc

This tax region was in the south of France between the rivers Garonne and Rhône. The pattern emerged by the mid-18th century and is an adaptation of the Auvergne pattern.

### Guyenne Pattern (*Portrait de Guyenne*)
*Kings*

All the kings look to their right and, except for the king of spades, carry strange sceptres in their left hand. The king of hearts' sceptre is surmounted by a fleur-de-lis, that of clubs has flames issuing from it and a heart-shaped base, and that of diamonds has a heart surmounted by an eye. The king of spades carries an axe in his left hand. In his right hand the king of hearts carries a harp, and that of diamonds a shield which sometimes features the maker's name.

*Queens*

The queens of hearts and clubs look to their left, with the queen of hearts being in profile, and both carry flowers in their left hands. The other two queens have the same designs in reverse. Sometimes the queen of diamonds is shown carrying a feather in her right hand.

*Jacks*

The jack of spades looks to his right, has his right hand on his hip and holds a halberd in his left hand. The other three jacks are shown in profile looking to the right-hand side of the card's face with those of hearts and clubs having their backs to the viewer. The jacks of hearts and diamonds hold their halberds in their right hand and that of clubs holds a halberd in his left hand and the hilt of his sword in his right hand. The jacks are all shown on ground, and sometimes there is a flower growing in the background of the jack of clubs' card.

### Languedoc Pattern (*Portrait du Languedoc*)

The cards made in Languedoc are slightly smaller than those of Guyenne. The main difference between the two patterns is that the Languedoc king of diamonds holds a money bag in his right hand and his sceptre is surmounted by a crescent. Also, the king of clubs now holds a shield in his right hand.

### Dauphiné Pattern (*Portrait du Dauphiné*)

This tax region in south-eastern France was

*Opposite above*: **Languedoc Pattern**

*Opposite belo w*: **Dauphiné Pattern**

**Auvergne Pattern**

bounded by the Alps, the river Rhône and the region of Provence, with the chief card-producing towns being Grenoble, Romans, Chambéry and Valence. Unfortunately very few cards have survived from this area.

*Kings*

The red kings look to their right and hold sceptres in their left hands. In his right hand, the king of hearts holds a dagger or small sword while the king of diamonds carries a hawk. The other two kings look to their left. The king of spades holds a sceptre in his right hand and the king of clubs holds an upright sword in his right hand and an orb in his left.

*Queens*

All the queens look to their left. The black queens hold long stemmed flowers in their right hand, while the red queens hold a flower in their left hand and a sceptre in their right hand.

*Jacks*

The jack of diamonds is the most interesting card in this pack. He is shown from a side view walking to the right-hand side of the card's face and the boots or socks he wears have human faces on them. He holds a

stick in his right hand and the card carries the title *Mais Bien Vous*. The jack of clubs looks to his left and has his left hand on his hip and with his right hand leans on a halberd. The maker's name is often written on the side of the card. The jack of spades is similarly positioned but looks to his right and the maker's name appears on a ribbon around the jack's legs. The jack of hearts also looks to his right and holds a sword in his right hand and points in the air with his left index finger. The inscription on this card usually reads *Toues Bien*.

**Auvergne** and **Limousin**

This tax region lay in central France and included the towns of Thiers, Clermont and Le Puy. The pattern is similar to the Paris pattern and often bears the same names as the Paris pattern on the court cards. Again the court figures usually touch the card's border, with part of the hats worn by the jacks of hearts, diamonds and clubs being cut off.

**Auvergne Pattern** (*Portrait d'Auvergne*)
*Kings*

The red kings look to their right and the black kings look to their left. The king of hearts is the same as in the Paris pattern, holding a sword in his left hand and

**Provence Pattern**

---

an orb in his right hand. The king of diamonds holds a sceptre in his left hand and a dagger in his right. The kings of spades and clubs hold sceptres in their right hand with that of clubs also holding a falcon or hawk in his left hand.

*Queens*

The queens of hearts and spades look to their right and hold sceptres in their left hand; the queen of hearts holds a flower in her right hand and the queen of spades a dog. The other two queens look to their left and hold a flower in their left hand and a sceptre in their right.

*Jacks*

The jacks of hearts and spades are shown in left profile and carry a halberd in their left hand and their sword hilt in their right hand. These designs are reversed for the other two jacks. The jacks all wear helmets and armour and their swords are curved and held behind them.

Packs have been made with the courts having the same names as in the Paris pattern and with the jack of clubs having an additional shield on his left.

**Limousin Pattern** (*Portrait du Limousin*)

The Limousin pattern is a second-class copy of the

Auvergne pattern and the main difference is that the jacks all face to their right.

**Provence Pattern** (*Portrait de Provence*)

This tax region lay in the south east of France and includes the card producing towns of Aix, Marseilles, Toulon, Avignon, Nîmes and Montpellier. The design originated in the late 15th century and was in use until the French Revolution.

*Kings*

Both the king of hearts and the king of spades are turned and look to the right-hand side of the card's face, with the king of spades being in profile. The king of hearts holds a hawk in his left hand and a sceptre in his right hand. The king of spades holds a sceptre over his right shoulder. The king of diamonds holds a sceptre in his left hand and looks to his right. The king of clubs looks slightly to his left and holds an axe in his right hand.

*Queens*

The queen of hearts is rather interesting as she is often shown wearing a scaly body stocking under her majestic robes and holds a flower in her left hand. She was originally shown as a fur-covered 'wild-woman',

Aluette Pattern: 2 of batons

as in the early Lyonnais packs. Later the fur was replaced by scales. The queens of spades and diamonds are shown in right profile and the queen of spades holds a flower. The queen of clubs also holds a flower but is shown in left profile.

*Jacks*

The jack of hearts looks to his right and carries a halberd in his left hand. The jack of clubs is shown in right profile. He has a banner carrying the maker's name around his legs and holds a halberd in his right hand. The other two jacks have their backs to us: the jack of spades is shown in left profile and holds a halberd in his right hand and the jack of diamonds has the same design in reverse. All the jacks are shown on rough ground.

## SPANISH SUITED

There are still two Spanish-suited standard patterns to be found in France – the Aluette and Catalan patterns. Both patterns are single-ended.

84

### Aluette Pattern (*Cartes d'Aluette*)

Aluette cards date from the late 14th century, although the modern design, still in use in Brittany and along the west coast of France, dates from *c*.1776. Pierre Sigogne of Nantes seems to have been among the first to produce the modern design. His trade mark of a stork is still found on several cards, such as: the 3 of cups, which shows storks sitting in two of the cups with one of the storks placing a laurel wreath on the bust of a young female found in the third cup; the 2 of cups, which has a human face superimposed on the suit sign and storks on either side looking like human ears or the handles of cups – underneath which is a cow; the ace of swords, which features two storks and a young naked boy with bows and arrows; the ace of cups which has two storks sitting on top of the cup supporting a crown.

Other interesting cards in this pack are: the ace of clubs which has a young naked Red Indian; the 2 of batons which shows a naked boy on a swing suspended from the two batons, with a dog underneath; the 5 of coins showing a man and a woman kissing – which legend has it are Ferdinand and Isabella; the 3 of coins which shows the bust of a man; the 4 of coins which shows two interlaced coloured triangles. Also, the 6, 7, 8, and 9 of coins have arrows somewhere on them.

Two unusual features of this 48-card pack are that it does not have the breaks in the card's border normally found in Spanish suited packs, and since 1776 the knights have been depicted as females. The knights ride horses, and both knights and jacks are on rough ground. The kings are crowned while the jacks and knights wear hats.

*Kings*

The kings of batons and swords look to their right. The king of batons holds his suit sign in his left hand and the king of swords holds his in his right hand. The other two kings look to their left. The king of coins holds an axe in his right hand and that of cups a sceptre in his right hand.

*Knights*

The knights of batons, coins and cups ride to the right-hand side of the card's face although the knight of cups has her back to us and has her head turned to the left-hand side of the card's face. The knight of batons holds her suit sign in her right hand and that of coins holds hers in her left hand. The knight of swords rides to the left-hand side of the card's face and holds her suit sign in her left hand.

*Jacks*

The jacks of swords and coins look to their right and

hold their suit signs in their right hands. The jack of batons also looks to his right but holds his suit sign in his left hand. The jack of cups looks to his left and holds a halberd in his right hand.

### Catalan Pattern (*Cartes Catalanes*)

The Catalan cards are still used today in a small area of south-west France. The pack comprises 48 numbered cards: 1–9 in the number cards and 10, 11 and 12 (jack, knight, king) in the court cards. As with the standard Spanish packs, the suit is indicated by breaks in the card's border. The maker's name is usually found on the ace of coins.

The kings wear long robes with big sleeves while the knights and jacks wear tunics, tights and boots. The kings wear crowns and the other court figures wear feathered hats. All the court figures hold their suit sign in their right hand and the knights and jacks either stand on grassland or are set against a low-level background with trees.

*Kings*

The king of swords looks to his left and the other kings looks to their right. The king of cups holds a long sceptre in his left hand.

*Knights*

All the knights ride horses. The knights of swords and clubs look and ride to the right-hand side of the card's face; the other two knights ride to the left-hand side of the card's face although the knight of coins looks to his left.

*Jacks*

The jack of batons looks to his left and points into the air with his left index finger. The other jacks look to their right; the jack of coins being in profile. The jack of swords has his left leg crossed over his right as though walking and the jack of coins holds a hunting horn in his left hand.

*Other Cards*

In some packs the 4 of batons and the 2 of cups have roses on them. The 4 of coins shows a crown surrounded by a wreath and the 5 of swords features two bunches of grapes.

# THE LOW COUNTRIES

## FRENCH SUITED

### The Netherlands Pattern

The Dutch version of the Paris pattern is similar to the German Berliner cards in artistic execution, with regal and rich designs on the court cards in reds,

Catalan Pattern: jack of coins

greens, blues, yellows and purples. The indices are H (Heer = King) V (Vrauw = Queen) and B (Boer = Jack), and packs usually contain 52 double-ended cards. Often (but not invariably) on both Dutch and Belgian modern cards only three-quarters of the suit sign is shown with the extreme left-hand quarter omitted to make room for the letter value.

Many packs have scenic aces which show two different named cities and buildings. These scenic aces first appeared in the 19th century and standard Dutch packs are also found with scenic background on the court cards.

All the kings and queens are crowned and the jacks wear feathered caps.

*Kings*

All the kings hold sceptres in their left hand. In the other hand the king of hearts holds an orb, that of spades a harp and that of clubs a shield. The kings of diamonds and clubs look to their left and those of hearts and spades to their right.

French-suited Belgian Pattern: queen of hearts

*Queens*

The queens of diamonds and clubs look to their right and in her right hand the queen of diamonds holds a mirror, while the queen of clubs holds a flower. The other two queens look to their left, with the queen of spades being in profile. In her left hand the queen of hearts holds a bird and the queen of spades a fan.

*Jacks*

All the jacks carry halberds in their left hand with those of hearts and spades holding their sword hilts in their right hands. The red jacks look to their right and the black jacks look to their left.

**The Belgian Pattern**

The most common standard pattern found in Belgium is practically identical to the French Paris pattern. Packs are found with both the French indices of R D V and the Flemish indices of H V B. As in the Netherlands only three-quarters of the suit sign is shown and the cards are double-ended.

From around 1880 manufacturers tended not to put their names or addresses on the cards; therefore identification can be difficult. One clue that can aid identification, however, is that the French Paris pattern is mainly printed in the colours of blue, black, red and yellow, whereas the Belgian Paris pattern packs are mostly (not always) printed in green, red and yellow.

## SCANDINAVIA

**FRENCH SUITED**

The Scandinavian countries use a French suited pattern similar in artistic style to the German Rhineland and Berliner cards. The pack comprises 52 cards and the indices are K D Kn. In Denmark the ace is lettered Es and in Sweden E. The largest Scandinavian manufacturers are J.O. Oberg of Eskilstuna, Sweden. Scandinavian cards are now all double-ended.

**The Danish Pattern**

This pack is usually very attractive and well produced. The predominant colours are rich and dark shades of petrol blue, maroons and reds, golds, and greens.

*Kings*

The kings wear crowns and carry sceptres: those of hearts and clubs in their left hand and the other two in their right hand. The king of hearts is full-faced and points in the air with his right index finger. The king of diamonds is shown in right profile and the king of clubs looks slightly to his left. The king of spades is rather interesting. He is shown from a left side view with his arms crossed as though he is either sulking or thinking deeply.

*Queens*

The queens wear simple crowns, with those of diamonds and spades also having veils and the queen of hearts a laurel wreath. The queen of clubs is the only queen without a necklace and all the queens wear their dresses off the shoulder.

The queen of hearts has her back to the viewer showing the right side of her face and holds a flower in her right hand. The other queens look to their left. The queen of diamonds holds a closed fan in her left hand and the queen of clubs holds a flower. The queen of spades shows an empty right hand.

*Jacks*

The jack of diamonds holds a halberd in both hands and the other jacks hold halberds in their left hand. The jacks of hearts and clubs look and face to the left-hand side of the card's face with that of clubs

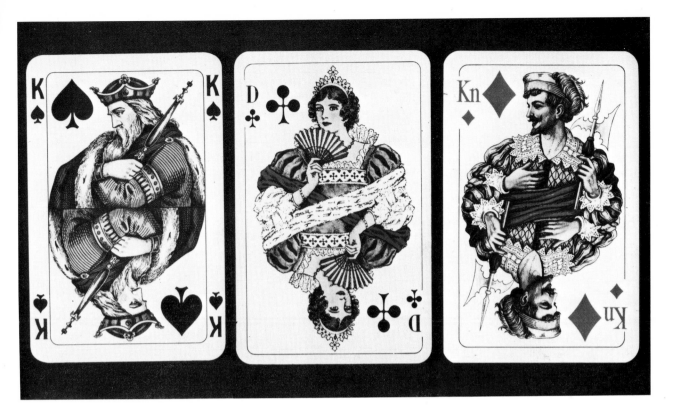

*Left to right*; Danish Pattern, king of spades; Swedish Pattern, queen of clubs; Piatnik's Swedish Export Pattern, knight of diamonds.

showing his back. The other two jacks look and face to the right-hand side of the card's face, with that of spades having an eagle embroidered on his tunic. The maker's name is on the jack of clubs and all the jacks wear feathered hats.

## The Swedish Pattern

In this pack each suit has a different main colour. In the clubs suit the predominant colour is purple; diamonds, blue; hearts, red; and spades, yellow and green. The kings and queens wear crowns and the jacks wear feathered hats.

### Kings

The king of spades holds a sceptre in his right hand and the other kings hold sceptres in their left hands. The kings of hearts and spades look to their left, with the king of spades being in profile. The other two kings look to their right with the king of diamonds being in profile. Above the indices there is a small crown.

### Queens

The queen of spades looks to her left and holds a closed fan in her right hand. The other queens look to their right, with the queen of hearts being in profile. The queen of clubs holds an open fan in her right hand, while the other two queens have their right hands raised to their necks. The queen of diamonds is the only queen who does not wear a necklace.

### Jacks

The jack of clubs looks to his left and holds a spear in his left hand. The other jacks look to their right with the jack of diamonds being in profile. In their left hand the two red jacks carry halberds; and in his right hand the jack of spades holds a sword.

## The Piatnik Swedish Export Pattern

Piatnik produces a standard export pattern for Sweden which varies from the aforementioned pack in a number of small ways. The indices are larger and there are no longer any crowns above the indices on

**Finnish Pattern, king of hearts**

**Russian Pattern, king of diamonds**

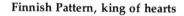

the kings. The queens have been given a more modern and less regal appearance and now all of them wear necklaces. The jacks have less frozen expressions and, except for the jack of clubs, are smiling. Other individual differences are:

*Kings*

All the kings carry an orb in their left hand and a sceptre in their right hand; except for the king of diamonds who holds a sword in his right hand.

*Queens*

The red queens now carry a flower in their right hand; and the queen of spades holds her closed fan in both hands. The queen of clubs' empty left hand is now visible.

*Jacks*

The jack of diamonds' empty right hand is now visible.

**The Finnish Pattern**

The most widespread modern pack used in Finland

today is one based on a non-standard design which originated at the turn of the century. Packs contain 52 double-ended cards (king, queen, jack, ace, 10–2) and the courts bear the indices K D Kn and the ace E.

*Kings*

All the kings have beards and moustaches and wear regal clothes and crowns. The king of diamonds holds an orb in his right hand while the other three kings hold a sceptre in their right hand. The king of diamonds looks to his left and the king of hearts is full-faced. The other two kings are in profile, the king of clubs in right profile and the king of spades in left profile.

*Queens*

The queens are in costumes and are found with or without crowns. The red queens look to their left and in their left hands the queen of hearts usually holds a bird and the queen of diamonds a fan. The queen of clubs usually looks into a mirror held in her right hand and fixes her hair with her left hand. The queen of

88

spades also looks to her right and has her left hand raised to her necklace.

*Jacks*

The jacks all have moustaches and wear head-gear. The jack of hearts is slightly turned to the left-hand side of the card's face. He twiddles his moustache with his right hand and holds a pike in his left hand. The other three jacks look to their left. The jack of diamonds is found either sounding a horn held in his left hand or holding a halberd in his right hand. The jack of spades holds a halberd in his left hand. The jack of clubs is dressed in armour and carries a shield in his left hand and a sword or halberd over his shoulder in his right hand.

# RUSSIA

## FRENCH SUITED

Early standard Russian playing cards had German suit signs but later a double-ended French suited variety of the Paris pattern was adopted. The artistic interpretation is akin to the German French-suited packs. The indices used are К Д В and Т (phonetically KDV and T). One of the distinguishing features of this pack is the indices which appear on the halberds held by the jacks and on necklaces or robes worn by most of the other court figures; also, the king of diamonds is a turbaned Moor. The other kings wear crowns, the queens wear crowns and veils, and the jacks wear hats with the jack of spades having a feather in his. The Pelican of Piety and the Imperial Eagle motifs on the aces ceased to be used after the Revolution.

*Kings*

The kings of hearts and clubs look to their left; the king of clubs holds a sceptre in his left hand and a shield in his right, and the king of hearts a sword in his left hand and an orb in his right. The king of spades also holds a sceptre and orb but looks to his right. The Moor king of diamonds is shown in left profile and holds a sceptre surmounted by a crescent in his left hand, while his right hand is on his sword hilt.

*Queens*

The queens of diamonds and clubs look to their left and hold flowers in their left hands. This design is reversed for the other two queens, although the queen of spades is in profile.

*Jacks*

All the jacks hold halberds in their left hand. In his right hand the jack of spades holds the hilt of his sword and the jacks of hearts and clubs have a shield on their right arms. These three jacks look to their left while the jack of diamonds is shown in right profile.

The maker's name is usually found on the ace of diamonds.

**Great Britain**

BRITAIN was one of the last European countries to receive playing cards and today, unlike the rest of Europe, uses only one standard pattern throughout the country.

The first reliable mention of playing cards in England was in an Act of Parliament passed by Edward IV in 1463 prohibiting their importation. Playing cards must have been familiar in England some time before this date to necessitate such an Act; and as the Act was intended to protect home markets, card makers must have established themselves already in England. An earlier Act of 1409 banned certain games, but did not refer to playing cards, so playing cards probably first appeared in England between 1409 and 1463.

As it was the French-suited cards that England adopted, it is reasonable to suppose that England received her first cards from France. Indeed it is thought that English cards are the descendants of the pattern used in the large card-producing town of Rouen. However, although England adopted the French-suit designs, the suit names of diamonds, clubs and spades are different. The English spades and clubs suits derive their names from their Italian and Spanish equivalents (the translation of the French suit names is *spades* 'pike staffs' and *clubs* 'trefoils'). For *diamonds*, the English chose a name which suited the design, whereas the French name for the diamonds

suit 'carreaux' is roughly translated as 'paving tiles'. Again, since diamonds suggest wealth, the suit sign is more akin to the Italian and Spanish coin suit sign. The only suit sign name which is the same as the French is hearts.

Cards quickly became popular in England and in one of the Paston letters, written by Margery Paston to her husband John Paston *c*.1443, we learn that they were an integral part of the Christmas festivities. In fact, gaming became so popular that both Henry VII in 1495 and Henry VIII in 1541 prohibited servants from playing cards except during the Christmas festivities; although a nobleman having a £100 a year estate could license servants to play on his property. In 1526, Henry VIII made an unsuccessful attempt to ban gaming altogether, causing 'Tables, Dice, Cards and Bowles' to be 'taken and burnt'.

These laws proved ineffective and gaming continued to thrive, but unfortunately, few packs of English playing cards prior to the late 1600s have survived. The blame for this mostly lies with Oliver Cromwell who propagated many puritanical attitudes. For, although under his aegis the manufacture of playing cards was not prohibited, staunch attitudes against gaming resulted in many thousands of packs being destroyed.

Like other countries, England eventually realized

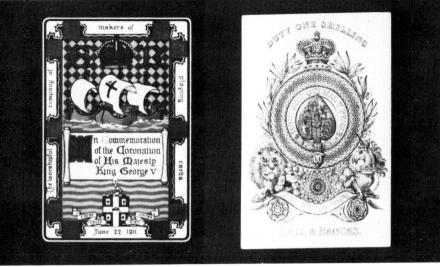

*Left to right*: two back designs of packs made by the Worshipful Company of Makers of Playing Cards, the first of 1943 and the second of *c*. 1911 showing King George V's coronation; 'Old Frizzle' duty ace of spades by Thomas Creswick, *c*. 1830.

---

that much revenue could be raised from taxation on playing cards. One of the earliest records of taxation is from Elizabeth I's reign, and concerns her granting a playing card monopoly to Ralph Bowes. On July 20, 1615, James I made Sir Richard Coningsby the 'Inspector of all Playing Cards Imported' upon which was a duty of five shillings on every gross imported.

Later in 1628 the Worshipful Company of Makers of Playing Cards was founded by Royal Charter to protect the interests of English playing card makers and in exchange for royal protection against imported cards, a duty of a farthing a pack was placed on cards. This Company, whose full title was 'Master Wardens and Commonalty of the Mistery of Makers of Playing Cards of the City of London' was given the power, within a ten mile radius of London, to make laws and impose punishments and fines in order to protect their trade. No one except a Freeman of the company who had served a seven-year apprenticeship could manufacture cards, and all members were required to use a trade mark by which they could be officially recognized. Every year a new master and two wardens were appointed to lead the company, the first clerk of the company being Thomas Watkins.

In 1792, due to financial difficulties, the company became a Livery and from 1882 the practice began of presenting each Livery member with a specially printed pack of cards. These cards feature a commemorative back showing an important event of the year in question, such as a coronation, and usually a portrait of the Master on the ace of spades.

The playing card duty of a farthing a pack remained constant until the reign of Queen Anne. In 1711 the large revenue required for war led to a tax of 3d. being levied on every pack made in or imported into England. This new tax rate caused many arguments as at that time card makers sold packs to retailers at 1½d. with only ½d. profit. The tax was double the retail price and six times the profit!

Despite these protests, on June 11, 1711 the tax was again raised to 6d. per pack of cards. A small concession was that cards made before 12 June 1711 were taxed at only ½d.

To prove that tax had been paid, one of the cards was stamped by the Stamp Office for the Vellum Parchment and Paper Duties. From 12 August 1712, however, it was ordered that both a card and the wrapper should be sealed and stamped or marked. Many people, it seems, tried to get around the new tax, for in 1719 George I imposed a £10 penalty for anyone re-issuing an already used stamp and seal.

In 1756, under George II, the duty went up to 1s. and in 1765 George III implemented a new system of paying taxes whereby the Stamp Office supplied makers with a specially made ace of spades bearing the maker's name. The wrapper was also still stamped.

This new ace of spades motif had the conventional spade design in the centre, surrounded by the Garter Wreath, with a crown above the motto 'Dieu et mon Droit' below on a ribbon. Beside the crown was written 'Geo. III Rex'.

In 1776 the duty was raised to 1s. 6d. and the wording 'Sixpence Addl Duty' was added on to the ace of spades, while in 1789 the duty was again raised to 2s. and a further 'Six-pence Addl Duty' was incorporated at each side of the spade design.

In 1800 a duty on cards imported to Ireland from Great Britain was fixed at 1s. 5d. per pack with an additional 2¼d. per pound weight. A year later in England the duty was increased once again to 2s. 6d., when yet another 'Addl Duty Sixpence' was added to the bottom of the ace of spades.

This design for the ace of spades was mainly used until 1820, after which other designs were introduced, including one used from 1820–28 where the 2s. 6d. duty was denoted by the wording 'Duty One Shilling and Sixpence' and 'Geo IV' on the ace of spades and two sixpenny stamps on the wrapper.

The worst was at last over. In 1828 George IV reduced the duty to only 1s. A new ace of spades was designed by Perkins Bacon for the occasion which, because of its intricate pattern, reminiscent of bank note engravings, was nicknamed 'Old Frizzle'. The ace itself contained the royal heraldic quarterings supported by a lion and a unicorn. Above the spade is 'Duty one shilling'.

In 1862 Queen Victoria further reduced the tax on cards to 3d., which was marked only on the wrapper – denoting the end of the 'official duty' ace of spades. Manufacturers began to design their own fanciful aces of spades and in 1960 the duty of 3d. was abolished altogether.

Further information on duty stamps and ace designs can be found in Catherine Hargrave's book and in a booklet by Sylvia Mann on English playing cards.

The standard design of English playing cards stabilized by the early 18th century. Designs varied only slightly from maker to maker and in the main remained true to the Rouen mother pattern. Three early changes, however, were:- the cross of Lorraine normally found on the French king of clubs' orb was transformed into a leaf design; the king of hearts' axe became a sword; and the jack of hearts was given a leaf to hold.

Until the end of the 16th century card makers placed their names on the jack of clubs as in France. But when in 1628 the Worshipful Company declared that makers must register trade marks, various designs appeared. At first these were incorporated into the card's design, but later appeared on the wrapper.

These trade marks afford a fascinating and lengthy study in themselves and many reflect the history of the day. For instance in 1654, four years after Cromwell's death, the following royal-sounding marks were registered: The Lion Rampant by Mr. Matthias Miningkin. The Royal Oak by Mr. John Evans; The Prince's Arms and Crown by Mr. John Wilson; and the Queen's Head by Thos. Havard. In the following years appeared: 1677 Prince of Orange by Thomas Chapman and the Royall Barge by Richard Davy; 1680 Royal Woods and Duchess of Monmouth by John Woods; 1710 Dr. Sacheverell; 1717 The Queen Anne. Tavern names were also chosen as marks, such as The Leopard and the Three Nags' Heads.

Eventually the same trade marks were used by many different manufacturers both in England and abroad. At this stage they tended to denote quality rather than maker, with the most used mark being variations of Henry VIII and The Great Mogul.

Playing cards went through another series of changes in 1850 when manufacturers adopted double-ended courts. Because there was less space on double-ended designs, the effect was more cramped than before and the court figures lost much of their personal charm. Other innovations of this period include the introduction of rounded corners, indices (c.1880), patterned backs (first used by Thomas De La Rue), and the joker, which was initially introduced from America and at first used as an extra blank card.

Although English standard cards may seem rather dull in comparison to those of other countries, her early non-standard political packs are undoubtedly the most imaginative and fascinating in all the world.

A long series of these packs was issued during the late 17th and early 18th century, mostly centring around alleged Catholic conspiracies and attempts to overthrow monarchs and governments. The cards usually follow the same format. Most of the card's face is taken up with an engraved illustration, underneath which is a caption or rhyming couplet with the suit mark, number, letter or word in a panel at the top of the card.

Following is a list of these political packs arranged in their historical sequence, which is not necessarily the order in which they were made.

### The Spanish Armada Pack c.1680

This pack illustrates the main events connected with the Spaniards' attempt to overthrow Elizabeth I with the Armada, and of the eventual Spanish defeat. In

*Left to right*: King of spades from the first pack made by De La Rue, *c*. 1832; Queen of spades from an early wood block printed and stencil-coloured pack of standard cards by Josiah Stone, *c*. 1812; jack of hearts from what is thought to be the first pack printed by the typographic process by De La Rue in 1840.

this pack the courts have a medallion bust portrait at the top of the card.

The Pope's participation in the Armada plot is a very strong anti-Catholic point in this pack and the jack of hearts shows the Pope consulting his cardinals about contributing a million of crown towards the project.

### The Knavery Of The Rump 1647–1653 or A Complete Political Satire Of The Commonwealth

This pack was designed by Francis Barlow *c*.1681. It satirizes the Rump Parliament and the Commonwealth period, together with the political events that resulted in the king's execution. Cromwell is shown on the ten of clubs praying all night after signing the king's death warrant.

### All The Popish Plots 1588–1678

This pack was also probably designed by Francis Barlow (1626–1704) and covers the four plots of: the Spanish Armada, Dr. Parry's Plot, the Gunpowder Plot, and the Popish Plot.

### The Horrid Popish Plot 1678 – *also known as the Titus Oates Plot*

Designed by Francis Barlow this was one of the most popular of the political packs and deals with the plot to murder Charles II, Titus Oates and the murder of Sir Edmondbury Godfree. Again strong anti-Catholic currents run through the pack and the first card, the

ace of hearts, shows 'The plot first hatch't at Rome by the Pope and Cardinals'.

Three variations of these cards exist: where the value is shown by a suit mark and Roman numeral or word at the top of the card; the courts also have a medallion bust portrait to the right of the card; and where pip card values are shown by a small panel in the top left corner of the card with only the suit mark and Roman numeral.

### Meal Tub Plot 1679–80 – *also known as the Presbyterian Plot*

These cards were probably based on drawings by Francis Barlow, although at one time Sir Andrew Fontaine was accredited with the designs.

The Meal Tub plot was Thomas Dangerfield's and Mrs. Cellier's attempt to fabricate a Presbyterian plot against the government.

### Rye House Plot 1683

The events which led to the discovery of the Rye House plot uncovered two separate groups of traitors. One group was known as the Council of Six (4 of diamonds) and headed by the Duke of Monmouth, aimed to prevent James Duke of York succeeding Charles II.

This group, however, was not involved in the Rye House plotters' attempt to kill the King and James,

The 'Popish Plot' pack, *c*. 1679.

Duke of York, although both groups were eventually implicated together. The various attempts on the King's life by the Rye House plotters began on the queen of diamonds.

### Monmouth's Rebellion 1685

This pack shows the plot to place James, Duke of Monmouth, the illegitimate son of Charles II, on the throne at the death of Charles II instead of the Catholic James II. This pack is full of scenes of bloodshed, hangings, and executions, with the eight of hearts showing 'bonfires made the 26 of July at night being the thanksgiving for the Victory in 1685'.

### Reign Of James II 1685–1688

This is one of two packs concerning James II. It opens with the Earl of Essex (king of hearts in the Rye House Plot) ripping his stomach open with a razor and the speculation that it was not suicide but murder (8,9,10 of hearts). The main theme of this pack however is James II's attempts at establishing Catholic rule in England and the unpopular criticism and outbursts that followed.

### Orange Cards

This pack again deals with events prior to and during the reign of James II, with special emphasis on the birth of his child and the revolution.

The birth appears on the king of spades and the baptism on the ten of spades.

### The Reign Of Queen Anne 1702–1704

This pack was made *c*.1704/5 and features the coronation and public appearances of Queen Anne, together with the European war and the Scottish troubles. It is numbered from 1–52.

Card No. 1 shows 'Her Majesty proclaimed Queen of England, Scotland, France and Ireland March 8, 1702', with her official crowning on 23 April on card No. 6.

### Marlborough's Victories 1702–07

Although Marlborough features prominently on the Queen Anne cards, another pack was made *c*.1707 revolving around the Spanish succession and Marlborough's victories. This pack is often acclaimed as one of the most finely engraved of the early English political cards and features a 'rogues gallery' of the monarchs involved with the war.

Other cards deal with the various battles and the denunciation of Louis XIV and the French. The four of spades is captioned 'Give him blood to drink' and shows Louis ill in bed.

### Dr. Sacheverell 1709–1711

This pack was made by the card-maker Gabriel Pink and is the first pack in this political series to use miniature playing card indices – positioned at the top right-hand corner of each card. Most of the cards relate to the court case against Dr. Sacheverell, although other court and political intrigues of 1709–1711 creep in.

The last two of the political packs deal with the many Bubble Companies which burst in *c*.1720. Both packs were first published by Thomas Bowles.

### All The Bubbles or The Bubble Companies, 1720

This pack deals with the more famous of the dubious enterprises which sprang up and were nicknamed Bubble Companies.

The cards again have a miniature playing card in the top left-hand corner and a panel beside it giving the name of the enterprise. The caption is at the bottom of each card.

One of the most interesting cards is the eight of spades showing the 'Puckles Machine'. James Puckle, the inventor, was born in 1667 in Sussex and practised as a lawyer. He wrote several books and patented his now famous 'Portable Gun or Machine called a Defence' on 15 May 1718. Although at the time, the gun was laughed at, it could fire 100 shots in ten minutes and pre-dated the Gatling gun of the 19th

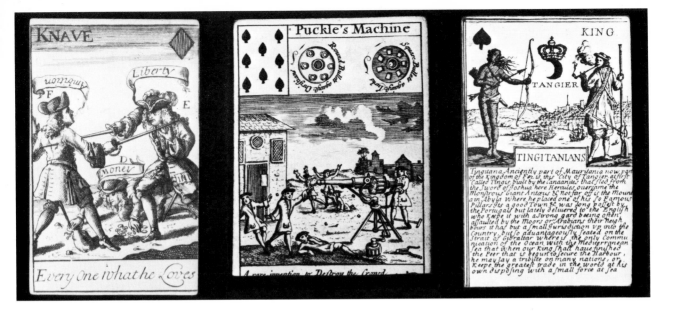

*Left to right;* **The knave of diamonds from the political pack 'Marlborough's Victories',** *c.* **1708; the 'All Bubbles pack,** *c.* **1720; a reprint of the Winstanley Geographical Cards,** *c.* **1676.**

century by 140 years. A quaint innovation was that the gun was designed to 'Fire round bullets at Christians and square bullets at Turks and Infidels'.

The gun was demonstrated for the first time at Woolwich in November 1777 and Mr. Peter Hartopp set up a company to sell the gun, with shares being sold at 2s. per share. However, the machine was far too advanced for its time and the 8 of spades reads:

'A rare invention to Destroy the Crowd
Of Fools at Home instead of Foes Abroad
Fear not my Friend, this Terrible Machine
They're only wounded that have Share's therein'

Two examples of this gun are now in the Tower of London.

### The South Sea Bubble 1720 or Stock Jobbing Cards

These cards deal specifically with the South Sea Company. They feature a miniature playing card index and caption at the bottom of each card together with speech balloons coming from the personalities' mouths – a rather strange effect in all.

Some of the more amusing cards in this pack read:

4 of diamonds
'Some Officers of Land grown Rich and Great, By Pay and Plunder in the Wars of late; Decoy'd by some, behind the South Sea Curtain Are wishing for New Wars to mend their Fortune.'

6 of diamonds
'A certain Lady when the stocks run high, Put on Rich Robes, to Charm her Lover's Eye, But South Sea falling, Pawn'd her fine Brocades, And now appears like other homely Jades.'

5 of clubs
'Three Merry Doctors, meet in Consultation, To Cure the South Sea Plague, that Spoils the Nation. But all agreed, the Fools should still endure it – Till Smarting Poverty alone should Cure it.'

Turning aside to other forms of educational cards, H. Brome issued one of the earliest English geographical packs in 1675. The four suits represent different regions while the main part of each card lists various cities, with their longitudes and latitudes. The hearts are devoted to Europe, diamonds Asia, spades Africa, and clubs America. On each court card is a medallion portrait of a monarch, including Queen Elizabeth for the English Plantations on the queen of clubs; a cannibal for the Caribbean Islands on the jack of clubs; and Rhea Silvia for Spain and Portugal on the jack of hearts.

The value of each card is indicated by a suit mark and a Roman numeral. Several editions of this popular pack were made with either script or block lettering.

Packs were also made where the cannibal on the jack of clubs wears a hat or (later) a crown of feathers. Other editions substitute Queen Mary for Elizabeth and George I for Charles II.

The next year saw the appearance of a number of geographical packs, one of the most celebrated of which was made by Henry Winstanley. Again the pack affords instruction in the various countries of the world with each card split into two sections. The top half shows a beautiful and detailed scene of the inhabitants and below is an extensive account of the land. As with the previous pack the four suits represent: hearts Europe, diamonds Asia, spades Africa, and clubs America. The value of each card is shown by a suit sign, Roman numeral and a word, together with the extra suit signs of: roses on hearts, suns on diamonds, moons on spades, and stars on clubs. In this pack the king of hearts represents London and the English; that of spades, Tangiers; that of clubs, James Town; and the knave of diamonds, Babylon.

The geographer Robert Morden issued a geographical pack in the same year relating to the counties of England and Wales. This time each card showed an actual map, along with the name of the county, suit sign and Roman numeral. Medallion portraits feature on the court cards. There are many editions of this pack, including one in book form produced in 1750 by H. Turpin. W. Redmayne also produced a similar pack in 1676 of inferior quality and design.

To illustrate how popular geographical cards were at that time, the plates for Emanuel Bowen's *Atlas Minimus*, which conveniently comprised 52 maps of the world, were actually modified to include a miniature playing card in one of the corners and then sold as playing cards. More unusual was an actual map of the British Isles by James Moxon which was cut up into 52 pieces to form a pack of cards.

Many of the geographical packs of the 17th and early 18th century, including the ones by H. Brome, Morden, Redmayne and Winstanley were reprinted by the publisher, Lenthall. He also produced the Sanson geographical cards and the Spanish Armada and the Reign of Queen Anne political cards.

Lenthall was based at the Talbot against St. Dunstan's Church in Fleet Street where he was an apprentice to William Warter. He later took over the business and many of his reprints can be recognized by what was at the time a novel decorative border. Some of his advertisements have survived to this day and list such packs as:

1. An English edition of Brianville's heraldry cards.
2. Astronomical cards, which were originally issued by Moxon in 1676 with the Lenthall edition appearing c.1717. The cards show various constellations, together with details about their positions, colour, nature and size.
3. Mathematical cards c.1770 by T. Tuttle. The cards were designed by Boitard and engraved by J. Savage and called 'Cards-English Arts & Sciences 1700'. Each card illustrates a type of mathematical instrument, together with the traders who used it. T. Tuttle himself made mathematical instruments for the king.
4. Geometrical cards, showing geometrical and mechanical principles.
5. Cookery and Pastry cards – with instructions on how to dress fish, fowl or flesh and how to make complementary sauces. c.1716.
6. Carving cards. Similar to the last pack, it shows the correct way to carve food with fowl on diamonds, flesh on hearts, fish on clubs and baked meats and pies on spades. These were published in several editions between 1677 and 1717 with various accompanying booklets.
7. Grammatical cards. First published by John Sellers in 1676, they show the general rules of Lilly's grammar, with Syntaxis on the hearts suit, Prosodia on the diamonds; Etymologia on the clubs and Orthographia on the spades.
8. Arithmetic cards which show questions and mathematically worked out answers, involving addition, subtraction, multiplication, division, reduction, the rule of three and practice. One of the more unusual questions posed is: how many lashes will a malefactor receive in total if he is tied to a cart and dragged through seven streets, in each of which are nine kennels, and at each kennel he is dealt twelve lashes? They were made c.1710.
9. Proverb cards – first made by William Warter c.1698. Each card illustrates a witty saying. The 2 of spades shows a wife on one side of a door and her husband with a lover on the other side of the door with the caption 'Out of sight, out of mind'. As with many of these packs, three editions are known, with a). outline suit marks, b). suit mark outlines and another stencilled suit mark superimposed on top, c). black and red filled in suitmark.
10. A similar pack called Delightful cards.
11. Frost Fair cards.
12. Instruction cards – teaching children to read and spell.
13. Forest cards or Birds and Beasts. The hearts and diamonds show various birds and the clubs and spades show animals. Some of the cards are rather amusing with the ten of spades showing a 'cat a-fiddling and mice a-dancing'.
14. Pastime cards, which relate various morals and

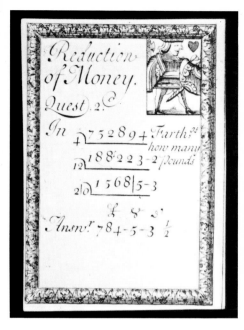

*Left to right*: The 'Arithmetic' pack made in the late-18th-century by J. Lenthall; the queen of hearts from 'Love Mottoes', by John Lenthall, *c.* 1710; the 'Lives of the Saints' satirical pack, possibly by Carrington Bowles, *c.* 1725.

precepts.

15. Love Mottoes, which feature illustrations of romantic situations, with a somewhat satirical rhyming couplet underneath.

Lenthall also sold the following imported French packs which he claimed were 'designed for the more easy and expeditious Attainment of that Language'.

16. Fortification and Military cards which are based on the French *Jeu des Fortifications* and *Jeu de Guerre*.

17. Political and Philosophical cards showing effigies taken from statues and medals.

18. Chronicle cards.

19. Ladies cards.

20. Classical cards, showing scenes from the fables in Ovid's *Metamorphoses*.

21. Roman cards, which feature and give information about various Roman emperors and empresses.

22. World cards, which are probably a reprint of Mortier's *Jeu des quatre Partes du monde*. They show the 12 months and 4 seasons of the year, the 5 senses, the 4 elements and several liberal arts, the 4 parts of the world and other curiosities.

23. Heraldry cards, showing the coats of arms of all the princes and states in the world. This is probably a French-language edition of Brianville's pack.

24. Historical cards, describing the cities of the world and the habits of their people.

25. Geographical cards, describing all parts of the world and showing maps of each country with a title and suit mark at the top of the card and reference scale at the bottom. This may be a reprint of Mortier's *Jeu de Géographie*.

The rest of the cards are in Dutch and French.

26. Masquerade cards.

27. Entertaining cards, describing the fashions of various countries.

28. Scaramouch cards, showing ways of distorting the body.

29. Turkish cards, showing the costumes and habits of people in that country.

30. Habit cards, showing the costumes worn in Holland and Augsburg.

This list is not complete and it should be remembered that many of these cards are reprints of other packs and come in many editions with slight modifications in design. For instance the carving, astronomical, geometrical and geographical cards were originally produced by James Moxon.

In 1675 Richard Blome issued a pack giving instruction on the art of heraldry. Blome also wrote a book on the subject in 1685. At the top of each card is a shield giving an example of a particular aspect of heraldry

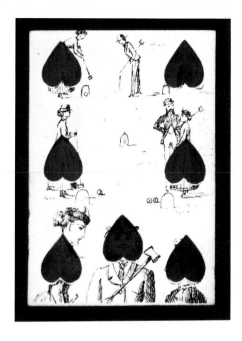

This Scottish heraldry pack is the only known pack with Scottish origin, engraved by W. Scott, Edinburgh, *c.* 1693.

Transformation pack by MacClure, Macdonald and Macgregor, *c.* 1865.

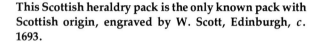

with information below. In the hearts suit the king, queen and three to ten show armorial bearings of ten different ranks from king to squire, while the ace and two show 'Military Things' and the jack 'Naval Things'! The title, suit sign, Roman numeral and court figure are shown in the top right hand corner. The pack was reproduced in 1885 and presented to the members of the Worshipful Company.

The Arms of the English Peers was issued in 1677 and in the first edition has the arms of the four kingdoms of Britain on the four kings. It was printed for John Nicholson and sold by E. Evatts of St. Pauls. A second edition of 1686 has a blank shield on the queen of clubs, while a third edition of 1688 reverts back to the original design.

Another similar pack was issued in Edinburgh by the goldsmith Walter Scott in 1691. The full title of this pack is 'The Blazoning of the Ensignes Armorial of the Kingdoms of Scotland, England, France and Ireland and of the coats of arms of the Nobility of Scotland'. This is the only known Scottish-made pack and was produced from copper plates, and coloured by hand. The pack contains two extra cards: one bearing the title and Edinburgh city arms and the motto *Nisi Dominus Frustra*; and the other bears the seal of the Lyon office impaled with the arms of Sir Alexander Ereskin of

Gambo. The kings show: spades, the Arms of France; hearts, the Arms of Scotland; clubs, the Arms of England; and diamonds, the Arms of Ireland. In the same order the queens feature: the Duke of Gordon, the Duke of Hamilton, the Duke of Lennox Scott together with the Dutches of Buccleuch and lastly Dowglas Duke of Queensberry. The 'princes' show: the Marquess of Athol, the Marquess of Dowglas, the Marquess of Montross and on the prince of diamonds the three coats of arms of Argile Campbel, Crawfurd Lindsay and Errol Hay.

A number of memorable packs were also made in England with light-hearted and whimsical subject matter – many of which have already been mentioned in the Lenthall lists. One 'Proverbs' pack (not made by Lenthall) of *c.*1710 has an illustration of a well-known proverb on each card with the 11 of diamonds showing a ship braving a stormy sea and the saying 'The more Danger the more honour'.

After the success of John Gay's *Beggar's Opera*, John Bowles in 1728 offered cards for sale showing the tunes and lyrics of the various songs performed in the opera and the name of the singer. For instance, the two of spades reads 'Tunes of Tunes when the Sea was roaring, etc., sung by Lucy Lockit.' A miniature playing card is featured in the top left-hand corner of each card.

Another musical pack (a copy of which is in the British Museum) dated at the second quarter of the 18th century has lines of music at the top of each card, a verse in the centre, and some more lines of music for flute accompaniment at the bottom. A miniature playing card is in the top left-hand corner. The cards mainly relate to the good and bad aspects of love with the queen of diamonds showing 'The Lover's Treasure'.

Another interesting 18th-century pack has allegorical figures and emblems on the court cards. The ace of hearts shows a personification of 'Religion' together with the description 'A woman veiled, a Book in her right hand, and a flaming fire in her left. The Veil informs us that Religion has its mysteries. The book expresses the Divine Law and the flaming Fire the utmost ardency of Devotion'. The jack of clubs is 'Deceit' which is 'A monstrous old man, with tails of serpents twining instead of legs; three hooks in one hand, a bag of flowers with a snake issuing from it; and behind him, a panther hiding his head, and showing his beautiful back. His Humane shape and Flowers denote his specious pretences; the Serpents' tails, the Hooks and the Snake, his villainous intentions; the Panther hiding his ugly head, his subtlety'.

One of the first packs of transformation cards to be made in England was by W. Fores of Piccadilly in 1805 and 1808. Later, in 1811, S. & J. Fuller issued their 'Metastasis – Transformation of Cards' with L. Cowell producing a similar pack a few years later. A pantomime transformation pack was made c.1810 showing Beau Brummel on the king of hearts, Three-Fingered Jack from the pantomime of Obi on the ace of clubs and Mother Goose on the four of spades. Other characters included are Shylock and Romeo and Juliet. Count d'Orsay later designed a pack in pen and ink drawings for Lady Blessington which refers to events of that period. A departure from the usual transformation pack was one by Alfred Crowquill where the pips are conventionally placed but have characters' faces inside them.

In c.1865 the Manchester firm of Maclure, Macdonald and Macgregor produced a rather amateur pack, which was nevertheless popular in its day and printed in three different versions. But the most famous English transformation card designs are those by William Makepeace Thackeray, which appeared in the first edition of his book *The Orphan of Pimlico*. In the pack the 3 of spades is headed 'Mr. Gibbon, Mr. Boswell, Mr. Johnson', the 10 of clubs is 'An Assyrian bas-relief *see* Herodotus' while other cards are examples from Shakespeare, Byron and various non-sense rhymes.

Apart from these packs mentioned, most of the English transformation packs were copied from European ones, such as Müller's Fracas pack which was printed in England by Ackermann, and Cotta's cards which were copied by E. Olivatte of London under the name of 'Kaloprosopian – Beautiful Disguise' in 1828.

Baker's Eclectic cards, printed by Theodore Page, Blackfriars Road, c.1813, is one of a series of historical cards produced in England in the 19th century. The suits are swords, hearts, acorns and diamonds. Each suit also has a secondary suit mark which relates to the country to which the suit is devoted, with: swords – leek and mistletoe for Wales; diamonds – a thistle for Scotland; hearts – a shamrock for Ireland; and acorns – an oak leaf and rose for England. The court cards represent various historical people in the costume of their day. The clubs show the English with Arthur as the king, Elizabeth as the queen and Sir John Falstaff as the jack. In the same order the other court figures are: hearts – Gathelus, the Grecian prince and the king of Ireland, Scotia his wife and Ossian a warrior and poet; diamonds – Achajus, Mary Stuart and Merlin the magician; spades – Camber, the third son of Brute, king of Cambria, Elfrida the queen of Mona and Thaliesson, the Welsh bard.

Offering more general information is a pack called 'Moral and Instructive Playing Cards' by Dean & Son of Ludgate Hill, London. Dated at the late 19th century the cards are double-ended with a different piece of information at each end of the card. The ace of diamonds states that 'Diamonds were formerly called Adamant' and 'Diamonds are the most costly of gems'.

Most English playing cards were made in London, although Birmingham made a big contribution to playing cards in the 1800s when the Kimberley firm produced a series of 'Royal National Patriotic Playing Cards'. The firm was set up by William Kimberley, son of David Kimberley who had been established in Birmingham as a carpenter's plane manufacturer since 1865. William was more interested in his own playing card designs than his father's business and in 1898 father and son amalgamated to form the Kimberley Press of Lancaster Street.

The cards they produced were of high quality and very attractive but due to severe competition the company was forced to close in 1906.

All the Kimberley cards follow the same theme of devoting one nation to each suit and portraying their rulers on the court cards. The diamonds suit represents England, the hearts U.S.A., the clubs Germany and the spades France. On the aces are found the flags

*Left to right*: **Hand-drawn transformation pack of 1870 – many of the designs show animals and circus performers and some of the cards are initialled with 'M.W' and 'C.S.W.'; an 'Historic' pack showing royalty from the Stuart, Elizabethan, Hanoverian and Plantagenet House, by Goodall & Son, *c*. 1893.**

of each nation. Due to printing costs the actual card designs went through a series of modifications. Trevor Denning identifies four different types of Patriotic Playing Cards made between 1893–1902, although a fifth 'back' variation has since been discovered. The distinguishing points between each edition are:

A. *c.*1893. Made by chrome-lithography in eleven colours and the only pack to use gold. The colours of the suit marks are black, blue, vermilion or crimson. There are no indices on the number cards but the words 'king' 'queen' and 'jack' are written in full on the court cards. The backs are dark blue and gold on white and show 41 clocks with the hands positioned at different times. Each ace shows four flags.

B. *c.*1896. Again the aces show four flags but with the aces of clubs, spades and hearts having a cloud effect background. The cards are more liberally coloured, using only red, yellow and blue. Corner indices have been introduced and the clocks on the back are in black on a single colour background.

C. *c.*1899. The colours now used are yellow, blue, red and pink, and the designs have been changed. In both C and D the English jack of diamonds, formerly a sailor, becomes George V and the jack of clubs is now Crown Prince Frederick of Germany and Prussia and the jack of spades carries a sword instead of a rope and

represents Napoleon Eugène of France. The jack of hearts is inscribed 'typical representative of the United States Navy'. The clocks on the back have elongated and simplified dials and only two flags are shown on the aces. As in A, the words 'king', 'queen' 'jack' and 'ace' are written in full.

D. *c.*1902. Almost the same designs as C, although corner indices are now used on all the cards. Also the dresses of the queens of hearts and spades are now red. The backs show a heraldic shield.

The fifth 'back' design must have been produced in-between C and D for the pack is identical to D except that the backs still show clocks.

## MODERN CARDS

Most of the smaller English card makers had disappeared by the beginning of the 20th century, with the only surviving producers of any consequence being De La Rue and Goodall & Son. After the First World War the two Leeds firms of Waddington and Alf Cooke (Universal Playing Card Co.) entered the scene.

It would seem, however, that the market was not big enough to sustain everyone. In 1921 De La Rue

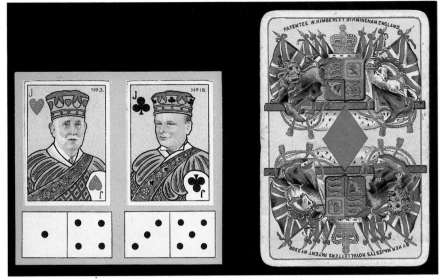

*Left to right*: One of the few 20th century British political packs, combining both a playing card and domino; the first edition of 'Royal National Patriotic Playing Cards' by W. Kimberley, Birmingham, *c*. 1893; a non-standard pack by De La Rue, London, showing Iranian suit symbols and court figures. This pack was later reproduced by H. Fournier of Spain.

took over Goodall & Son (although they used the Goodall imprint until 1960) and later De La Rue and Waddington joined forces to form the Amalgamated Playing Card Co. Ltd. Waddington quickly gained sole control and in 1971 also absorbed Alf Cooke and changed their name to Waddingtons Playing Card Company Ltd.

Among the non-standard packs produced this century, one of the earliest was a Shakespeare pack manufactured by Chas. Goodhall & Son in 1900. The courts depict named characters from four Shakespeare plays, with their names on the aces. About ten years later, C.W. Faulkner and Co. of London issued a similar pack where the kings are: Richard III, Henry V, Claudius of Denmark and Henry VIII. The backs show an advertisement for Hotels of the Midland Railway. Another Shakespeare pack by Bemrose & Son of Derby, *c*.1914, has a scroll on the court cards giving the act and scene from which the court figures represented are taken, together with a quotation from the text.

Two identical packs, called 'Fennel Heroic Cards' with figures from Irish history on the kings and queens and charioteers on the jacks were issued in 1935 by Goodall & Son and the Irish Playing Card Co. At about the same time, the Irish Playing Card Co. also produced the 'Fennel Historic Playing Cards' which has named Irish monarchs on the kings and queens and harp players on the jacks.

Thos. De La Rue issued a historical pack of *c*.1930 which has the kings and queens representing English monarchs, such as Queen Victoria, and the jacks showing famous English personalities such as Robin Hood and Shakespeare. The joker shows Oliver Cromwell.

Another interesting pack by De La Rue was issued in 1957 to mark their 125th anniversary. Called 'Picart le Doux Playing Cards' (after the designer) the four suits symbolize the four elements. In 1960 Waddingtons got Siriol Clarry to design a pack on the same theme, with spades representing fire, diamonds water, clubs air and hearts earth. In this pack the courts are reminiscent in style of some of the modern Fournier issues and are on a dark background with the indices on a white surrounding border.

Commemorative packs have always been popular with collectors due to their historical interest. As well as the usual cards produced to commemorate various coronations, weddings and silver jubilees, a pack was specially produced in 1970 for the British-American Bicentenary Group to celebrate the crossing of the Delaware, Christmas 1776. Called 'Grand Slam', 2,400

**Cigarette card by W.D. & H.O. Wills, Ltd., Bristol, c. 1890.**

double packs were issued, the same number as American troops who took part in the exercise. In one pack the courts show prominent American leaders (blue backs) and in the other British military leaders (red backs). The cards are single-ended and the personalities are pictured against a scenic background with a caption underneath.

To cater for the film-going population, De La Rue issued an M.G.M. Film Stars pack in c.1935. A semi-advertising pack called Sebastian Sed Playing Cards was specially printed for the Peter Lumley photo model agency in 1969. It features photographs of models on the cards with their statistics on the jokers.

Other advertising packs include one by Thomas De La Rue c.1935 which had J. Lyons' waitresses on the queens and the question 'Where's George?' on the joker. Waddingtons advertised the Hoover firm in a pack where the court figures are shown holding Hoover vacuum cleaners. A rather more artistic pack was designed by André François for Simpsons of Piccadilly. It has Eros on the aces and a scene of Piccadilly on the backs, while the modernistic courts appear on

different coloured backgrounds.

During this century, various unsuccessful experiments were made at modifying the suit signs and designs. In 1930 the Ormond Printing Co. of Dublin issued a four-colour pack, with the diamonds suit in yellow and clubs in green. Arpak of Liverpool made a pack in 1920 with yellow spades, red hearts, white diamonds and green clubs. In 1936 Waddingtons modified the clubs and diamonds suits and later added an extra blue crown suit to the standard pack for five-suited bridge. On the subject of bridge, Goodall issued an interesting pack which had added text, giving suggestions for playing whist and bridge. Another novel pack was a domino pack printed in c.1930 under the name 'Triplicate'. Each card is divided into three parts, the top part shows the playing card, the centre shows a domino, and the bottom shows a letter of the alphabet and the domino value in Arabic numbers. A circular pack was made by Waddingtons in c.1930 called 'Cir-Q-Lar cards, which was reissued in the fifties.

W.D. & H.O. Wills Ltd. of Bristol and London have probably issued the greatest number of cigarette cards in England. They cover a wide variety of subjects, young ladies being the most popular, and feature either a miniature playing card in one of the top corners or just the suit sign, letter or number. Two of the earliest Wills' series were Military Uniforms 1893–1902 and Animals 1897–1902. A Jockey series ran from 1904–1927 and The Young Ladies series from 1904–1927 with a different edition appearing in 1912. From 1924–1928 they issued a Birds series which was originally used by Ogden's of Liverpool in 1912–1914.

Variations on the Young Ladies' theme were made by Richmond Cavendish Co. of Liverpool 1899–1906; Gallaher Ltd., Belfast and London 1898–1906 and Ogden's of Liverpool 1890–1903. Other cigarette insert card themes were: Japanese Military Uniforms by Muratti 1900–1908; Soldiers and Indians by Ogden's 1890–1903; Sovereigns and Princes by Cope Brothers & Co. of Liverpool and London 1875–1907; Natural History by Swectule Products Ltd. 1961 and Fortune Telling by Carreras Ltd. in 1926.

Carreras Ltd. also made a combination playing card and domino pack in 1929. The courts depict famous personalities such as Churchill and Lloyd George and are perforated to separate the playing cards from the dominoes. Packs were made with and without playing card indices.

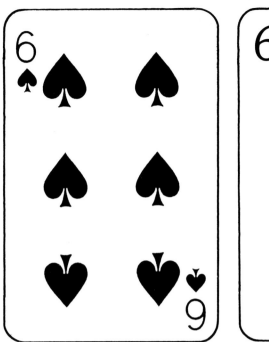

# America

AMERICA holds a somewhat unusual place in the history of playing cards, as in contrast to other countries, it did not start producing cards until comparatively recently. However, despite initial setbacks and delays, once the card producing industry was firmly established in North America, it contributed greatly to the development of cards by way of new patterns and improvements in basic designs.

At the time of the continent's discovery, in 1492, the vogue for cards in Europe was well under way, and they were beginning to be produced in large quantities. It is without doubt that the Spanish sailors on board the *Santa Maria* would have had cards packed among their kits, and have passed their time or calmed their fears by playing the odd hand.

It is from the Spanish that the native Indians adopted their own playing cards, termed by the early Mexicans as 'amapatolli' (paper game). Originally they had taken the same form as Spanish cards, with the four suits of Copas, Oros, Espadas and Bastos, and the court cards of Rey, Caballo and Sota; but as time went on, the various tribes added some of their own cultural and artistic interpretations.

Stuart Culin, in his book on playing cards, identifies a pack of forty cards, hand-painted upon tanned hide, as those of the Apache Indians. With great similarity to the early Mexican cards, they call the suits: Copas, Escudos, Espadas and Bastones or Polos. Two of the courts, Rey (also called Inju or Inshu – Good) and Sota are the same as the Spanish, with the addition of Jliv or 'Horse'. The Ace they call As and the numerical cards: Naqui 2, Taqui 3, Tingui 4, Irosh Klay 5, Custan 6, Cusetti 7. Their game they call 'Con-quien' ('With whom'), or Daka – Canitnun – ('Cards ten').

The history of card manufacturing in the English colonies set off badly right from the beginning; but it was not from lack of interest. Cards were as popular in America as in Europe, and there are many records of laws against card-gaming in the colonies.

As early as 1624 the ministers in Virginia were banned from gaming both with dice and cards. In Plymouth, a law of 1656 fixed fines against card playing at 40 shillings for adults, while punishment for children and servants was left to their parents' or master's discretion, on promise of a whipping at the second offence. In the same year the burgomaster of Newfoundland passed a law forbidding drinking, sewing, dancing and card playing, etc., on Sundays. In New Amsterdam, where cards were introduced by the Dutch, it was forbidden to play at cards during the time a church service was in progress.

But despite the many laws, gambling flourished, and there is an account of how, in June 1699, Judge Samuel Sewall of Boston suppressed a card game only to find, a few days later, packs of cards strewn across his lawn, as if to mock his efforts.

Hand-drawn and coloured on hide, Apache card of 1840–1890.

stationer. Following tradition, Samuel started his career as a stationer and began to produce cards *c.*1849.

Two of Hart's most notable innovations were the joker and round corners. He first featured the joker with an ace reading 'London Club Cards'. When he introduced round-cornered cards they were usually 'satin finished', double-ended and had either Mogul or Steamboat wrappers.

It seems that Hart was typical of many American card manufacturers in adopting two policies. On the one hand he produced mock English cards, with English names and grades, for an apparently conventional market. On the other hand he introduced innovations and new designs, such as the American jokers, and ace of spades featuring the eagle and stars.

Another important company, which is amongst the biggest card producers in America today, is the New York Consolidated Card Company, which was founded in 1833 by Lewis I. Cohen.

In 1835 Cohen contributed a major breakthrough to the playing card industry, when he invented a machine for printing at one impression the four colours on the face of playing cards.

In his early days he produced cards with an ace of spades showing an eagle and often 13 stars. In the eagle's beak is a fluttering ribbon inscribed *E Pluribus Unum* or 'New York' rather than the common 'American Manufacture'. Sometimes the street address is also given, and a shield inside a laurel wreath with the words 'L.I. Cohen' at the bottom of the card. One of his better quality packs of early cards has the ace with sixteen stars and the words 'New York', and the shield as described above. The cards are square-cornered, rather large and bear no indices. The large pips and courts are laced in gold and the backs are patterned in blue, white and gold.

In 1850 Lewis I. Cohen sold the stationery end of his business, and in 1854 he retired, leaving the playing card company in the hands of his son Solomon L. Cohen and nephew John M. Lawrence under the name of Lawrence and Cohen.

The cards of Lawrence and Cohen were very much like English cards of that period. They had typical English wrappers and often did not feature the eagle. However, they retained the artistic and much acclaimed backs of Owen Jones, which is mentioned

The early playing cards used in the English colonies were exported from England, as was everything else, and bore no novel designs, or inscriptions, to set them apart from ones used in the 'mother country'.

Card manufacturing started in America after the Revolution, when the middle colonies, where the first traders and businessmen settled, started in earnest to set up industries. It is interesting to note, however, that for some time after playing card industries were set up in America, the cards produced still followed English patterns. In fact, in many cases American manufacturers would put the word 'London' on the ace of spades, even though the cards had not even crossed a river – let alone an ocean.

One of the most important individuals of American card history in the 19th century was Samuel Hart. He came from a background of printing; his father Abraham was a bookseller and his mother Sara a

*Opposite above*: 'Union Playing Cards' made to promote the Republican cause during the Civil War by the American Card Co., New York, 1862.

*Opposite centre & below*: A selection of standard patterns by A. Dougherty, New York, showing their development in the mid-19th century, *centre, left, c.* 1870, *right, c.* 1860; *below, c.* 1880.

*Left to right*: Jack and ace of spades from a standard pack by L.I. Cohen of the mid-19th century, with gold edging around the designs and pips; standard pack by Lawrence Cohen & Co., of the mid-19th century.

on the wrapper and ace of spades.

They later used the steamboat wrapper and double-ended designs, and the corner indices which they called 'squeezers'.

On 5 December 1871, the business became a stock company and included three nephews of Lewis I. Cohen, Samuel Hart and Isaac Levy of Samuel Hart and Co., Phil., and John J. Levy of N.Y. The new company was called the New York Consolidated Card Company.

The joker they entitled the 'Best Bower', and they used two types of aces to indicate quality. The lower grade wrapper shows a picture of a factory.

For the Paris Exposition in 1878 they issued the 'American Playing Cards', although it is uncertain whether they were issued to be sold at the Fair, or at a later date. The courts depict the European rulers of the day, with the kings being Humbert I of Italy, Alexander III of Russia, Franz Joseph of Austria and Wilhelm II of Germany.

The ace of spades is a multicoloured version of their standard ace of spades, with cherubim and laurels.

Another pack made by the company in 1898 was for use by the troops in the Spanish-American War. Its interest does not lie in its standard designs, however,

but in its packaging. The case is made in imitation of the soldier's knapsack then in use. The cards occupy the body of the knapsack, while a supply of poker chips fill the roll above. Unfortunately this exercise has not been repeated.

Cohen's main competition came from another leading and prolific card company owned by Andrew Dougherty. Established in 1846, Dougherty's early cards were stencilled and distinguishable by the suit signs and court card faces which are often askew.

Dougherty brought out a similar version to Cohen's cards, with gold edging, called 'Illuminator Great Mogul'. In the late 1870s he also introduced indices to his cards which he called 'Triplicate' (later to be called Indicators) and were used with a special ace, showing cherubim and a laureated spade inside which is a display of the 'improved cards'. The wrapper, which shows a picture of his factory, mentions the 'improvements'. His un-indexed cards were still called Excelsior.

There is a pack of cards, issued in 1877, with backs showing two dogs chained; one is called Trip and the other Squeezer, and they represent the sales treaty between the two companies of Cohen and Dougherty.

Some of the most interesting non-standard cards

Standard pack by Andrew Dougherty, *c*. 1870. The miniature playing card index in the corner was a novel introduction and forerunner of modern indices.

produced in America feature war as a subject matter. The earliest of these packs were made by Jazaniah Ford, who was born in Milton in 1757, where he had a flourishing card-making business for over 50 years. The cards were made in honour of Stephen Decatur, commander in the Tripoli War at a time when the American naval officer was experiencing great popularity among the masses. The court cards show figures dressed in pseudo-Algerian costume, while on the ace of spades is the American eagle with a ribbon in its claw stating American manufacture, and Jazaniah Ford's name below. Above, is a picture of the frigate *United States*. This picture also appears on the wrapper.

Ten years later Jazaniah Ford used the same pack, but with a different ace of spades, to commemorate the return to America of the Marquis La Fayette. The new ace of spades features a central medallion portrait of General La Fayette, above which are an eagle, a bough of bay, an oak and a flag. A cannon and the maker's name are below.

Another famous early commemorative war pack was made *c*.1819 by J.Y. Humphreys. The pack is hand-coloured with stencilled pips and the suit signs are in four colours: spades, blue; hearts, red;

diamonds, yellow; and clubs, green. Called the 'Seminole' war pack, the jacks are Indian chiefs, the kings represent Washington, Jefferson, General Andrew Jackson (commander of the action against the Seminoles), and John Quincy Adams (secretary of State who ordered the invasion of Florida). The queens are Venus, Justice, Ceres and Athena.

A long series of war packs was produced during and after the Civil War. The first of the Civil War packs is the 'Union Playing Cards' of 1862, made by the American Card Co. of New York. The pack features National Emblems as suit signs, with the red suits showing stars and the American flag, and the black suits printed in blue and featuring shields and the American coat of arms with eagle crest. The four jacks show Majors, and the kings Colonels, with a befitting 'in the field' background. The queens appear as goddesses of Liberty. These cards lack corner indices or marks of value and on the backs feature a shield, anchor and flag. The next year the same company issued another similar 'Union' pack, but this had full figure courts with no background scenes. M. Nelson of New York decided he could monopolize on both sides of the Civil War, and in 1863 issued a 'Confederate Generals' pack as well as a 'Union Generals' pack. Both packs are identical except for the changed personalities featured on the court cards. Each court has a bust portrait of an officer or high government official, with his name printed underneath. In the corner is a miniature playing card to denote value, the same as was used later by A. Dougherty for his 'Triplicate' cards.

In 1865, Andrew Dougherty issued his famous 'Army and Navy Cards'. This is one of the most original Civil War packs, and employs novel suit signs. The red suits are drummer boys and zouaves, representing the army. The black suits, again printed in blue to give the red, white and blue effect of the flag, are Monitors and Merrimacs, representing the navy. The latter were named after a 40-gun screw frigate built in 1855. It had been sunk in 1861, but the Confederates renovated it along the lines of the *Monitor*, and gave it a four-inch iron plating and renamed it the *Virginia*. The ace of Monitors reads 'To Commemorate the greatest event in Naval history, the substitution of iron for wood'.

Russell Morgan & Co., although not issuing a complete pack dedicated to war, instead used the army and navy as brand names and designs for the ace of spades. Originally printers, they built an addition for making cards to their printing factory in Race Street, Cincinnatti. They produced their first cards in 1881. Their first trade mark was either Army or Navy.

In 1891 they changed their name to the United States Printing Company, and in 1894 to the world famous United States Playing Card Company (U.S.P.C. Co.). As the U.S.P.C. Co. they excelled themselves in producing a number of world-famous transformation packs. The first was 'Hustling Joe' of 1895. In this pack the courts are not truly transformed but superimposed on a scenic background. Two issues of this pack are known, the first had Hustling Joe in red on the ace of spades. The cards have a solid background in which the colour runs to the ends of the cards. The second issue, dated the same year, was published for the sake of the gambler. As all the court cards had coloured edges and the number cards white edges, a card-sharp might be able to determine when a court card was coming. The re-issued pack had a coloured background on the courts which did not extend to the borders, but left an irregular white border.

Hustling Joe is portrayed in a yellow costume on the ace of spades. The number cards in both packs are the same, with the spade suit showing various balancing and meditation postures. The diamonds show various professions, and the hearts young ladies dressed for sport. The club suit tells the story of how someone breaks a safe, gets caught, tried and sent to jail, while the policeman involved finds a girlfriend and eventually gets married. Maybe this is a satirical interpretation of the two types of sentence – both for life!

Equal in fame and ingenuity is the U.S.P.C. Co. 'Vanity Fair' transformation pack, also made in 1895. This time all the pip cards are transformed, but the courts are just double-ended amusing caricatures. The following year they produced 'Ye Witches' fortune cards. Again only a partial transformation pack, the ace of spades shows a knave in costume with the name and address. The ace of clubs is a wedding bell, while the other two aces show respectable gentlemen suitors. The backs of the cards show witches astride broomsticks.

The U.S.P.C. Co. did not, however, produce the first transformation packs in America. This dubious honour goes to Charles Bartlett of New York. Known as the 'Bartlett Transformation Pack', it was published in 1833 but sadly bore no original features. The cards are suspiciously similar to three packs produced about 15 years earlier in Vienna by H.F. Müller, in France by Gide Fils and in England by Ackermann. The distinguishing point is that in comparison with the other three packs, the Bartlett cards are gaudy and garishly coloured, with purples, bright greens and reds. The number cards show various soldiers and knights of all nations, both on and off duty. The court cards show various nationalities with the spades suit in Bohemian costume, the hearts in Roman garb, diamonds in Turkish dress, and the clubs being a mixture, with the queen a Sultana, the king Alexander, and the jack a Saxon chief.

The first totally original transformation pack to be produced in America is the 'Eclipse Comic Playing Cards' by F.H. Lowerre of New York, in 1876. All the court cards are framed in gold, as are the crowns worn by the court figures, and this is also the first transformation pack to use a joker. Acrobats feature promi-

---

*Opposite above, left to right*: 'Columbian Exposition' souvenir pack by G.W. Clark, Chicago, 1893; the 'Vanity Fair' transformation pack by the United States Playing Card Co., 1895.

*Opposite centre, left to right*: 'Harlequin' transformation pack designed by C.E. Carryl for Tiffany and Co., 1879, here in a cigarette card size; 'World Fair Souvenir' pack, with courts showing a bust protrait of King Ferdinand, Queen Isabella and Columbus. Made for the Columbian Exposition in 1893 by Winters Art Litho Co.

*Opposite below, left to right*: One of a series of tobacco insert cards by Moore & Calvi, c. 1890.

nently in the designs, as do soldiers, but in some cases the suit signs are not truly transformed but merely superimposed on a scene. The name of the cards is on the ace of spades, while the American eagle and the price of one dollar, appear on the king of hearts.

Around 1860 Samuel Hart published a transformation pack called 'Pictorial Cards' whose designs, except for the ace of hearts, are identical to a pack printed by William Tegg of London. Tegg in turn, copied the designs from a pack by Braun and Schneider of Munich made c.1850.

One of the few transformation packs designed to advertise a product was made by A. Dougherty on behalf of the Murphy Varnish Co. Called the 'Murphy Varnish Transformation Advertising Pack' of c.1883, the pack is rare and much sought after by both playing card collectors and advertising ephemera collectors. It contains 52 cards plus a joker, called 'The Best Card', and each card is cleverly converted into a comical cartoon advertising the company's product.

During the 1860s/70s a new trend in advertising was born in the United States. This was the *insert* card. The most popular use of the insert card was in tobacco products, and in time advertisers began to use playing cards as inserts. After all, what better way to tempt people to buy the same pack of cigarettes than the need to complete a pack of 52 cards?

Because of the difficulty of collecting a whole series, these packs are extremely rare. One of the most popular subjects for cigarette insert cards was that of glamour girls. Most of these packs are similar, showing beauties of the day dressed in theatrical costumes. The suit sign and number are in the top right-hand corner and the advert is on the backs and sometimes on the front of the cards as well. The first known pack issued was for Lorillard's 5 Ante-Chewing Tobacco c.1885. They were printed by Donaldson Brothers, Lithographers, New York, with a size of 1¾in. × 3½in. The same company issued an identical pack for their snuff, only changing the wording of the advert.

Two quite novel insert playing cards were produced by the Kinney Brothers. They were the 'Kinney Transparent' cards of c.1890 and c.1892. The first pack had 52 cards (no joker), which when held up to the light revealed a picture and a 'fortune'. The second issue included a joker and had slightly different back designs. Another craze the American card manufacturers quickly catered for was the souvenir and commemorative packs.

The first known American cards to commemorate a fair or exhibition are those of Victor Mauger of New York. Called the 'Centennial Playing Cards' of 1876, they have a standard face, but featured corner indices, which were still very new in those days. For a dash of originality they also had four different coloured suits: spades black, hearts red, diamonds yellow and clubs blue.

Issued for the same exhibition were the 'Centennial' playing cards by A. Dougherty in 1876. Again the faces are standard, but the backs have an oval portrait of George Washington, surrounded by a patriotic motif, and the words 'America's Centennial, July 4th, 1876'. Just so as not to be missed out, the Continental Card Co. issued a pack for the same event, under the same name. It was made to be sold at the fair with the backs, wrapper and ace mentioning the occasion.

The Columbian Exposition of 1893 can boast at least seven different souvenir packs, mostly with Columbus featuring somewhere or other. One of the most unusual of these packs is *Columbiano Naipes* by U.S.P.C. Co. These are Spanish playing cards issued for the exhibition, with South American Indians featured on the courts. The suits are changed to Suns – coins, Earthern bowls – cups, Arrows – swords, and Indian War Clubs – clubs.

Advertisers also took the opportunity of designing cards for exhibitions, with the Enterprise Brewing Co. having cards printed by Winters for the Midwinter Exposition. The pack is identical to another one sold in the Exposition, also by Winters, except for two cards – the jack of diamonds and queen of spades which feature brewery advertisements and 'Compliments of Enterprise Brewery Co'. The rest of the cards have colour sketches of the Fair, and bust portraits of Uncle Sam, Liberty, etc. The backs show state seals of California, Oregon, Washington and the Exposition.

Railroad souvenir packs were also produced. Now, these are highly prized collector's items and are difficult to come by as they cut across many collecting fields, such as railroad and advertising collectors. Thousands of packs were issued featuring the name of the line on the backs. A smaller percentage of them actually had a different scene of the route on each card. Some of them also advertised the rail line on the back of the cards and on the ace of spades.

In time, as souvenir cards became more and more popular, there was not an amusement arcade, park or city that did not issue its own souvenir pack. Although one cannot be specific, and there are many exceptions, a general trend can be seen among the designs.

The earliest type, of around 1895, shows black and white or sepia tone, oval shaped scenes which have no outlines. A few years later, in c.1898, a fine ornate type outline was added. With the advent of the 20th century the mono-colour oval photo-scenes were introduced. It is not unusual for each suit to be printed in a

*Left to right*: Railway souvenir pack with the reverse showing 'Crossing the Great Salt Lake' by the United States Playing Card Co., Cincinnatti, *c.* 1906; 'Indians of the South West' souvenir pack with oval photo scenes made for Fred Harvey, *c.* 1905; 'The Championship Fight' souvenir pack showing famous boxers and matches, by W.P. Jefferies & Co., Los Angeles, *c.* 1909.

---

different tone, with an outline around the photo scene in the same colour. Many modern cards with photo-scenes are the round-cornered rectangular card variety, which first appeared *c.*1915.

The close of the 19th century brought with it a new fashion among non-standard American playing cards – the political cards. A.H. Caffee of New York issued the 'Comic Political' pack in 1892. It was designed for the Presidential Campaign of Grover Cleveland in his effort to regain the Presidency from Benjamin Harrison. The courts are political figures of the national scene, with the king of hearts as Cleveland and that of spades Harrison. As was common, an extra card was issued identifying all the personalities. The joker shows a boxing scene where Cleveland has just knocked down Harrison.

## MODERN AMERICAN CARDS

It has often been a criticism of the card manufacturing industry world-wide, that with the birth of the 20th century came the death of the 'original' playing card: this is aptly reflected in modern American cards.

Although their modern cards are of great interest as items in their own right, when viewed as an extension of their earlier cards, they contribute little by way of new designs or ideas.

Apart from souvenir cards, which have still continued to be produced in ever increasing numbers, the bulk of American non-standard cards again fall into the two broad categories of war and politics. Most of the war cards perpetuate the use of novel suit signs, and feature the services and front-line leaders or rulers, while the political cards reflect the U.S.A.'s preoccupation with either bolstering or demolishing their respective Presidents. Also, whereas the card designers of by-gone days regarded their craft as a minor art form, this seems to have been replaced by a dedication to the 'hard sell' techniques of advertising and propaganda.

The romantic notions of war, as were experienced by most nations – until they actually found themselves in a trench – were a constant feature of the packs produced during the First World War.

The Liberty Playing Card Co. of New York issued their 'Liberty Playing Cards' in 1915 in an attempt to rouse public support for U.S. involvement in World War I. The joker shows Uncle Sam rolling up his

Two cards (*left* and *right*) from the 'Trumps Long Cut' cigarette insert cards, *c*. 1886; in the *centre* a court card featuring four contemporary actors and actresses from 'The Stage Playing Cards' by the United States Playing Card Co., *c*. 1896.

sleeves and the title 'Invincible'. The aces are replaced by bullets, kings by commanders, queens by nurses and jacks by soldiers and sailors.

In later packs the slogans became more forceful. The 'Freedom Playing Cards' of 1917, by the company of the same name, has a joker showing a soldier, a sailor and a donkey with the statement 'No Kings or Queens for Me'. The courts show Uncle Sam, Liberty and Infantry soldiers.

Even more to the point are the messages on the 'Democracy Playing Cards' produced a year later: 'Patriotic Americans Insist on Democracy Playing Cards in your home and club.' 'Out with Kings and Queens. Four million brave American boys and girls willingly answered the call to put down autocracy. They did their work well and Democracy's banner has been unfurled to the world forever.' 'Our hero Aces of the Air who, facing death above the clouds, guided our boys on land and sea to a glorious victory for the world.' One gets the impression they fought the war single-handed! With this pack the nurses feature on the queen cards, jack tars on the jacks and infantrymen on the kings. The air force is immortalized on the aces. The backs show battleships, planes and howitzers, while the joker shows a sailor nailing up the

pennon 'Democracy' to a flagstaff surmounting a globe of the world. Beneath, a soldier ceremoniously blows the bugle while a nurse dutifully stands by.

Another pack issued before the U.S.A. stepped into the war was by the Montreal Lithograph Co. Called the 'Allied Armies' pack of 1916, it was issued in two versions both with backs showing the flags of France, Belgium, Serbia, England, Japan, Russia and Italy. The first version dedicates the suits to: spades Italy, hearts Belgium, diamonds England and clubs Russia, with the kings and queens showing the respective monarchs, and the jacks privates in uniform. The other rulers are mentioned on the aces.

The second version promoted Japan to the spades suit, with the ousted Italians having to be satisfied with a mention on the ace of diamonds.

By way of a refreshing change, Levis and Cook of Chicago produced 'Playanlearn' in 1918, which in the author's opinion, has to be acknowledged as one of the most sensible and industrious uses of playing cards throughout that period. Except for the ace of spades, all the cards are printed in light grey with a French lesson superimposed on them. Its purpose was to teach French to troops stationed in France on the principle of one learns faster while having fun.

'Victory' pack by Arrco, *c.* 1945.

A very rare and much sought-after war pack is the '26th Yankee Division', issued in 1933 by the Press of the Woolly Whale. A total of less than 400 packs was issued by Melbert B. Cary Jr. (who also wrote a book on war cards and owned a fine collection of cards), in commemoration of the signing of the Armistice on 11 November 1918.

The jacks illustrate the three branches of the combat services, all armed appropriately, while the kings represent officers of infantry and artillery, and hold useless weapons such as a fountain pen. The queens are based upon the popular First World War song, 'Parlez-Vous'. The queen of spades is the Mademoiselle of Gay Paree and holds a bottle of champagne; the queen of clubs is Mlle. of Orleans and holds a bottle of red wine; the queen of diamonds is a typical German Fräulein and holds a stein of beer, and the queen of hearts is the winking Mlle. from Armentières. The joker honours the 103rd Field Artillery.

Moving on to the Second World War a most unusual pack is the 'Anma' pack by the Anma Card Co. in 1941. The name is derived from the initials of: Army, Navy, Marines and Air Corps. The courts are: kings, Lt. Colonels; queens, Nurses; jacks, Majors and aces, Colonels. Each number card is given a rank with Cap-

tain as card no. ten. The joker is the Commander-in-Chief.

Victory in Europe was commemorated by 'Victory Playing Cards' by Arrco, 1945. Predictably the kings show Uncle Sam, queens Liberty and jacks have a soldier and sailor. The joker is a caricature of Hitler and Mussolini.

'The President Suspender Deck' of 1904, by C.A. Edgarton Co., is one of the more ingenious packs using a political theme for advertising a product. Each king and jack shows two different Presidents, with the queens showing their First Ladies. The joker is George Washington. The backs carry an advertisement for their product – President Suspenders.

The tragic death of President Kennedy affected the whole world in some form or another, including The Humor House card producers. In 1963 they produced their 'Kennedy Kards', in which all the courts are members of the Kennedy Family or Administration. The Kennedy assassination took place just before the cards were scheduled to be released, consequently they were not put on the market until a respectable period of time had elapsed.

President Nixon was not so fortunate, and can claim at least three packs produced for his ridicule. The

*Left to right*: 'Kennedy Kards' produced in 1963 by The Humor House; 'Politicards' the 1980 Presidential Elections pack produced by a Washington lawyer and political adviser to the labour unions, Victor Kamber; non-standard transformation type pack by Sutherland-Brown of Santa Cruz, *c*. 1977.

'Politicards' by Politicard Corp., Los Angeles, which were also made in Japan, show caricatures of the personalities in the political scene. The black suits are devoted to the Republicans, with the spades showing Nixon and his Administration, while the red suits show the Democrats.

A year later in 1972, the Alfabet Co. commissioned U.S.P.C. Co. to print the 'Presidents Deck', which has caricatures of Nixon on the kings, Mrs. Nixon on the queens and Agnew on the jacks. The jokers are Wallace and Humphreys. The third pack, called 'Executive Deck' by Merser and Smith, was printed in Japan in 1973 and repeats the same theme but varies the politicians on the jacks.

Aside from war and political packs, an amusing and now rare modern pack made in a limited edition of 600 copies was designed by Dick Martin for the Chicago Playing Card Collectors in 1961. The cards are humorously designed and portray the history of playing cards, featuring the different types of cards and the famous people associated with them. Called 'Fact and Fancy', the 52 cards have an additional title card and the booklet *Six Centuries of Famous Card Players and Famous Playing Cards*.

Another limited edition was issued by U.S. Games Systems Inc., N.Y., in 1976 entitled 'American Historical'. Two varieties of the pack were made, one to be sold ordinarily, and a limited edition of 200 presenta-

tion packs which were signed by the author and artist. All the cards show historical persons from U.S. history, with an accompanying book by Stuart Kaplan.

Since the U.S. is a conglomeration of all nations, card manufacturers have produced, and still do, not only French- and Spanish-suited cards, but also cards which can be used by different speaking nations. This includes the 'O Shlemiel Cards', which are standard except for Yiddish wording, and their English equivalent overprinted on the card faces. In addition each card has a letter and number, making a very versatile pack suitable for a number of games.

Another feature of modern American card making is the rise of many small craft communities which have produced some quite original playing card designs. One of the most notable of the new packs is one designed and produced by Sutherland-Brown Playing Cards of Santa Cruz, California. The cards are printed in black, white and red, and are an interesting development of the transformation pack. Whereas on most transformation packs the pips remain in their usual position and the pictures are drawn around them, with this pack the reverse applies. The designs have been drawn and then the pips suitably placed on the card. Many of the cards portray stories or puns, such as a heart attack on the 4 of hearts, where it shows four soldiers storming a castle.

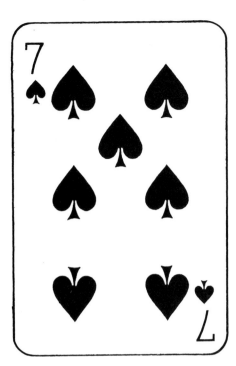

# The Orient

ONE could be forgiven for not recognizing an Oriental playing card when one saw one. The shape, and subject matter are totally different from Western cards, and even the pronunciation of their names is enough to put most people off studying or collecting them. However, perseverance would be well rewarded, for as well as their physical beauty, this complex group of playing cards has some fascinating history attached to it – much of which has yet to be unravelled. With Indian playing cards, we have Rudolf von Leyden to thank for most of the information on the subject, but in all areas of Oriental playing cards there is still a great deal of research to be done and the following can be taken only as a brief introduction.

## INDIA

Indian playing cards, termed as Ganjifa, are traditionally round, varying from 1 to 5 inches in diameter. They are usually hand-made from lacquered paper, although examples are known made from thin wood, woven cotton fibres, leather and animal skins, ivory, fish scales, mother of pearl, tortoiseshell, enamel and with gold and silver inlay. Packs can comprise anything from 36 to 384 cards of different suits, which usually have different background colours. Since the cards are hand-made, a certain amount of artistic licence is present with regard to the suit designs, background colours and the amount of detail and ornamentation used, even with recognized standard patterns. Because the methods and designs on Indian playing cards have remained unchanged for centuries it is often difficult to tell a 20th-century example from one of the 19th or even 18th centuries.

The quality of Indian cards can vary greatly. Well produced packs are clear in detail and are contained in equally beautiful hand-painted boxes. At the other end of the quality scale are the 'bazaar' cards. These are made from lacquered paper in dull colours and because they are hurriedly put together the suit signs often get distorted out of recognition.

The many different types of cards used in India are usually localized to certain areas, with the two predominant packs being 'Dasavatara' and its sub-groups (Hindu tradition) and 'Ganjifa' and its sub-groups (Moslem tradition – the word ganjifa is here used to describe a specific game). Four other main groups of Indian cards exist which are: 'Ganjappa' – used in Orissa; 'Chad' – which was used in Mysore and of which there were fourteen different types; military based packs; and European-derived packs. As well as the military, the subject matter used on Indian cards comprises structure of palace life, religion, astrology and mythology.

Indian 'Mogul Ganjifa' pack of 96 cards from the Deccan.

Indian 'Dasavatara Ganjifa' pack of 120 cards from Sawartwadi.

The actual origins of Indian cards are still unknown, although it is generally thought that they appeared in the form we know them during the 15th or 16th century. One theory suggests that Indian cards evolved from chess, for like chess some of the earliest Indian cards were based on a military format and manoeuvres.

The first reliable mention of cards in India, however, was in 1527. It tells of how the first Mogul Emperor Baber sent a pack of 'Ganjifa' to Sind. Later, in 1590, Abul Fazl Allami, Secretary of the Emperor Akbar, recorded how Akbar played a 12-suited card game which he found cumbersome. He therefore reduced it to an 8-suited game called 'Mogul Ganjifa', in which the suits represent different departments of the Imperial court. Like many Indian packs the cards are divided into weak and strong suits. The suits are:

*Weak Suits*
Dhanpati – Master of the Gold Mint and Treasury (Surukh suit)
Firman or Bharat – Master of the Chancellery
Quimash – Master of the Stores
Chang – Master of the Royal Music

*Strong Suits*
Sadid or Safet – Master of the Silver Mint
Shamser – Master of the Sword

Taj – Master of the Crown and Royal Insignia
Ghulaman or Golam – Master of the Servants of the Royal Household.

Originally each card in the pack featured detailed pictures of the activities of the various departments. Gradually the designs became more and more diluted until now the pips just act as symbols. The Golam suit, for a time continued to show a number of men and women corresponding to the card's value, performing tasks or sitting around. Later, this suit also developed uniform pips which usually depict busts of men.

Like most Indian cards (the exception is the Chad cards) two court cards are present in this pack: the Mir or king and Vazir the minister. The distinctive features of the pack are that the Mir of the Surukh suit is shown as a sun riding a lion or surrounded by lions. The Mir of the Golan suit rides an elephant and the Vazir a bullock. The Vazir of the Chang suit usually shows a woman riding a camel. The other court figures ride horses, although occasionally the Mir and Vazir are shown sitting on thrones surrounded by servants holding umbrellas, punkahs or fly whisks. Many variations and sub-groups of this pack exist.

Packs made in Orissa have the Mir as the god Rama and his Vazir as one of the supporting gods Lakshman, Virupaksha, Arjun or Vishnu.

Indian Ganjappa pack.

The 'Dasavatara' pack is one of the most interesting and decorative of the Indian packs and contains 120 cards of 10 suits of 12 cards. Each of the suits represents a different incarnation of the god Vishnu. The highest card, the Avatar, shows Vishnu himself performing some deed or sitting on a throne and the second court card, the Pradhan, shows him on horseback or on a chandeli (foot stool). The remaining cards of each suit are valued from 1–10 or 10–1 with pips that are symbolic of the 'suit-incarnation' or with the corresponding number of Krishna figures as the value of each card.

The ten incarnations of Vishnu are split into five Ages, with the fifth Age, represented by the 10th suit, still to come. The first Age is called Satya Yuga or Age of Truth and has Vishnu appearing on earth in the guise of various animals and tells the story of the 'new creation'. The legend begins when the earth was at the height of corruption and the gods had caused a mighty deluge to engulf the earth. The suits are as follows:

*Matsyavatara* – the Fish. In the form of a fish Vishnu saved the seventh law-giver and founder of present-day humanity Manu Styavarata by towing his ship, containing all the sages, plants and animals to safety after the flood.

*Kourmavatara* – the Tortoise. Legend has it that the Indian continent rests on the back of a tortoise. Originally however the tortoise served as a support for the Slow Mountain which the gods and genii used as a churning rod when recovering valuables lost in the deluge.

*Varahavatara* – the Boar. The wild boar killed the demon Golden Eyes and recovered the earth from the bottom of the sea, re-floated it on the ocean and divided it into the seven continents.

*Narasinhavatara* – the Lion. This is the last incarnation of the first Age and the purpose was to establish the worship of Vishnu. Taking the shape of a man-lion Vishnu destroyed the evil king Prahlad who had threatened the worship of the deity.

*Vamanavatara* – the Dwarf or Water Vases. The second Age was called Treta Yuga and started with Vishnu as a dwarf tricking Bali, the king of the genii, out of his dominion of the three worlds: heaven, earth and the nether world.

*Parasou-Rama* – the Axe. This incarnation represents Rama with an axe who re-established the social order that had been disturbed by the attempts of kings to gain spiritual control from the priest sect.

*Rama-Ichandra* – Bows and Arrows or Monkeys. In this incarnation Vishnu mercifully killed the demon king Ravana who had abducted his wife Sita. The monkeys sometimes depicted probably represent the monkey headed demi-god Hanuman, the selfless helper and devotee of Rama.

*Krishna* – Quoit Shaped Thunder Bolts (sometimes Cows in remembrance of the time Krishna spent with the cowherds). This incarnation begins the third Age of Krishna. It is said that he came to establish the religion of love before the fourth Age of Strife.

*Buddha* – Umbrellas or Conch Shells. Our present age, Kali Yuga, is represented by this incarnation when Buddha replaced ritual by moral values and established the importance of the individual. This is intended to hasten the ruin which will complete the present cycle.

*Kalki-Avatar* – The Swords or Horses. This last suit represents the incarnation to come. Vishnu will return triumphant riding a white horse and wielding a mighty sword. He will punish the evil, comfort the righteous and then destroy the world. From the ruins a new mankind will emerge.

A variant Dasavatara pack from Rajputana has: 22 suits or Avatara illustrating the usual but extended incarnations of Vishnu, eight Dikpalas suits (guardians of the quarters), and two extra suits. Each suit has ten cards and two court cards of a Divinity and a Pradhan totalling in all 384 cards. Only one example of this pack is known, which is painted on wood and dates from the 18/19th century.

'Ganjappa' (sometimes called Ramayana Ganjifa) is the Rama pack of Orissa and is based on the military exploits of the god Rama. It contains 144 cards of 12 suits of 12 cards. Again there are six weak suits devoted to Rama and six strong suits belonging to Ravana – the demon king of Ceylon. The two court cards in each suit are either Rama and a Vazir or Ravana and a Vazir. The suits are: Rama, or the weak suits: an Arrow, Quiver, Monkey, Bear, Hill, Shield, and Sword.

Ravana, or the strong suits: a Club, Spear, Noose or Snake, Pica (tail-less hare) and a Sword.

Examples of a different military pack exist which also comprise 144 cards divided into 12 suits of 12 cards and two court cards in each suit. The first eight suits are based on the departments of imperial life with the last four suits devoted to the different forms of the deity Shiva. It could well be that this is the pack the Mogul Emperor Akbar reduced into the eight-suited Ganjifa pack. The six strong suits are: Ashvapati – Master of Horses, Gajpati – Master of Elephants, Narpati – Master of Men (the foot soldier suit), Gadhpati – Master of Fortresses, Dhanpati – Master of Treasures (the jars of coins suit) and Dalpati – Master of Hosts (the warrior suit). The six weak suits are: Nawapati –

Master of Ships, Tipati – Queen with her maids (women suit), Surapati – Master of Divinities, Asurapati – Master of Demons, Banpati – Master of Beasts (animal suit) and Ahipati – Master of Serpents.

The largest group of cards in India is formed by the 'Chad' packs of which there are fourteen different types. They are mainly found in southern India and their subject matters include mythological and astronomical elements. Most of these Chad packs of Mysore were invented by Krishnaraja Wadiyar, ruler of Mysore, after he was deposed by the English in 1831. The number of cards in a pack ranges from 36 to 360 with four to eighteen suits. The court cards usually feature elephants, chariots, horses, foot soldiers and fortresses. Six of the Chad packs have special cards, including 'bird' cards, which are similar to tarot trumps and jokers.

One 'Chad' pack called 'Chamundeshvari' has sixteen suits of eighteen cards (six court cards and twelve number cards in each suit). The court cards show different mythological figures in various poses in litters, chariots or on horseback and even sitting on palace roofs waving banners. The number cards show the signs of the zodiac. The court cards are: Nayak – Presiding Deity, Shakti – Consort, Rath – Chariot, Mantri – Horse-rider, Yoddha – Warrior, Dhwaj – Fortress/Flag. The zodiacal signs are: Mesha – Aries, Vrishaba – Taurus, Mithuna – Gemini, Karaka – Cancer, Simha – Leo, Kanya – Virgo, Tula – Libra, Vrischika – Scorpio, Dhanus – Sagittarius, Makara – Capricorn, Kumbha – Aquarius, and Meena – Pisces. Each of the suits represents a different deity including: Chamundi, Ganesha, Shiva, Kumar, Virabadhra, Vishnu, Venugopala (Krishna), Rama, Kama, Mohini, Brahma, Indra, Surya, Varuna, Vayu and Naga. The total is 320 cards.

Another 'Chad' pack called 'Krishnaraj Chad' has four suits of eighteen cards. Again each suit has a presiding deity of either Vishnu-Krishna, Shiva, Brahma or Indra. The second court cards are: Shakti – Consort, Mantri – Horse-rider, Yoddha – Warrior and Dhwaj – Fortress/Flag. Another four cards are related to Vishnu and show: Garuda – Bird Man, Hanuman – the Monkey god, Chakra – Vishnu's quoit weapon, and Shanka – Vishnu's conch. The rest of the number cards show animals or birds with: Hati – Elephant, Aswa – Horse, Simha – Lion, Varaha – Board, Gaja-Virala – Lion Gryph, Makara – Crocodile, Matsya – Fish, Jalayus – Vulture, Ganda-Bharunda – Double-Headed Eagle. The total is seventy-two cards.

The first European cards to be introduced into India were the Portuguese-type cards. They contain three court cards of which one is always a horseman. Origi-

**Mah Jong cards made in Japan.**

nally they depicted the Portuguese Dragons on the aces, but this has gradually changed into a crocodile. Most of the Portuguese-based packs and the French-suited Indian packs are rectangular in shape. Some of the French packs have special aces (called a 'marriage') which combine the qualities of king and queen. The European-type cards are often known as: 'Spades', 'Taz', and 'Chiridia' or little birds. The French suits are called Hukm (spades), Paan (hearts), Eent or Brick (diamonds) and Chiri or Bird (clubs).

## PERSIA

It is thought that Persian cards first appeared in the Safawiden Dynasty of *c*.1700. They are similar to Indian cards in as much as they are hand-made from lacquered paper, wood or ivory and the suits are distinguished by different background colours. They differ from Indian cards, however, in their subject matter

and composition.

Although many variant packs exist in Persia the most common pack is known as 'As Nas'. It is made up of five suits, each containing any number of cards divisible by five, e.g. five suits of five, totalling twenty-five cards. Each suit repeats the same design on each card. The suits are: Padishah showing the Shah or King on a green background, Bibi – showing the favourite wife of the Shah on a throne against a red background, Lakkat – a dancing harem girl on a yellow background, Sarbaz – the archer, later the soldier, on a golden background, and the As suit – showing the lion from the Persian coat of arms and the rising sun on a black background (sometimes an eagle or dragon).

Three other main groups of Persian As Nas cards exist which depict various flowers, various ornaments or figures and scenes from sagas. The cards which only depict objects are probably the ones used by strict Moslems who in accordance with the teachings of the Koran do not play with ordinary cards that depict

European-type, French-suited Indian cards.

Persian card from Asnas game.

figures. Rectangular Ganjifa-type cards are also sometimes found in Persia.

## CHINA

Chinese cards are long and thin with modern cards being made from flimsy paper. The exact date of their origin is again unknown, but some people are of the opinion that they existed in China as long ago as 618–907 A.D. in the T'ang Dynasty. Detailed authentic information about playing cards, however, did not appear in China until the 17th century in the Ming Period. Some of these early cards figure literary scenes; either showing just figures from novels or plays by themselves or coupled with quotations. Other packs show different hierarchies. One known example from the 18th century has the suits of: W'en (civil), Wu (military), K'o (science) and Yiuan (academy). The various offices of each department are

arranged in order of importance on the number cards in each suit.

Modern Chinese cards can be classified into five main groups: Mah Jong cards; Word, Phrase or Number cards; Domino or Dice cards; Chess cards; and Money cards.

The 'Mah Jong' cards are simply a paper version of the Mah Jong tiles, and are based on money cards. Packs contain 136 cards of three suits of nine cards repeated three times and a 'four winds' suit and a 'three dragons' suit repeated four times. The suits are: Bamboos, Circles, Characters, East, South, West, and North Winds and Red, Green and White Dragons. Sometimes two sets of four flower cards are added to the packs. These two sets comprise 1. Summer, Autumn, Spring, Winter, and 2. The Fisher, The Woodcutter, The Farmer and The Scholar.

The word, phrase or number cards are similar in principle to Western game packs such as Happy Families. Each pack has two sets of cards arranged in

**Chinese domino cards**

categories (e.g. words, sayings or numbers) and the player has to collect as many cards in the category as possible. The categories can be repeated a number of times to give packs of thirty cards upwards. Sometimes joker cards are added such as the Five Blessings of Posterity, Promotion, Long Life, Happiness and Health.

The 'Domino cards', called 'Tien Chiu Pai', feature one of the twenty-one possible values obtained from throwing dice. Sometimes they are illustrated and have miniature domino cards at the top and bottom of the card denoting the card's value. The domino values are divided into a military and civil section and the one and four spots are usually coloured in red with the remaining spots in black. The twenty-one basic cards can be repeated four to six times forming packs of 84 or 126 cards.

The other packs based on an existing game are the Chinese Chess cards. Packs are made based on both two-sided and four-sided chess and the idea of the

game is to collect as many related cards as possible. Cards based on the four-sided chess are called 'Soo Sik Pai' and contain twenty-eight basic cards repeated a number of times. Each suit has a different coloured background and contains seven number cards which represent the chess pieces. The green and white suits include: Chiang – General, Shih – Official, Hsian – Elephant, P'ao – Cannon, Ma – Horse, Chu – Cart, and Ping – Soldier. The red and yellow suits have: Shuai – General, Shih – Official, Hsiang – Minister, P'ao – Cannon, Ma – Horse, Chu – Battlewagon and Tsu – Soldier.

The two-sided chess cards are called 'Hung Pai'. They have two suits, one white and one red or black, which contain the same cards as the respective suits in the four-sided chess game. The basic cards can be repeated several times to a maximum of 112 cards. Sometimes jokers are added to the pack.

The Chinese cards based on money are found in most parts of China and South-East Asia although

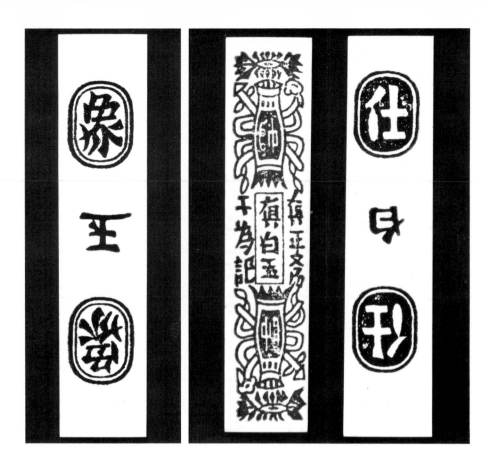

Chinese chess cards.

many variations exist. Packs include a basic number of 30 or 40 cards repeated three or four times. In each pack the three or four suits have nine number cards and a court card. The suits are based on Chinese money called cash and are variations of: single coins, strings of coins and myriads of coins. The single coin suit shows a single coin with a hole in the middle. The string of coins suit shows coins tied together with string and the myriad of coins suit shows portraits of wealthy gentlemen and the coin's value in figures. Sometimes packs have jokers and extra cards such as the White Flower, Red Flower and Old Thousand.

## KOREA

Korean cards are very similar to Chinese cards and are usually made on card, leather or oiled paper with orange as the predominant colour. The Korean word for cards is 'Fighting Strips'. Packs contain 60 or 80

cards of six or eight sets of nine cards valued from 1–9 and six or eight 'General' or court cards valued at ten. One side of the card has Korean characters describing the suit and the other side is blank or has a feather or arrow-head design. Because of the 'arrow' design it was at one time believed that Korean cards were derived from arrows. In the 80-card pack the suits represent: Men, Fish, Crows, Pheasants, Antelopes, Stars, Rabbits and Horses.

## JAPAN

Japan's standard cards can be divided into two main sections: the 'Awase' type of composition games which have a purely Japanese heritage and can be traced back to the shell game of the Heian Period (794–858); and the Western-influenced cards which evolved from the first Portuguese examples introduced into Japan in the 16th century.

**Chinese-suited money cards.**

It would seem that, like early Chinese packs, Japanese cards were originally very reliant on literature and poetry for their subject matter and illustrations. One of the most famous of the Japanese packs, the 'Hundred Poets' cards (and other related packs), works on the same principle and probably evolved from poem shells which are known from at least the 15th century. One half of the shell had one line of verse and the second shell had the lower line of verse and the purpose was to match the two shells and poems.

Today a variety of traditional Japanese games exist based on this concept, including:

### Hana Fuda Cards

Packs contain 48 cards (about 54mm × 35mm or 2¼ × 1⅜in.) which in the Japanese tradition are printed or hand-painted on thick cards. Hana players use two sets of cards, one of which is black-backed and the other brown-backed. The pack comprises twelve suits of four cards each. The suits represent the months of the year and the cards in each suit feature the flower which is peculiar to each month with: January, Pine; February, Plum; March, Cherry; April, Wisteria; May, Iris; June, Peony; July, Clover; August, Pampas-grass; September, Chrysanthemum; October, Maple; November, Willow or Rain; and December, Paulownia – the crest of the Emperor. Each card is worth a point and some of the cards have special features which earn them extra points.

### Hyakunin Isshu or The Hundred Poets Game

Packs contain 200 cards divided into two sets of 100. A classical collection of the works of a hundred different poets from the 7th to 13th centuries are featured on the cards (again part of the poem is on one set of cards and the remainder of the poem on the other set) together with a portrait of the poet in question. Related packs are:

'Ise Monogatari' or Stories of the Ise which contains 400 cards of short classical poems.

'E-Awase' or picture-matching cards with a varying number of cards to a pack.

持統天皇

春すぎて夏きにけらし白妙の衣ほすてふ天の香具山

山部赤人

田子の浦に打ち出でてみれば白妙の富士の高嶺に雪はふりつつ

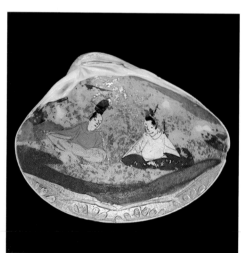

*Above, top*: 'Hana Fuda' the Japanese flower cards; *bottom, left to right*: two cards from the Japanese 'Hyakunin Isshu' or the 'Hundred Poets' game; an illustrated shell from the 'Hundred Poets' game which is thought to be the forerunner of the card game of that name.

*Opposite, top and centre*: Japanese 'Unsun' pack.

*Opposite below, left to right*: 'Ukiyo–E' non-standard pack showing pictures of Japanese ladies by such artists as Utamaro and Hiroshige; two Japanese 'Kabu Fuda' cards.

京　都

松井天狗堂

**Japanese Mekuri cards.**

'Iroha', a 96-card alphabet pack where half of the cards show a picture and the other half have text.

Through the passage of time the European-based games have changed almost out of recognition and it is only just possible to recognize the suits of: cups – koppu, swords – isu, coins – oru, and batons – ho. Examples of European derived games are:

## Unsun Cards

This pack comprises 75 cards of the four above-mentioned suits and an additional Tomoe – or 'whirligig' suit. There are fifteen cards in each suit, 1–9 in numerical cards and the six court cards of: king – koshi, knight – uma, jack – sota, dragon – rohai, god of good fortune – un, and the Sun (Dignatory).

## Kabu Cards

These packs have one basic suit repeated a number of times and sometimes additional shingo cards. Packs have 40 or 48 cards with nine numerical cards and one

to three court cards. The various Kabu cards include:

*Kabu Fuda.* This 42-card pack uses the batons suit with 1–9 in numerical cards and one court card repeated four times. One of the suits has overprints on the four and occasionally on the ace and three. There is also a demon or shingo card and an extra blank card.

*Daini.* This pack has a similar composition to the Kabu Fuda cards but uses the coins' suit repeated four or five times.

*Komaru.* This pack uses the coins suit and the usual cards repeated four times; although in the fourth suit there is a four of batons (ho) and the ace shows a dragon. Packs usually contain 40 cards.

*Kudosan.* This 50-card pack uses the coins suit with three court cards. Each suit is repeated four times although the fourth suit is overprinted and again includes a four of batons. Also featured are the demon and blank card.

*Irinokichi.* This pack has up to 49 cards featuring the batons suit and three court cards. The suits are repeated four times with the last suit having a different ace and four cards overprinted in silver. There is also a demon card.

*Kinseizan.* This 50-card pack uses the batons suit and three court cards repeated four times. Japanese numerals appear on all but three cards and the fourth suit has silver overprinted court cards, ace and two. This pack also includes a demon and blank card.

## Mekuri Cards

These packs are similar to the 'Kabu' cards but feature four different suits of twelve cards each.

*Akahachi.* This 50-card pack has the four suits of cups, swords, coins and batons, 9–1 in numerical cards and three court cards. The most distinctive card is the 2 of swords which features Buddha. Also, except for the 2 and 3, all the cards in the sword suit bear Japanese numbers. Silver overprints appear on the 8 of swords and 2, 3, 4, 5 and 6 of batons and money. Packs include a demon and blank card. A similar pack is called 'Komatsu'.

*Fukutoku.* This is similar in composition to the last pack but all the batons suit are overprinted in silver, as are the 2, 3, 4, 5 and ace of swords. The last four of the numerical cards in the batons suit and the 4 to 9 in the sword suit have Japanese numbers and the 2 of swords shows a human face. The pack includes a demon card. A similar pack is 'Kurofuda'.

'Kabu' and 'Mekuri' cards are usually printed in red, black, silver and sometimes dark blue with plain backs in red or black.

# MODERN CARDS

Over the last 20 years or so the Japanese playing-card industry, like many other Japanese industries, has thrived. Most of their Western-type standard and non-standard cards are mass produced and one gets the impression that they are only made to supply a vast world-wide demand and have commercial rather than artistic merit.

A full listing of all the Japanese modern non-standard cards is beyond the scope of this book and would be rather monotonous. Most of their packs only differ from each other in the subject chosen to adorn the card's face, with some of the Japanese favourite themes being different animals, birds, flowers or vintage and new motor cars. Japan is also probably the world's largest producer of pornographic and 'pin-up' playing cards.

There is one section of modern Japanese non-standard playing cards however which is of high artistic quality and can rival packs produced in any other country of the world. In this group are found the traditional Japanese paintings and souvenir packs which feature paintings of people or views by famous Japanese artists. One of the most beautiful of these packs was made by the Braun Playing Card Co. Ltd. of Tokyo. Called Ukiyo-E, each card shows a painting by a famous Japanese artist from the 17th to 19th century, including Moronobu (17th century), Harunobu (1725–1770), Kiyonaga (1752–1814), Utamaro (1753–1806), Sharaku (c.1786), Hokusai (1760–1849), Toyokuni I (1769–1825) and Hiroshige (1797–1858). The subjects of the Ukiyo-E are mainly devoted to active figures of profiles of Kabuki actors and beautiful women, Musha-e (warrior pictures) as well as ordinary life and landscape pictures.

The paintings by the celebrated artist Ando Hiroshige (1797–1858) feature on two different packs of cards, the first of which was made by the ACE Playing Card Co. and shows various landscape views. The second pack was made by the Nintendo Playing Card Co. of Kyoto in 1967. Each card has a landscape view of the 'Tokaido', or shrines, along the 496-kilometre highway between Tokyo and Kyoto.

Nintendo Playing Cards are in fact one of the biggest Japanese playing card producers. They made a series of souvenir packs showing views of various cities and islands, including two of the city of Kyoto, one just showing scenes (c.1960), and the other having additional Japanese and English text. The firm also made packs featuring the islands of Kyushu and Hokkaido, with the latter again having a descriptive text in Japanese. Their Tohoku pack of 1972 features views of the

とうさんいぬは、いさましい とらんぶです。とらんぶと れでぃーは、いつまでも なかよく しあわせに くらしました。

**Disney Television deck by Nintendo Playing Card Co., Kyoto, c. 1968.**

whole of Japan and an advertising pack they made for a brewery in 1971 called Suntory Beer Playing Cards has world-wide scenes.

Between 1964 and 1970 the firm produced the Ukiyoe-S pack where the courts show drawings of Japanese people in traditional and folk costume. The pack was designed by Eisho and the card backs show Japanese women. Earlier in 1960, they produced a pack showing mildly erotic drawings of geisha girls called Ontamaro Engravings. The scenes are in a central oval with a miniature playing card index in two of the four corners of the card and standard indices in the other two corners.

The Nintendo Playing Card Co. also produced various costume and historical packs including one featuring the Wild West. Called Torys, the pack was made in 1966–77 for a distillery firm and depicts various legendary characters from the Wild West, including Wyatt Earp on the king of clubs. The designer was Ryohei

The 'Hiroshige' pack showing the 53 stations of the Tokaido Road from Tokyo to Kyoto.

Modern Japanese pack showing landscape views by the artist Ando Hiroshige.

Yanagihara and the card backs show whisky glasses and the firm's name. A few years later the Nintendo Playing Card Co. produced an advertising pack centred around Greek mythology for the firm of N.T. Cutter.

In recent years Japan has produced a number of experimental packs with different coloured suit signs, card shapes and pip arrangements. Round cards are the most popular of the different shapes. They either show standard designs or pictures of dogs or scenic views as in the pack devoted to Kyoto by the Nintendo Playing Card Co. This firm made an advertising pack for a Japanese brewery of Mexican Oval cards in 1966 where the cards are in the shape of beer kegs. They produced a convex shape pack for another brewery in 1968 called the Asahi Beer Playing Cards. This pack also has two-colour suits, with hearts and diamonds in red/orange and spades and clubs in green/violet.

The firm produced two other packs with non-standard colours. The first was made in 1966 and called Sharp Oracle. It was made for a television manufacturing industry and all the cards have a black background with modernistic courts. The diamonds are coloured in orange, hearts red, spades blue and clubs green. The other 'Rosier' pack was made a few years later and has red diamonds, lilac hearts, violet spades and green clubs. This pack is round and pictures mythological characters on the court cards.

Among the packs made by the Nintendo Playing Card Co. with unusual pip arrangements is a series made c.1965 showing the texts of stories from: a Walt Disney production, a space programme, and a jungle or other adventure story. Each card features a scene from the story in the centre and Japanese text underneath and indices in the top left-hand corner. In the top right-hand corner are the relevant number of suit signs arranged in rows, e.g. the king of clubs has two top rows of five clubs and a bottom row of three clubs. The pack with the most unusual pips and indices, however, is one made for a computer firm in 1971 called Yamatake Data. In addition to the normal suit signs, the card values are indicated with extra pips based on the binary system.

# 8

# Tarot Cards

T AROT cards have always been popular collectors' items with the playing card collector, the occultist and the collector of the unusual. But unfortunately, the mass of literature that has accumulated over the past 200 years about the tarot cards, has resulted in many misconceptions and romantic notions about the subject; and indeed many people no longer regard the tarot cards as playing cards at all.

The most popular idea about tarot cards is that they pertain either to fortune-telling, or some other equally mysterious branch of occultism. These magical connotations were first introduced in 1781 when Count de Gébelin published a treatise on the subject in the eighth volume of his book on civilization, *Le Monde Primitif Analysé et Comparé avec le Monde Moderne*.

De Gébelin claimed that the tarot cards were devised some 2,204 years before the birth of Christ, and that they contain the secret doctrine of the Egyptian priesthood.

The late Roger Tilley, in his book on playing cards, pursues a similar line of thought, but places the date of the origin of tarots in the 15th century and their country of origin as Italy! Agreeing that the tarot cards must conceal sacred teachings, Tilley states that they were the invention of an exiled band of heretics, known as the Waldenses, and were used as a means of communication with their followers which was capable of

avoiding detection at the hands of the Spanish Inquisition.

Although many of these theories about the origin of tarots make fascinating reading, there is usually little evidence to support them; and it must be remembered that for the greater part of their existence tarot cards were used for the sole purpose of playing card games. As to their place of origin, the general concensus of opinion now agrees with Sylvia Mann's proposition that they are of North Italian origin, from around the area of the Taro river.

The earliest existing tarot cards were all commissioned, hand-painted works of art for wealthy families such as Visconti-Sforza and Este, and it has been suggested that they developed because of the fashion for miniatures at that time. Since most of the figures are dressed in 15th century costumes, it is assumed that they evolved during the mid-1400s. As ordinary playing cards had been in existence since at least the late 14th century, the tarot trumps must have been an independent, and later, addition to the standard pack for a game requiring 78 cards.

This seemingly simple explanation poses its own problems. If they had been invented for a game with 78 cards, why not just extend the number cards, instead of employing such elaborate designs? Even more puzzling is the reason for choosing such con-

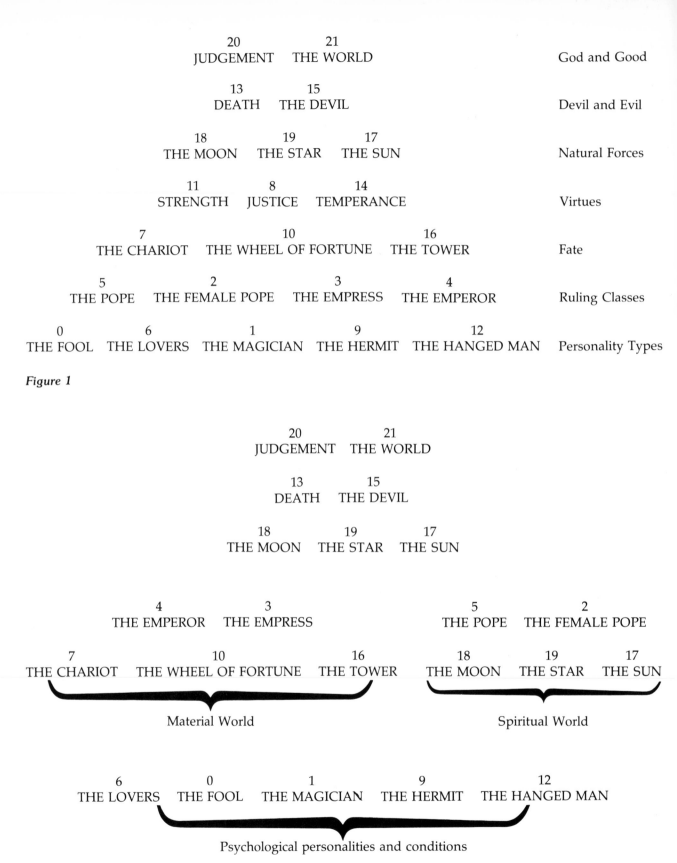

|  |  | God and Good |
|---|---|---|
| 20 | 21 | |
| JUDGEMENT | THE WORLD | |

| 13 | 15 | Devil and Evil |
|---|---|---|
| DEATH | THE DEVIL | |

| 18 | 19 | 17 | Natural Forces |
|---|---|---|---|
| THE MOON | THE STAR | THE SUN | |

| 11 | 8 | 14 | Virtues |
|---|---|---|---|
| STRENGTH | JUSTICE | TEMPERANCE | |

| 7 | 10 | 16 | Fate |
|---|---|---|---|
| THE CHARIOT | THE WHEEL OF FORTUNE | THE TOWER | |

| 5 | 2 | 3 | 4 | Ruling Classes |
|---|---|---|---|---|
| THE POPE | THE FEMALE POPE | THE EMPRESS | THE EMPEROR | |

| 0 | 6 | 1 | 9 | 12 | Personality Types |
|---|---|---|---|---|---|
| THE FOOL | THE LOVERS | THE MAGICIAN | THE HERMIT | THE HANGED MAN | |

*Figure 1*

20     21
JUDGEMENT    THE WORLD

13     15
DEATH    THE DEVIL

18     19     17
THE MOON    THE STAR    THE SUN

4     3         5     2
THE EMPEROR   THE EMPRESS      THE POPE   THE FEMALE POPE

7     10     16      18     19     17
THE CHARIOT   THE WHEEL OF FORTUNE   THE TOWER     THE MOON   THE STAR   THE SUN

Material World            Spiritual World

6     0     1     9     12
THE LOVERS   THE FOOL   THE MAGICIAN   THE HERMIT   THE HANGED MAN

Psychological personalities and conditions

*Figure 2*

troversial and carefully defined subject matter; and from where did their inspiration arise? Gertrude Moakley, in her book on tarot cards, suggests that the characters on the trumps were the same as those on the carnival processions that were popular in the 15th century.

My own belief is that the tarot trumps were used by the rich both for a game of cards, and for some secondary educational purpose; and that the trumps portray both a hierarchy of life and the different conditions of life.

If, for instance, we study the trump arrangement in Fig. 1, we find that the top two rows signify the absolute Christian properties of death, with their two results. Consider how similar in design the Death card is to the Judgement card. But whereas the Death card implies Hell and the Devil, the Judgement card suggests resurrection and heaven, i.e. if you follow God's path you inherit the World. Moving to the third row, the next step in the Universal Hierarchy is the natural forces which are essential for the survival of the planet. The fourth row represents ruling principles or virtues.

The remaining cards relate more directly to people, with the Wheel of Fortune in the fourth row signifying birth and the embarkation on the journey of life in a naive and pure state. The surrounding two cards imply the two main directions in which one can go – to poverty and misfortune, or riches and power. Below this, can be seen the ruling classes. The bottom row brings us to the ordinary man, and the many different situations and personalities of life.

Naturally, the cards could form a number of different arrangements, each telling a different story. Another quite plausible arrangement is shown in Fig. 2. While the top three rows remain unchanged, I have separated the earthly leaders and their characteristics, and the spiritual leaders and their related properties; all of which have their influence on the ordinary man in the bottom row.

The stubborn purist may adamantly say that if the tarot trumps contained some message, then there should only be one true arrangement. I would suggest that the purpose of these educational playing cards could be to see what lesson is learnt from a certain combination of cards left in a player's hand – their versatility therefore being their virtue. After all, with this method of teaching, the pupil would be both enjoying himself, as well as using his ingenuity and imagination. Also, rather than the lesson being limited to a particular age group, cards could be used with equal value as the pupil matures and progresses.

It is interesting to note, that c.1450 there existed a similar pack of cards in Italy, known as the Mantegna cards, that were definitely used for educational purposes. Containing 50 cards in five groups of ten, the lower group depicts the ten conditions of life. After this, in order, comes Apollo and the nine muses; the sciences; the virtues, time and light; and lastly the seven planets, heaven the Prime Mover and the First Cause (*see* Fig. 3).

The Mantegna Tarot: The pack is divided into five groups of ten cards, numbered 1 to 50 and lettered E to A:

| E | | D | | C | |
|---|---|---|---|---|---|
| 1 | Misero | 11 | Caliope | 21 | Grammatica |
| 2 | Fameio | 12 | Urania | 22 | Logica |
| 3 | Artixan | 13 | Terpsicore | 23 | Rhetorica |
| 4 | Merchadante | 14 | Erato | 24 | Geometria |
| 5 | Zintilomo | 15 | Polimnia | 25 | Aritmetricha |
| 6 | Chavalier | 16 | Talia | 26 | Musicha |
| 7 | Doxe | 17 | Melpomene | 27 | Poesia |
| 8 | Re | 18 | Euterpe | 28 | Philosofia |
| 9 | Imperator | 19 | Clio | 29 | Astrologia |
| 10 | Papa | 20 | Apollo | 30 | Theologia |

| B | | A | |
|---|---|---|---|
| 31 | Iliaco | 41 | Luna |
| 32 | Chronico | 42 | Mercurio |
| 33 | Cosmico | 43 | Venus |
| 34 | Temperancia | 44 | Sol |
| 35 | Prudencia | 45 | Marte |
| 36 | Forteza | 46 | Jupiter |
| 37 | Justicia | 47 | Saturno |
| 38 | Charita | 48 | Octava Spera |
| 39 | Speranza | 49 | Primo Mobile |
| 40 | Fede | 50 | Prima Causa |

*Figure 3*

Despite their beautiful appearance, tarot cards were not very popular outside Italy during the 15th and 16th centuries. One of the reasons for this was probably the high expense of their production. In fact, it is doubtful whether some of the early tarots, which were made from copper plates, ever saw a gaming table, but were kept as curiosities and show pieces. When they were used to play a card game it was known as *trionfi*, or 'trumps'.

The most famous tarot pack, still produced today, is the French Tarot de Marseille. This is the only Italian-suited tarot in use in France, and came into general circulation around the 16th/17th century. It is thought that the varied original 'archaic' Italian tarots must have travelled into France at that time, and the French simply standardized them into their present-day

*Left to right*: Trump No.13 from the French Marseilles' tarot; Trump No.15 from the Milanese tarot; Trump No.3 from the Italian Lombard tarot.

order and designs, and added French captions on the trumps.

In the late 16th century, due to the taxation on playing cards, some French card makers moved to southern Switzerland, taking with them the Tarot de Marseille. Once they were in Switzerland, the French card manufacturers did not change the style or design of the Marseilles' tarot, so identification can be very difficult, unless the maker's name and address is printed on one of the cards.

Totalling 78 cards, the Tarot de Marseille has 56 'standard' cards divided equally into the four Italian suits of *coppe* (cups or chalices), *spades* (swords), *denari* (coins) and *bastoni* (batons). Within each suit are ten numerical cards and the four court cards of *re* (king), *regina* (queen – omitted from ordinary Italian packs), *cavallo* (knight) and *fante* (jack). The rest of the pack is made up of twenty-two trump cards. In order, the twenty-two trumps read:

| | |
|---|---|
| 1 The Juggler | 12 The Hanged Man |
| 2 The Popess | 13 Death |
| 3 The Empress | 14 Temperance |
| 4 The Emperor | 15 The Devil |
| 5 The Pope | 16 The Tower |
| 6 The Lovers | 17 The Star |
| 7 The Chariot | 18 The Moon |
| 8 Justice | 19 The Sun |
| 9 The Hermit | 20 Judgement |
| 10 The Wheel of Fortune | 21 The World |
| 11 Strength | |

The Fool

These trumps bear no suit marks and are found numbered in either Roman or Arabic numerals.

At various times in history the tarot cards have come under close scrutiny by the authorities and the Church, who disapproved of some of their subject

*Left to right*: Trump No.7 from the Epinal tarot, which is a variation of the Marseilles' tarot. The pattern features Jupiter and Juno on trumps Nos. 5 and 2 and on the card shown the horses are turned to their left as opposed to facing straight ahead; Trump No.5 from a Besançon tarot *c*. 1860; Trump No.29 from the Italian Minchiate tarot.

matter. In some French Tarot de Marseille packs the words Pope and Popess have been erased and re-written as the High Priest and High Priestess. The Pope has also occasionally been changed to *Le Printemps* (Springtime). Sometimes the Pope and Popess were replaced by Jupiter and Juno, including in Constance *c*.1680, Mannheim *c*.1750, and Besançon *c*.1800. This pack became known as the Besançon tarot and a version following 19th century styles is still produced today in border areas of France, Germany and Switzerland. Strasbourg during the Revolution, eager to wipe away all traces of imperialistic rule, portrayed a Grandfather and Grandmother instead of the Emperor and Empress.

During the 1700s the Marseilles' tarot design was re-introduced into Italy and produced there under the name of the Piedmont tarot (*tarocco Piedmontese*).

The Piedmont and Marseilles' tarots are identical; although a slightly different design has been disco-vered, now called the Lombard tarot. The distinguishing features between the Piedmont and Lombard tarots are that the Lombard tarot always has single-ended courts and trumps, whereas the Piedmont tarot adopted the double-ended designs during the mid-19th century. Also, the Lombard tarot is narrower in format and the paper on the back of the card has been folded over to form a raised border over the card's face (known as a turn-over edge).

The card making firm of Gumppenberg in Milan, *c*.1830, produced another tarot based on the Lombard tarot which differs in artistic interpretation. Called the Della Rocca tarot, the designs were widely copied and are found in the single-ended narrow Lombard format as well as the double-ended broad Piedmont format. In 1976 this tarot was reproduced and named the *Tarocchino Milanese*.

One of the oldest and most attractive of the original Italian tarots is the Florentine Minchiate tarot, dating from the early 1500s.

Of all the European tarot cards the Florentine Minchiate contains the greatest number of cards – a total of 97 cards made up by the usual four suits of fourteen cards plus 41 trump cards. In addition to most of the traditional 22 trumps have been added the twelve signs of the zodiac, the four virtues and the four elements. The first 35 trumps are numbered in Roman figures, the remaining six are unnumbered, and all are unnamed. The first four trumps are known as Papi, and were not given separate identities until a later date. In order, the trumps now read:

| | | | |
|---|---|---|---|
| 1 | The Mountebank | 24 | The Scales |
| 2 | The Grand Duke | 25 | The Virgin |
| 3 | The Western Emperor | 26 | The Scorpion |
| 4 | The Eastern Emperor | 27 | The Ram |
| 5 | The Lovers | 28 | The Goat |
| 6 | Temperance | 29 | The Archer |
| 7 | Fortitude | 30 | The Crab |
| 8 | Justice | 31 | The Fishes |
| 9 | The Wheel of Fortune | 32 | The Water Carrier |
| 10 | The Chariot | 33 | The Lion |
| 11 | The Hermit | 34 | The Bull |
| 12 | The Hanged Man | 35 | The Twins |
| 13 | Death | | |
| 14 | The Devil | | Following on |
| 15 | The Tower | | unnumbered are: |
| 16 | Hope | | |
| 17 | Prudence | | The Star |
| 18 | Faith | | The Moon |
| 19 | Charity | | The Sun |
| 20 | Fire | | The Angel |
| 21 | Water | | The World |
| 22 | Earth | | The Fool |
| 23 | Air | | |

The Minchiate tarot are smaller than the Piedmont cards, slim in format and have turnover edges. They bear Italo/Portuguese suits, which are characterized by the swords on the sword suit, which are straight, long and slim, crossing each other to form a delicate trellis design rather than the curved and large-size swords on the purely Italian suits. Also the batons are shown as clubs.

Other novelties of this popular tarot lie with the court and number cards. The knights of cups and money are shown as half-human, half-dragon like creatures, and those of swords and clubs as centaurs. The jacks of swords and clubs are aggressive young men, while those of cups and money show young females. On many of the number cards can be seen small vignettes of animals, some of which seem to portray old European folk tales. For instance, on the two of batons there is a fox and a stork reminiscent of a story by Aesop of how a fox invited a stork to dinner, but as the food was served on flat plates the stork could not pick up the food. A little later, the stork in turn invited the fox to dinner. This time the food was served in long pitchers. Naturally the stork with her long beak could reach the food, but the ill-equipped fox had to go hungry.

During the 17th century the Minchiate tarot spread to Genoa where it was known as Ganellini and to Sicily where it was called Gallerini. It became less popular in Sicily during the 18th century although it was produced in Florence and Rome until the second half of the 19th century. Unfortunately this beautiful tarot is now no longer produced, with the last known example dated 1929. This 1929 edition is identical to 16th-century tarots except that it no longer has turn-over edges, but a border of dots. Although the maker's name rarely appears on Minchiate packs, most of them were manufactured in Florence, Bologna and, later, Genoa.

A reproduction was made in 1977 of forty trumps of an alleged 15th-century Minchiate tarot (now thought to be 16th century) from the Rothschild collection. Only twenty-five packs were made, each being hand-stencilled and having a different back and box design.

Another Italian tarot is the Bologna tarot (*tarocco Bolognese*) which is thought to have originated in the early 16th century. Containing only 62 cards, the pack still retains the 22 trump cards, but the twos, threes, fours and fives of each suit are omitted (hence its reference as a tarocchino or little tarot). The cards are long and narrow and early examples had turn-over edges. At first the courts and trumps were single-ended, with the double-ended design introduced in the late 1700s. Only trumps 5–16 are numbered in Arabic numerals and all the trumps are unnamed. Originally the trumps were the same as for the Marseilles tarot, but due to papal intervention and objection, the Emperor, Empress, Pope and Popess were replaced in 1725 by four Moors. The unnumbered trumps are: The Mountebank, the four Moors, The Moon, The Sun, Judgement or The Angel, The World and The Fool. The numbered cards in order are:

| | | | |
|---|---|---|---|
| 5 | The Lovers | 11 | The Hermit |
| 6 | The Chariot | 12 | The Hanged Man |
| 7 | Temperance | 13 | Death |
| 8 | Justice | 14 | The Devil |
| 9 | Fortitude | 15 | The Tower |
| 10 | The Wheel of Fortune | 16 | The Star |

Trump No.9 from the Italian Minchiate tarot.

One of the four Moors from the Bolognese tarot.

---

The last of the Italian tarots to be discussed is the Sicilian tarot (*tarocco Siciliano*), which again has only been recently identified. It is thought to have evolved in the mid-1600s although the modern, slightly changed design probably appeared in the early 19th century. Because of its small size, it is also sometimes known as a *tarocchino*. It originally contained 78 cards but during the 18th century it was reduced to 64 cards with the 2 and 3 in the coin suit and ace to 4 in the other suits omitted. Although, in its early stages, the 22 trumps were probably the same as for the Marseilles' tarot, the Pope, Female Pope and Devil have now been replaced with Constancy, a ship (representing the water element in the Minchiate tarot) and a beggar. All the trumps are numbered except for the last two – the Beggar and the Fool. In order the trumps read:

| | | | |
|---|---|---|---|
| 1 | The Juggler | 13 | Death |
| 2 | The Empress | 14 | The Ship |
| 3 | The Emperor | 15 | The Tower |
| 4 | Fortitude | 16 | The Star |
| 5 | Temperance | 17 | The Moon |
| 6 | Constancy | 18 | The Sun |
| 7 | Justice | 19 | The World |
| 8 | The Lovers | 20 | Judgement |
| 9 | The Chariot | | |
| 10 | The Wheel of Fortune | unnumbered are: |
| 11 | The Hanged Man | The Beggar |
| 12 | The Hermit | The Fool |

This pack is still precariously produced today, and its unusual designs give it an original character. The Sun card shows a Cain and Abel scene, with two men

*Left to right*: **Trump No. 19 from the Sicilian tarot; Trump No.5 from a Belgian tarot, known as** *Capitano Eracasse –* *Le Spagnol* **pack, by Van Den Borre; French-suited tarot.**

fighting and one ready to strike the other over the head. The Hanged Man is hanging from his neck rather than his feet. The mighty Atlas supports a globe of the world on the World card and on card No. 20 can be seen the god Jupiter holding rods of lightning. In early examples trump No. 2, now the Empress, featured a moustached king.

An interesting variation of the 78-card Italian-suited tarot pack was once produced in the Low Countries. It is sometimes known as the *Capitano Eracasse – Le spagnol* pack, after trump No. 11. The Pope of card five has been replaced by Bacchus, where the god is seen merrily astride a barrel in his usual intoxicated state. The Tower card shows a tree struck by lightning and is called La Foudre. The Hanged Man is shown the wrong way up – standing on tip-toe. It is interesting to note that although this tarot uses most of the subject matter of the Marseilles' or Piedmont tarot, three of the cards – The World, The Moon and The Star – have designs characteristic of the Italian Bolognese tarocchini cards. All the trumps, except the Fool, are named in French in very bad spelling.

Recently a reproduction of this 18th-century pack was made in a limited edition of around 400. Unfortunately it is now proving hard to come by. But since this tarot is invaluable for its historical implications it is well worth the hunt.

Around the 1750s drastic changes occurred to the face of the tarot cards. Until that time, all tarot packs bore the Italian suits, but then packs began to be made featuring the traditional French suit signs. Moreover, not only were the suit signs changed but the actual designs and subject matter used on the trump cards were completely revised.

The standard French-suited tarot, still in use in France today, originated just over a hundred years ago, possibly from Germany or Austria. The pack still totals 78 cards, with 22 trumps and four suits of king, queen, knight, and jack and ace to ten in numerical cards, but now the trumps and courts are double-ended. The subjects on the trumps are contrasting pictures of pleasure and work and town and country 19th-century scenes. All the rich symbolism has gone, and there is no mystery in the simple actions performed by the characters on the cards, such as going to the theatre, fishing and dancing. Although there are

*Left to right*: an animal tarot with 78 cards by F.D. Mühler, Regensburg, *c*. 1771; a 78-card animal tarot from Luxembourg, *c*. 1780; the 'Fool' card from a Belgian animal tarot by Daveluy, *c*. 1870.

variations in subject matter on the cards, the Fool is always shown playing a lute.

Despite their new appearance, these tarots were still met with indifference by the French, being used mostly along their eastern borders. The Swiss, however, received the new tarot designs with greater warmth, and again they are indistinguishable from their French counterparts, except for slight variations in designs of the pictures shown on the trumps. Both the French and Swiss card makers included a scroll design or monogram of the maker's name at each end of the trump cards, which are numbered in Arabic numerals and unnamed.

Apart from a small number of specially imported examples, tarot cards did not become widespread in Germany until the late 17th century. The pattern adopted at that early time was similar to the 78-card Besançon pattern, with bad spelling of the French names. This pattern was relatively short-lived. In *c*.1750 the Germans introduced a totally novel French-suited tarot which showed various animals on the trump cards. Aptly entitled the 'animal' tarot, the trumps were single-ended and bore Roman numerals.

A wide variety of animals was featured, including unicorns, camels, turkeys, deer, lions and performing bears. At that time there was a vogue for Chinoiserie and Eastern art in Europe, which is reflected in these tarot designs. On some of the cards can be seen peacocks fanning themselves beside flowing fountains, or elegant gentlemen riding camels or elephants and carrying parasols, while palm trees sway in the background.

The 'animal' tarot also spread to Belgium where the order and subjects were more standardized than those of Germany.

At the turn of the 19th century, Germany, like France and Switzerland, adopted double-ended designs, and the trumps of the 'animal' tarots now featured either two completely different animals, or two animals of the same species at each end of the trump cards. Trump No. 1, the Fool, however, was always portrayed as a stage musician.

Because of the inconsistency of the trump cards on animal tarots, it has been very difficult to distinguish between the various patterns and to know where they were made. Recently three such patterns have been

*Left to right*: **Austrian Tarock Pattern: Style A; Style B; Style C.**

defined and can be identified by certain characteristics on the court cards. One of the first of the stabilized animal tarots to emerge is now called the Bavarian Animal tarot. This single-ended pattern appeared in Bavaria during the 1750s and was also used in Alsace, Belgium, Luxembourg, Sweden and Russia. It died out during the early 19th century. Numbering 78 cards, the courts are based on the Bavarian version of the Paris pattern with some of the distinguishing points being the king of spades carrying a harp; the queen of spades in profile and the jacks of hearts and clubs holding a shield.

The second identifiable pattern is the 78-card single-ended Belgium Animal tarot. This is best recognized by the kings who expose bare legs underneath their long robes and wear thonged sandals.

The last variation, known as the Upper Austrian Animal tarot was, despite its name, also made in Bohemia until at least 1858. Early packs were made with 78 double-ended trumps and courts which had the same pictures on both ends. The distinguishing feature is the king of spades, who no longer holds a harp as in the Bavarian pattern. Also unlike the other two patterns, the Upper Austrian Animal tarot trumps do not have a panel at the top and bottom of the card and the numerals are on the left-hand side of the cards, as opposed to the centre.

Sadly 78-card packs are now no longer produced as, during the 1850s, the 54-card game of Cego became popular, and German card makers began producing animal tarots with only 54 cards. The trumps still number 22, and have the same designs, but are now numbered in Arabic numerals; while the five to ten in the red suit and ace to six in the black suit have been dropped. The Upper Austrian Animal tarot is among the many 78-card tarots to be reduced in this way. This 54 card tarot pack became known as the 'Adler Cego'.

Shortly after, the Germans started producing tarots with trumps showing double-ended scenes of work and play. Originally produced with 78 cards, they were again reduced to 54 cards, and are known as a Cego pack (sometimes referred to as the Standard Cego), after the game of the same name. The maker's name is usually shown on the ace of hearts and the 22 trumps are numbered in Arabic numerals, except for the traditionally unnumbered Fool. Both the Cego

*Left to right*: non-standard War tarot by Josef Glanz, Vienna, *c*. 1880; non-standard 54-card French-suited tarot with trumps, depicting Alpine scenes by F. Piatnik & Sons, Vienna, *c*. 1910.

packs are still being produced today.

The Austro-Hungarian Empire adopted the French-suited tarot, with its industrious scenes, around 1800, although they are known as Tarock cards. At first they used a 78-card pack, later being replaced by the 54-card version. In the latter variety there are the usual four courts and four numerical cards: ace to four in the red suit and seven to ten in the black suit. The courts are similar in style to those of the Bavarian tarot but with more detailed and ornate designs. The 22 trumps are double-ended and, except for the unnumbered Fool, are numbered in Roman numerals.

Today, three varieties of Tarock cards are still in existence, which can be identified by the pictures on trump No. 3. In style A trump No. 3 shows a well scene; in style B a gondolier scene and in style C a soldier with a corn sheaf. The rest of the trumps portray people in regional and national costumes in a variety of work and leisure situations. With a truly international flavour, sultans can be seen smoking pipes, peasants working in the fields, and Scotsmen mingling with Danes. The order and details of the

trumps differ with the three varieties, except for card No. 1 which in all styles shows at one end a young boy dancing with either a zither or harp, and at the other end a young girl dancing with a tambourine.

The Austrian Tarocks are by far the most beautiful of the 'work and play' tarots produced in Europe, and are sometimes referred to as the Industrie und Gluck tarot ('Industry and Good Fortune'), because on trump No. 2 a crowned eagle sits, sword in claw, on a rock inscribed with those words. In the Czechoslovakian version, at one time, packs were produced where the eagle has lost its crown and the inscription reads *Audaces Fortuna Juvat*. In Hungary it reads *Szerencse Fel*. The maker's name and address are found on the jack of diamonds and his stamp and tax stamp on the ace of hearts. Style A has been made in Austria, Czechoslovakia, and Germany, Style B in Austria and Hungary, and Style C in Austria, Hungary and Poland.

As more and more card manufacturing industries were set up in Europe, competition became fierce to produce the most novel and bizarre card designs possible. The tarot cards became a prime target for experimentation and with their 22 trumps, a perfect canvas for the card designer's imagination.

C. Titze and Schinkay of Vienna, in 1885, adorned their tarot trumps with a selection of famous Austrian buildings, including: Parliament, the Mint, Town Hall, Opera House and University. Josef Glanz of Vienna made a famous war tarot in 1864. The double-ended courts portray famous characters such as Karl VII, Romeo, Othello, Lear, Lichtenstein and Mary Stuart. On the trumps can be seen barons giving orders for the troops to charge, soldiers receiving medals or keeping sentry duty.

An amusing tarot produced by Gassman of Geneva in 1873, has black and white trumps showing people in unfortunate and unflattering situations. On trump No. 7 can be seen a man holding a broken umbrella, standing thigh-high in rain water. On the other end of the card can be seen a man with a head the size of his body, riding on the back of a hare. Trump No. 15 shows a typical Punch and Judy scene, with a hooked-nosed man ready to be struck by a woman holding a huge log in her arms.

Another notable pack was made by F. Piatnik & Son of Vienna, c.1880, which has named trumps showing figures portraying various personalities, such as the 'conceited jester' or the 'drunken jester'. Trump No. 21 is particularly striking and shows a man with the body of a snail and the shadow of an ass, bowing to a medal which is held dangling in front of his nose. He is entitled the 'prudent jester'.

Among the many other types of tarot packs produced were ones issued as souvenirs showing the highlights of a country or town. One such Swiss pack features Alpine views of hotels, meteorological stations, watch towers and rest houses on various mountains together with their name, location and height in metres above sea level. But perhaps the most famous non-standard tarot is the one designed by Ditha Moser for a Viennese charity in 1906. The delightful double-ended trumps show scenes like a wooden toy town, while the court cards have a stained glass effect with a different time in history represented on each suit. The diamonds show Egyptians, the spades Assyrians, the clubs medieval knights and royalty, and the hearts personalities of the 18th century. Originally only 100 packs were made, and they were recently reproduced, but due to their popularity examples are now proving hard to come by.

As we approach the 20th century we find a completely new breed of tarot cards – the 'magical tarot' already mentioned at the beginning of the chapter. Although Court de Gébelin himself never issued a new tarot design, many of his predecessors did. The first on the bandwagon was a self-professed Parisian fortune-teller, alchemist and cabalist named Alliette. He published both a fortune-telling pack and a tarot pack, as well as an explanatory book on the subject. His pack the 'Grand Etteilla Egyptian Gypsy Tarot' can still be bought today.

The occultist Arthur Edward Waite, devised a completely new tarot based on his own magical beliefs, in which the suits are wands, cups, swords and pentacles. Designed by Pamela Colman Smith it is one of the biggest selling modern tarots. One of the most beautiful of the 'magical tarots' is one designed by Aleister Crowley and executed by Freida Harris. They are a complete departure from the traditional tarot and have some trumps re-named to No. 1 Magus, No. 5 Hierophant, No. 8 Adjustment, No. 11 Lust. The colours are stunning and vibrant and Crowley relates each card to the zodiac, elements, astrology, planets, Hebrew letters, and the ancient gods of Egypt.

In recent years, card manufacturers world-wide have probably produced more novel tarot packs than all the other types of playing cards put together. Now there are more than enough tarots to suit all tastes, whether one wishes to collect standard tarots, tarots by subject matter, country, or novelty factor. Because of their popularity, prices tend to be higher than for some other playing cards. However, as most of the traditional tarots are still produced today and are still identical to ones produced hundreds of years ago, a collector can form a collection of modern tarot cards relatively inexpensively. Most modern packs are priced at a few pounds.

Fortune-telling itself is as old as man and has taken a number of different forms. Not surprisingly, it was not

*Opposite above, left to right*: **Facsimile of fortune-telling cards first published in 1714 by Lenthall; fortune-telling pack by B.P. Grimaud, Paris, c. 1850; German *Lenormand* fortune-telling pack, c. 1850.**

*Opposite centre, left to right*: **French *Grand Etteilla* fortune-telling pack, c. 1900, with the original made in the late 18th-century by Alliette; Aleister Crowley's 'Thoth' tarot which is one of the most imaginative and original of the 20th-century magical tarot packs.**

*Opposite below, left to right*: **reprint of a non-standard tarot designed for a Viennese charity by Ditha Moser in 1906; the French *Grand Jeu de Mlle. Lenormand* pack of the late 19th-century by B.P. Grimaud.**

Queen of Disks

*Left to right*: The famous 'Narren Tarock' or 'Fools Tarot' by Ferd. Piatnik, *c*. 1815; non-standard 54-card, French-suited tarot showing dancers and actresses on the trump cards, by E. Knepper & Co., Vienna, *c*. 1880; the *Il Matto* card from a 22-card pack of tarot trumps, hand-engraved by Donato Lanzoni, 1980.

very long after their introduction that cards were used for reading the mysteries of the future. As already stated, it was not the tarot cards that were initially used, as most people suspect, but ordinary standard playing cards.

One of the earliest references to fortune-telling with cards in Europe is in a German divination book of the 1480s called *Eim Loszbuch Ausz der Karten*. The enquirer is instructed to shuffle the cards and withdraw one. He then consults the book of fate for the meaning of the card. A similar book was published in Venice in *c*.1550 which also describes fortune-telling and the different interpretations that can be made with ordinary playing cards.

Cards made specifically for fortune-telling did not appear until some time later, with some of the oldest examples being based on palmistry. France was the biggest producer of fortune-telling cards, with Germany and England following close behind.

In England one of the most famous early packs was one reprinted by Lenthall in 1712. The original pack was probably published in the late 1600s and is quite complicated in both the method and symbolism. A choice of questions is given on one of the kings, together with a number. In this pack the kings represent: diamonds, Nimrod; clubs, Pharaoh; hearts, Herod; and spades, Holophernes. Once the question has been chosen the enquirer turns to corresponding 'sphere' cards. These cards are on all the odd numbers and show a zodiacal wheel headed with the name of a famous sage, magician or scientist, such as Merlin on the ace of clubs, and Hermes Trismegistus on the ace of hearts. Finally the enquirer is directed to the even-numbered cards which show reputed sayings of famous sibyls of antiquity including those of S. Phrygia on the 2 of clubs and S. Lybica on the 4 of clubs.

Moving on to more modern times, probably the most famous fortune-telling pack is the one devised by Mlle. Lenormand. She was a celebrated sibyl of the 18th-century and is said to have read for Napoleon.

Late 18th-century British 32-card fortune-telling pack.

Japanese fortune-telling cards, *c*. 1930.

Her large-size cards comprise a central picture and three smaller pictures at the bottom of the card, the middle one of which is a plant or flower. A miniature playing card index is in the top left-hand corner and a letter and planetary sign are in the top right-hand corner, with a constellation or planetary arrangement in the top centre.

Another beautiful French pack was made by B.P. Grimaud *c*.1890 called 'The Book of Fate'. Most of the cards have a well-executed illustration and an English and French interpretation underneath. The cards represent such things as: king of hearts, a man of law; the queen of diamonds, hope; the jack of clubs, a dark haired young man; the 10 of diamonds, a trap or treachery; and the 7 of clubs, a love letter.

A very popular pack of German origin which is still being produced today is the 'Lenormand' fortune-telling pack. The cards are of a normal size and feature different meaningful pictures and interpretations. The cards are numbered and have miniature playing-card indices either in a square or oval design at the top of the cards.

Most other fortune-telling packs follow a similar pattern to the ones already mentioned and mainly vary only in the amount of symbolic detail used. Some of the more complicated packs have a picture, letter, number, Hebrew letter, planet, astrological sign and a palm reading. In contrast, other packs simply show a picture and a one-word caption such as 'love', 'sorrow' or 'marriage'.

143

# Children's Game Packs

CHILDREN'S game cards have been rather neglected in the past and have only recently come into their own. They are quite distinct from ordinary playing cards with their most obvious difference being the lack of any court cards or suit marks. Instead game cards are either numbered, lettered or grouped in some way.

Today the most common type of game cards are those like Snap or Happy Families. These are specifically made for children with no other purpose than to amuse, and as such are usually of inferior quality and cheaper to buy than ordinary playing cards. However, this type of pack is relatively modern. Originally game packs were of high quality, both in the materials used and in their designs and engravings, and they usually had some educational quality.

The actual design of game cards has also changed through the years. The earliest type belongs to the 'picture and story' category, where the top half of the card is devoted to a scenic picture or medallion bust portrait of a person with an explanatory text underneath. The card's number usually appears in one of the top corners. This card design probably evolved in France and became very popular in the mid-18th century, although of course the same design was used on non-standard suited playing cards from a much earlier date.

One of the earliest 'picture and story' packs was made by Mortier in c.1700, and called *Le Jeu des Hommes et Femmes Illustrés*. The cards feature such illustrious beings as Plato, Solon, Virgil, Sappho and Zenobia.

Another pack of this period *Le Grand Jeu de la Géographie avec Costumes Colorées* has twenty-four cards showing an inhabitant of a particular country with a description underneath. Among the countries featured is France on card No. 1, which states that *La France est le pays le plus agréable de l'Europe*, and China on card No. 9 saying that *La Chine est le pays le plus peuplé de l'univers*.

A long series of 'picture and story' game packs was made in the mid-18th century by the French maker, E. Jouey. The cards all have an educational theme and were sold mainly by Vanackère in Lille, Rénouard in Paris and Nicolle in Paris. They must have been issued in fairly large quantities as many are still easy to find today. His most popular titles include:

1. Roman history, where at the top of each card is a 'coin' portrayal of a famous Roman with text underneath, such as Romulus on card No. 1 and Julius Caesar on card No. 39. Similar packs were issued dealing with Middle Eastern and Greek history.
2. The Life of Christ, which on card No. 1 has the Angel Gabriel visiting Mary, the birth of Christ on No. 2 and his crucifixion on No. 36.
3. History of the Roman Emperors, with Caesar on card No. 1 and the last emperor, Romulus Augustus,

*Left to right*: a hand-coloured biblical educational card from the 'History of the Bible' pack printed for John Wallis, London, *c*. 1800; French geographical game pack of 84 cards, plus 4 title cards and instructions, *Analise Géographique des departments de la France, c*. 1770; from 'The Liliputian History of England' pack showing English kings from William I to George III, late 18th-century by John Harris.

on No. 47.

4. French monarchy, which begins with Pharamond the first king of France and ends with Louis XIV.

5. English history which begins with Egbert Ethelwolf and ends with George III.

6. A pack explaining the rudiments of music with lessons on how to play at the top half of the card and musical bars underneath.

7. Alphabet and grammar, in which each card is a lesson and begins with the alphabet written in different scripts and goes on to various maxims, phrases, numbers, morals, fables and anecdotes.

Also in this series are cards on mythology and astronomy, ancient and modern history, geography and natural history.

A number of interesting game packs were made in England, including the 'Prince of Wales Emblematic Cards'. These were published in 1788 by J. Wallis of No. 6 Ludgate Street, J. Binny of Leeds and L. Bull of Bath. Each card shows an object or emblem such as a

crown, ship, anchor or cannon in a large shield. Above the shield is the crest of the Prince of Wales, a motto scroll, curtain-like drapery and palm branches. Underneath each emblem is a four-line verse relating to the subject matter. John Wallis also published a 40-card pack on 15 July 1795, explaining 'The Elements of Astronomy and Geography'. The cards are beautifully engraved and coloured by the Abbé Paris and have a diagram on one side and explanation on the other.

In 1828 C. Hodges of 27 Portman Square, London, made a 36-card astronomical pack. Each card shows a constellation and its personification, such as a dog for Canis Major, a swan for Cygnus and a centaur for Centaurus; the four emblematic seasons; zodiac signs and planets. Later twelve court cards and the suit signs of red chalices, blue pike heads, green trefoils and golden diamonds were added to the pack.

During the 19th century the 'group' games became popular. England produced a large number of these

*Left*: 'The Royal Historical Game of Cards' from King John to Queen Victoria invented by Miss Jane Roberts *c*. 1850; and *right*; 'Our Kings and Queens – the great historical game', by the Mazawattee Tea Co., Ltd., London, *c*. 1910.

English early 20th-century game pack showing 'The Counties of England'.

which had historical monarchs as the subject matter. The usual format for these cards was to have either the head and shoulders or full-length figure of a monarch with his dates and some essential facts underneath.

The 'British Historical Cards' by E.G. Ludlow of *c*.1770 had 63 cards of which 8 were ancient cards giving narratives, 33 royal cards showing the various kings from the conquest, and 22 'children' cards showing the children of each king. In 1820 the 'Magna Charta' or 'Knight Errantry' cards were produced giving 'a synopsis of Chivalry by a Lady' and featuring full length portraits of the kings of England. The king's name is in the top left hand corner of the card and the date of the beginning and end of his reign at the bottom. A similar but more complicated pack called 'The Royal Historical Game of Cards' was invented by Miss Jane Roberts in 1836. The 45-card lithographed pack is comprised of nine groups of four cards showing full-length portraits of monarchs from William I to Queen Victoria. Each king and queen is dressed in state robes and stands on a low pedestal giving their name and century number. Separate cards give full accessional details of the monarchs century by century.

This pack was very popular and many makers made modified versions of it. In *c*.1910 the 'Game of Our Kings and Queens' appeared. Containing 38 cards, it again shows monarchs arranged in sets according to the century they ruled in, from William I to Queen Victoria. The monarch's name is in the top left-hand corner and his century in the top right. Underneath are the names of the other monarchs of the same century. The back of this pack advertised Mazawattee Tea, Cocoa and Chocolates. The aim with both the last two packs is to collect as many 'tricks' as possible. A 'trick' consists of all the cards showing monarchs of a particular century. Along the same lines was a long series of 'Famous Personages' packs which feature the head and shoulders of a famous person with textual instructions underneath. The pack was first issued by William Darton of Holborn Hill, London, in 1818, and re-issued in 1822, 1823, 1824 and 1825.

A similar card format to the historical cards was used for the geographical card games of the late 1800s and early 1900s. Packs were either split up into groups of countries and sub-divided into cities and the player had to collect all the cards of a particular country, or they were divided into counties. A typical example is a series made by John Jacques & Son of London which deals with various parts of England. Each card shows a picture capturing the essence of a town with the name underneath.

During the 19th and 20th centuries, 'combination' type cards became popular. In the British Museum is a multiplication pack where one card shows the body of an animal and a sum and a corresponding card shows the head of an animal and the answer to the sum. When the right cards were combined both a completed animal and sum were formed. In the 20th century Waddy Products made the 'Spelling Bee' game. The game has two packs of 56 cards each bearing letters of the alphabet, prefixes, suffixes and affixes and a number from which various words are formed.

Among the question-and-answer combination-type pack is one 'selected and arranged' by John B. Marsh of Manchester. Based on Shakespeare, the 30-card pack is divided into 15 riddle cards and 15 answer cards. The 'Conversation' cards of the 19th century follow a similar theme. Packs are usually formed of two sets of cards printed in two different colours; one has questions printed on them and the other answers to the questions. The idea of the game is for someone to ask a question and another person to find the most suitable answer from the cards in his hand. Among the many such packs made is one by Wattilliaux of Paris and another 'Poet's Conversation Cards' pack by Mrs. Alliston.

One of the most difficult of these 'active' games is the German Rebus pack. A standard example by I. Heller consists of 36 engraved and hand-coloured cards. On each card is a series of numbers, syllables, single letters, complete words and pictures. The player has to decipher the message contained on the cards by sound values. The game is made even more difficult by neither spelling nor sense being of any importance.

Rebus cards became widespread in the 18th and early 19th centuries, although the principles of rebus were used far earlier. In the Middle Ages, clerics in monasteries amused themselves by writing satirical chronicles using pictures and fragments of words. As early as 1466 P. Gall Kemli used rebus in his *Promtuarium Ecclesiasticum* which circulated in all German-speaking countries. The use of rebus did not break free of religious subject matter until the early 17th century when it experienced a revival as an amusing and witty pastime.

Another vogue in the 19th century, particularly in France, was the Alphabet cards. These were usually of high quality with delightful designs showing various, often comical, personalities together with letters of the alphabet and amusing verses. One pack features the adventures of M. Calicot, a rascal, and the lovely but foolish Mlle. Percale. Yet another series has a number of different stories with such titles as *'L'amour enchaîné'*, *'Le café tortonie'* and *'Famille anglaise en promenade'*. Some had caricatures on them such as *'Marie à la Coque'*, or *'M. Double Croche'* and *'Mme. La Joie'*.

Other types of alphabetical cards show full-length whimsical figures such as knights, harlequins, jugglers and two consecutive letters of the alphabet. The cards are divided into three by two horizontal lines and presumably one would cut the cards up and then try and re-assemble them. Similar series have birds, animals, tumblers and figures with grotesque heads on them.

The Snap and Happy Families type games became popular in the 1850s although earlier examples are known. At first many of these cards featured full-length figures of various named characters with an amusing verse underneath. An example in the Bowes Museum, Durham, has such characters as: Ned Crusty who says 'I won't and I will; And I don't and I do; I will have my own way; Well, and what's that to you?' and Master Ninny who admits that 'I'm such a ninnyhammer, I don't know a word of my grammar'. Also included are Billy Overall, Captain Swagger, Mrs. Midnight, Billingsgate Nell, Mrs. Platterface and Mrs. Dandle Puppy. Another English pack called 'Volunteers' of c.1840 has Sultana Fatina complaining that 'These English girls have lovers plenty, Whilst we have scarcely one for twenty' and Harry Couplet with the verse 'Of cake your Poet humbly craves his share, If you refuse, you'll drive him to despair' and Sr. Toper Tipple, Dick Spoutwell and Signora Squallini. A French example portrays the idiosyncrasies of English, German and American national characters with such people as the son of Harry John Bull who is shown in sailor's uniform blowing a sailing ship in a tub.

The 19th century Snap and related game packs were printed on thick card, boxed and had square corners. The same design was sometimes used for a great number of years, long after the fashions had changed, and so dating can be difficult. Two of the most charming series are the Victorian and Edwardian cards, many of which portray their characters with grotesque or large-size heads.

Packs contain a varying number of cards with the only real requirement being that they are made up of related groups (usually two or four cards in a group). Snap packs have the same picture repeated a number of times in each group, e.g. four Postmen, while Happy Family packs show the father, mother, son and daughter, etc. of a subject in each group, for example, the Fishmonger's family. Makers include J. Jacques

**36-card Rebus pack by I. Heller, Germany, *c*. 1829.**

**French Children's Alphabet game pack, *c*. 1810.**

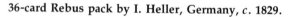

and Son, Pepys, Chad and Waddington.

The subjects used on Snap and Happy Family packs vary greatly, and so far a full listing of the various combinations of cards, designs and makers has not been attempted. Sometimes a maker would use the same subjects for twenty years and then suddenly change one of the figures. This of course is a principal point of interest with collectors of these cards.

Several advertising packs have been made along the 'Snap' format including one for Banks, English & Scottish Joint and C.W.S. Tea. The advert is on the back of each card and the card fronts form groups showing the processes involved in making tea from the initial planting to serving it at home.

Some Snap packs have an educational theme, such as one made *c*.1870 featuring four different shops and the goods for sale in them. Comprising 48 cards, each shop has 12 cards which are coloured in red, blue and black. Another German 40-card pack made for export to France called *Jeux Spear* (*c*.1930) has the history of transport on the cards. There are four cards in each set which show a different form of transport. A 54-card

pack of *c*.1850s has the rather obscure groups of fire-irons, seasons, cards, Great Britain, vowels, professions, meals, senses, days of the week and months of the year.

Among card games introduced in the 20th century is the 'Bobs y'r Uncle' game of *c*.1925 by Waddingtons. The 54-card pack contains 48 nursery rhyme cards, three uncle cards and three negro cards. The idea of the game was either to lose all your cards or to collect the three uncle cards.

'Forfeits' is another interesting game, made by J. & L. Randall, Ltd. As the name suggests each of the 48 cards has a humorous illustration and instruction which the player must perform, or forfeit an item. Among the commands given are 'Give a performance of a puppy drinking a saucer of milk' and 'Hop around the room with an imaginary Aspidistra balanced on your head'. Another game of *c*.1920 called 'The Matching Game' shows the head and shoulders of a person with either a different expression or facial action. The groups are: Sympathizing, Listening, Mashing, Asserting, Winking, Fearing, Bamboozling,

*Left to right*: **20th-century English snap pack; early 20th-century English 'Old Maid' game pack; late-18th-century French game pack,** *Grand Jeu des Aventures de Gil Blas,* **containing 25 engraved and coloured cards.**

Appreciating, Crying, Top-note-ing, Laughing, Joking and Depreciating. Presumably the players had to imitate the actions.

Before finishing this chapter on game cards mention should be given to a few more purely fanciful packs; a few of which could be loosely termed as game packs because they bear numbers instead of suit signs.

Back in the 18th century France produced a number of 'picture and story' packs which were either numbered or unnumbered and just told a complete story. A scene from the story occupies the top half of the card and the story is underneath. One of the most famous of these packs is the *Grand Jeu, Les Aventures de Gil Blas*. Produced in the late 18th century this pack consists of 25 engraved and coloured cards which relate a story based on Alain René le Sage's (1668–1747) masterpiece Gil Blas. The story is set in Spain and begins when Gil Blas leaves his home in Santillane in search of fame and fortune. With a strong humorous element, each card tells of Gil Blas's numerous adventures – of how he fell in with robbers, rescued maidens in distress and inherited fortunes and titles from noble families in whose service he was employed. Unfortunately his life was riddled with bad luck and misfortune and no sooner had he found happiness and wealth than, by trickery, it was taken away again. Other stories in this series are about Don Quixote *c.*1770, Cinderella *c.*1770 and Robinson Crusoe and his Man Friday which was produced in America by Crosby & Nichols in Boston, Santon & Miles in New York and Samuel Hart in Philadelphia.

Packs of cards were also produced which just featured a picture and title with no text and sometimes no number. This type of pack usually revolved around costumes of different countries and periods such as an Austrian edition of *c.*1750 which has 50 unnumbered and hand-coloured cards showing characters from different walks of life.

A French historical game pack of the 19th century has certain cards showing a scene involving a monarch such as Napoleon, Charles VII or Hugh Capet, together with his name on a plaque underneath. A few other cards have ornamental boxes just showing 'busts' of other kings with their names.

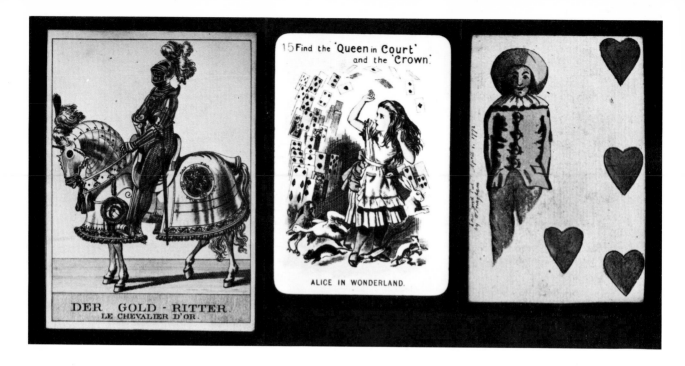

*Left to right: Le Chevalier d' Or,* a 13-card game pack showing different types of knight, by H.F. Müller, Vienna, *c.* 1810; 'Alice in Wonderland' pack of 48 cards by De La Rue, *c.* 1893; conjuring cards by W. Tringham, *c.* 1772.

A number of English packs have also used famous characters or stories for their subject, such as a pack of *c.*1850 which is based on Robin Hood. Sixteen of the cards have pictures only on them while another sixteen have pictures and titles.

Another delightful pack, again from England, features pictures from Sir John Tenniel's illustrations for *Alice in Wonderland*. Each of the forty-eight cards has a simple caption such as 'Find the "Queen in Court" ' and 'The Crown'.

Among the ranks of the miscellaneous must also be placed the various conjuring cards. One French pack was engraved from copper plates and coloured by hand. The cards are diagonally divided and have two different pictures on each including: an ostrich, pipe, goblet, violin, rooster, bagpipe, courtier, cavalier, parrot, guardsman, lobster, lady of the court, mountebank, monkey, lion rampant with a parasol and a sinister looking person with a ladder.

# Appendices

## APPENDIX I

### METHODS OF MAKING PLAYING CARDS

T HE EARLIEST method of producing playing cards was with woodblocks. This is called relief printing as the design to be printed is in relief.

First a piece of wood was taken and cut in plank (along the length) and the design drawn on to the wood. All the surplus areas which were not part of the design were then cut away to a depth of ⅛ to ¼ inch. The relief design left was then coated with ink and printed. Sometimes blocks were made using the end grain of wood which is termed wood engraving.

At first the actual printing was done by 'rubbing', i.e. the card was placed on the back of the inked woodblock and rubbed on the back. Later presses were invented where the inked plate was placed on a press and covered with the sheet of card. Several layers of fabric were placed on top of the card and the press was screwed down. When enough pressure had been exerted the press was unscrewed and the printed paper hung to dry.

Although an innovation in its time, this type of printing often produced quite crude results. Unless performed by skilled craftsmen it was very difficult to cut away the wood to leave a design line of equal thickness all the way through. The earliest woodcuts were therefore deliberately simple, with little or no shading.

The wood itself had a limited lifespan and cards are found with gaps in the outlines where the relief design has worn away. Also, because such great pressure was needed for printing, the ink was usually pressed out leaving a thinner impression in the middle of the line and thicker at either side.

During the early 1700s copper and zinc superseded wood, although the same methods for cutting away surplus metal were used. Later the metal was 'deep etched' by drawing the design directly on to the metal with an acid-resistant substance and then 'lowering', by exposing the undrawn areas to acid.

### Intaglio

Intaglio printing from copper plates was known in Germany and Italy before 1450 and was used extensively for high-quality playing cards by the end of the century. The principle of intaglio printing is the exact reverse of woodblock printing. A sheet of copper was taken and the design engraved into the copper, leaving a groove. The copper plate was then inked and wiped clean. The print was made from the ink left in the grooves.

The most common metals used were copper for line engraving, drypoint and colour printing, and zinc for

151

broad line drawing and deep etch techniques. In about 1820 steel plates began to replace copper as they gave a finer design and did not wear as quickly as copper.

The two basic methods for copper engraving were:

1. *Drypoint*, which was the most direct and sensitive of the intaglio processes and employed a strong needle to draw directly on to the plate so that the incised line was made just deep enough to hold the ink. As the needle was dragged through the metal, a 'burr' was ploughed at the edges of the line which gave the print a rich, soft linear quality. This burring quality gradually faded unless the plate was steel faced.

2. *Line-engraving*. This process was perfected by the Germans and Italians and employs a sharp burin with a cutting point at an angle of 40°.

During the 16th century the 'etching' technique was introduced into Germany, Italy and Spain. It was first used by gunsmiths and armourers and the basic principle is that the plate was covered in acid-resistant wax through which the drawing was made with a sharp instrument. The plate was then exposed to acid and the exposed metal was 'etched' while the waxen areas were left unaffected. The plate could be 'etched' or 'bitten' in varying degrees and stages to produce contrast, shades, tones, etc. from slightly etched lines to very deeply bitten lines. First the lighter tones were treated and when completed, protected with an acid-resistant material. The plate was then put back in the acid to form the next darker area and so on until the complete range of tones had been bitten.

Another method of achieving tones and shades on cards was the aquatint process. Acid-resistant powder resin was put on the area to be given a tonal effect and acid was applied. The acid only affected the resin-free areas and formed areas of grained tone. Another way of producing tones was by stippling or using cross lines and dots.

Under a magnifying glass it can be seen that an etched line ends abruptly while an engraved line tapers to a point.

The plates were printed in a similar manner to woodblocks but on specially modified intaglio presses.

## Lithography

The most modern printing method is lithography. It was invented by the German Aloys Senefelder in 1796; although lithography in its present state is far removed from Senefelder's techniques and is in fact constantly being improved upon and experimented with.

The main difference between lithography and other printing processes is that it is based on purely chemical properties – not mechanical.

Aloys Senefelder lived in Bavaria and came across lithography during his experiments to find a cheaper way to print his manuscripts. As copper was hard to come by at that time, he attempted to etch on the smooth limestone that was quarried in the area. During one of his experiments his mother asked him to prepare a laundry list. As he did not have any paper handy he wrote the list with greasy ink on a piece of stone. Later he realized the natural affinity of grease and stone and that it was possible to damp the stone so that the printing ink would only take on the greasy drawing and leave the white or unwanted parts of the design blank.

In the mid-19th century the stone was replaced by zinc plates and more recently by aluminium. Experiments were also made to link photographic processes with lithography, although the full implications and use of photo-lithography were not perfected until some thirty years ago. The use of lithography for colour prints was also used extensively and called chromolithography.

During the history of lithography various machines have been developed to mechanize the different processes involved. One of the most advanced of these processes is offset printing. With this method the original printing plate first prints on to a rubber blanket which then 'offsets' or reprints the design on to paper. This method reduces the wear on the original plate and enables printing to be done at high speeds.

Of all the printing processes lithography produces the most realistic impressions – similar to photography – and captures the most details with small graduations in tone and shading.

## Colour Printing

Until the 19th century playing cards were coloured by means of a stencil. A stencil is a piece of card from which a shape is cut out corresponding to the shape of the coloured area required. The stencil is placed on the sheet of playing cards and paint is applied to the cut out shapes.

The problem of finding a mechanical process of colouring cards had puzzled manufacturers for a very long time, and a commercially viable method was not fully implemented until the first half of the 19th century. In England Thomas De La Rue was the first to patent a colour-printing method for playing cards in 1832. Each colour was applied separately on to the wood block and printed on to the card. This idea of course was not totally new, but the problem until then had been to register the colours properly so that there were no overlaps or white gaps.

In the *American Mechanics Magazine* of September 17, 1825 there was an article on the then current methods used to produce playing cards. They were usually prepared from three separate sheets of paper: the 'belly' paper which comprises two thin sheets of paper pasted together, and the back and front which is made from pure white paper. When the sheets were pasted together they were placed in a press, the pressure of which was increased at regular intervals. Afterwards the edges were washed with a soft brush dipped in water, to get rid of the excess paste.

In the early 1800s the printing of French playing cards in America was done mainly on wood blocks. Usually two blocks were used, one for cards which included black, and the other for cards with no black on them. The numbered cards had a block for each suit. The colours were applied by means of a stencil of which the yellow was made from Turkey berries, with about an eighth of alum; the red from vermilion ground with gum water, the black from lamp black, mixed with glue, and left for five to six months before it was used; the blue of indigo mixed with size; and the grey was dilute blue. Each colour was applied by a separate stencil. The cards were then illuminated and heated in a stove to make sure the colours were dry. Next, the cards were 'soaped' by means of a rubber which was passed over a cake of dry soap, then over the cards. While hot, the cards were polished with a stone, and again placed under the press, after which they were ready for cutting.

# APPENDIX II

# SOCIETIES

T HERE are now a number of playing card societies which a collector can join. Most of these offer a list of other members' names with whom it is possible to correspond for information or to exchange and buy packs of cards. In addition, they publish a news letter and/or a regular society magazine containing authoritative specialized and beginners' articles on the various aspects of playing cards and current news and views. They also usually hold conventions or meetings where one can meet fellow collectors and, again, exchange information and packs of cards.

The following is a list of addresses of the main playing card societies and is correct at the time of writing.

**Great Britain**
The International Playing-Card Society
The Secretary
188 Sheen Lane
East Sheen
London SW14 8LF

This society has an international membership. Some of its members have formed branch groups in different countries. For full information on the various branches one should contact the International Playing-Card Society.

**France**
Another recently formed society is:
L'Association des Collectionneurs des Cartes et Tarots
M. Pascal Pette
c/o Madame Ravel
28 Rue Lauriston
75116 Paris
France

**U.S.A.**
A small and select organization in America which recruits members who are primarily concerned with contributing working knowledge and information was founded, and is run, by:
Playing Card Information 'Circle'
Emanuel S. Newman
8604 Julian Road
Richmond
Virginia 23229
U.S.A.

There is also:
The Chicago Playing Card Collectors Inc.
9645 South Leavitt Street
Chicago
Illinois 60643
U.S.A.

and

Playing Card Collectors' Assn. Inc.
1511 West 6th Street
Racine
Wisconsin 53404
U.S.A.

# APPENDIX III

## DEFINITIONS AGREED BY THE INTERNATIONAL PLAYING CARD SOCIETY AT THE CONVENTIONS OF RYE 1973.

| TERM | DEFINITION |
|---|---|
| PLAYING-CARDS<br>FACE OR FRONT &<br>BACK<br>PACK OR DECK | Any group of flat, regular shaped pieces of material bearing informative and comparable symbols or other visual presentations on one side only (known as the face or front) whereas the other side (known as the back) should be of uniform appearance throughout each group (known as a pack or deck) suitable for competitive play according to rules. |
| SUITED PACKS<br>  SINGLE-SUITED<br>  MULTI-SUITED<br>SUIT-MARK, -SYMBOL<br>  or -SIGN | Packs comprising a number of sequences of regular length and composition. Such packs can be single-suited, having one suit or sequence repeated, or may be multi-suited, in which each suit or sequence is differentiated by an individual suit-mark. (The terms suit-symbol and suit-sign are permissible alternatives). Such packs can be associated with up to six Jokers without losing their essential character. |
| AUGMENTED SUITED<br>  PACKS,<br>REGULAR SUITED PACKS | Packs conforming to the definition of suited packs but having, in addition, extra cards with a special purpose. Packs conforming to that definition but not having such extra cards are known as regular suited packs. |
| NON-SUITED PACKS | Packs which conform to the definition of playing-cards but which have no regular or recognized suits. These are usually designed for use in one specific game. |
| PERMANENT TRUMPS,<br>WILD CARDS | The additional cards of an augmented suited pack may be permanent trumps which will have a value higher than suited cards, or wild cards which can be used in different ways. The permanent trumps may have a special name under the rules of the game for which they are used. |
| STANDARD CARDS | These are packs which, having become widely accepted by playing-card users conform to a recognized pattern which, as a general rule, have been made by more than one maker and in any case are not completely restricted in principle to one maker, have been made over a period of years, may be redrawn from time to time, and of which it will be possible to formulate an overall generic description to which the examples of different cardmakers will substantially conform. |
| REGIONAL PATTERNS,<br>OFFICIAL PATTERNS,<br>OPERATIONAL PATTERNS | Standard cards as so defined may conform to: regional patterns, which will have emanated from a defined geographical area; official patterns, which will have emanated from Governmental or Religious decree; and operational patterns, which will have originated from a particular card game. |
| STANDARD VARIANTS,<br>NON-STANDARD CARDS | Standard cards as so defined may, however, in some respects vary from a recognized pattern to a slight but noteworthy degree. Such cards may be known as standard variants (and the variation shall be specified). They are still to be included within the general classification of standard cards. All other playing-cards shall be considered as non-standard. |
| FRENCH SUIT SYSTEM,<br>LATIN SUIT SYSTEMS,<br>GERMAN SUIT SYSTEM,<br>SWISS SUIT SYSTEM, | The four suits of the French suit system are: Hearts, Spades, Diamonds and Clubs. The four suits of the Latin suit systems are: Cups, Coins (to be abbreviated D), Swords and Batons. There are four distinct suit types within the Latin suit systems – Italian, Italo-Portuguese, Spanish and Archaic Italian. The four suits of the German suit system are: Hearts, Bells, Acorns and Leaves. The four suits of the Swiss suit system are: Shields, Acorns, Bells and Flowers. |
| SUITS<br>  COURT CARDS<br>  PIP CARDS | In suited packs (whether regular or augmented) each sequence or suit usually comprise court cards, usually presented pictorially, and pip cards, which usually show or imply the relevant number of suit-marks according to the value in play of the card. |

| | |
|---|---|
| NAMES GIVEN TO<br>COURT CARDS | The names by which the court cards of packs are known vary according to area and the game played. In the French suit system these are: King, Queen, Jack (or Knave) and Cavalier. In the Latin suit systems these are King, Queen, Jack (or Knave), Cavalier, Female Cavalier, and Maid. In the German suit system these are: King, Ober, Unter, Cavalier and Banner. In the Swiss suit system these are: King, Ober and Under. |
| COMPLETE PACK,<br>INCOMPLETE PACKS | A complete pack is one in exactly the same state in terms of number of cards and composition as when it left the maker. (Note: as extra cards such as Jokers and title-cards are often and easily mislaid, it will be in order to describe a pack incomplete only in such a particular as 'complete except for extra cards'. Incomplete packs other than those coming within this proviso will be known as incomplete packs.) |
| FULL PACK,<br>SHORTENED PACK,<br>EXTENDED PACK | A full pack is a reference to the basic composition of a pack indicating that it has, when complete, the same number of cards as its prototype. A shortened pack, therefore, would be a subsequent version of the same prototype, with certain cards having been omitted. Similarly an extended pack would be a subsequent version of the same prototype with certain additition al cards. |
| SIZE | Size refers exclusively to the dimensions of the cards. These should be given in millimetres, the height, and width, or diameter being stated. |
| SINGLE-FIGURE,<br>DOUBLE-FIGURE,<br>VARIABLE DOUBLE-<br>FIGURE,<br>INDEX | The face or front of a court card may show the pictured figure once (known as single-figure) or with a design incorporating reversed figures or half-figures so that the card is recognizable whichever end is uppermost (known as double-figure). In these latter cards, the two halves of the design are usually divided horizontally or at an angle. If the two halves of the design are substantially different, the expression variable double-figure is appropriate. In cards whose value is shown by incorporating a letter, numeral or other symbol, that letter, numeral or other symbol is an index which may be in single, double, quadruple or multiple form. |

**APPENDIX IV**

# BIBLIOGRAPHY AND FURTHER READING

ALLEMAGNE, HENRI RENÉ D'. *Les Cartes à Jouer du XIVe au XXe Siècle*. Hachette, Paris, 1906.

AUTENBOER, DR EUGEEN VAN. *The Turnhout Playing Card Industry 1826–1976*. Preceded by a History of Belgian Playing Cards from 1379–1826: by Louis Tummers in collaboration with Jan Bauwens. Aurelia Books, Brussels, 1975.

BEAL, GEORGE. *Discovering Playing Cards and Tarots*. Shire Publications, Ltd., Buckinghamshire, 1972.

BEAL, GEORGE. *Playing Cards and Their Story*. David and Charles, Newton Abbot, 1975.

BENHAM, W. GURNEY. *Playing Cards: Their History and Secrets*. Ward Lock, London 1931, reprinted by Spring Books, London, during 1950s.

CARY, MELBERT B. JR. *War Cards. A Prolusion*. Press of the Woolly Whale, New York, 1937.

CASTELLI, ALFREDO. *Viaggio Curioso nel Mondo delle Carte*. Fratelli Fabbri Editori, Milan, 1975.

CAVENDISH, RICHARD. *The Tarot*. Michael Joseph Ltd, London, 1975.

CHATTO, WILLIAM ANDREW. *Facts and Speculations on the Origins and History of Playing Cards*. John Russell Smith, London, 1848.

DENNING, TREVOR. *Translucent Playing Cards*. Published by the author, Birmingham, 1976.

DUMMETT, MICHAEL. *The Game of Tarot*. Duckworth, London, 1980.

DUMMETT, MICHAEL. *Twelve Tarot Games*. Duckworth, London, 1980.

FOURNIER, HERACLIO. *Museo de Naipes (catalogue of)*. Heraclio Fournier S.A., Vitoria, 1972.

GRUPP, CLAUS D. *Spielkarten und ihre Geschichte*. ASS Verlag GmbH, Leinfelden, 1973.

HAICH, ELIZABETH. *Sagesse du Tarot*. Dervy-Livres, Paris, 1972.

HARGRAVE, CATHERINE PERRY. *A History of Playing Cards and a Bibliography of Cards and Gaming*. Dover Publications, Inc., New York, 1966.

HASE, MARTIN VON. *Spielkarten aus aller Welt*. Staatsgalerie, Stuttgart, 1968.

HOCHMAN, GENE. *The Encyclopedia of American Playing Cards, Vol. I and Vol. II*. Published by author, New Jersey, 1976.

HOFFMAN, DETLEF. *Spielkarten des Historischen Museums Frankfurt am Main*. Detlef Hoffman, Frankfurt, 1972.

HOFFMAN, DETLEF. *Spielkartensammlung*. Piatnik, Vienna, 1970.

HOFFMAN, DETLEF. *The Playing Card: An Illustrated History*. Edition Leipzig, 1973. Distributed in U.K. by George Prior Publishers, Ltd, London.

HOFFMAN, DETLEF & ERIKA KROPPENSTEDT. *Die Cotta'schen Spielkarten-Almanache 1805–1811*. Deutsches Spielkarten Museum, Bielefeld, 1969.

HOFFMAN, DETLEF & ERIKA KROPPENSTEDT. *Französische Spielkarten des XX Jahrhunderts*. Deutsches Spielkarten Museum, Bielefeld, 1967.

HOFFMAN, DETLEF & ERIKA KROPPENSTEDT. *Inventar-Katalog der Spielkarten-Sammlung des Stadtmuseums Linz*. Deutsches Spielkarten Museum, Bielefeld, 1969.

HOFFMAN, DETLEF & ERIKA KROPPENSTEDT. *Wahrsagekarten*. Deutsches Spielkarten Museum, Bielefeld, 1972.

INNES, BRIAN. *The Tarot*. Orbis Publishing Limited, London, 1977.

JANDIN, CÉCILE DE. *Catalogue de la Donation Paul Marteau*. Bibliothèque Nationale, Paris, 1966.

JANSSEN, HAN. *Spieelkarten*. C.A.J. van Dishoeck, Bussum, 1965.

KAPLAN, STUART R. *The Encyclopedia of Tarot*. U.S. Games Systems Inc, New York, 1978.

KOHLMANN, THEODOR & SIGMAR RADAU. *Das Preussische Bild*. Museum für Deutsche Volkskunde, Staatliche Museum Preussischer Kulturbesitz, Berlin, 1978.

KOPP, PETER F. *et al. Schweizer Spielkarten*. Kunstgewerbemuseum der Stadt, Zurich, 1978.

LÉVI, ELIPHAS. *Dogme et Ritual de la Haute Magie*. Paris, 1856.

LEYDEN, RUDOLF VON. *Chad, The Playing Cards of Mysore*. Published by the author, 1973.

LEYDEN, RUDOLF VON. *Indische Spielkarten*. Deutsches Spielkarten-Museum, Bielefeld, 1977.

MANN, SYLVIA. *Collecting English Playing-Cards*. Stanley Gibbons Publications Limited, London, 1978.

MANN, SYLVIA. *Collecting Playing Cards*. Howard Baker, London, 1973.

MANN, SYLVIA. *The Dragons of Portugal*. Playing Card Society, London, 1973.

MANN, SYLVIA. *The William Penn Collection of Playing Cards*. Published by the author, Rye, 1966.

MAYER, L.A. *Mamluk Playing Cards*. E.J. Brill, Leyden, 1971.

MERLIN, R. *Origine des Cartes à Jouer: Recherches Nouvelles Sur les Naibis, les Tarots et sur les Autres Espèces des Cartes*. Paris, 1869.

MILANO, ALBERTO. *Carte Milanesi da gioco nell'Ottocento*. Gianluigi Arcari Editore, Mantua, 1978.

*In de Kaart Gekeken: Europese Speelkarten van de 15de Eeuw Tot Heden*. Museum Willet-Holthuysen, Amsterdam, 1976.

O'DONOGHUE, FREEMAN M. (compiler). *Catalogue of the Collection of Playing Cards Bequeathed to the Trustees of the British Museum by the late Lady Charlotte Schreiber*. Longmans Green and Co. and others, London, 1901.

'PAPUS'. *Absolute Key to Occult Science; The Tarot of the Bohemians; The Most Ancient Book in the World* (3 titles) Chapman and Hall, London, 1802.

PRUNNER, GERNOT. *Ostasiatische Spielkarten*. Deutsches Spielkarten Museum, Bielefeld, 1969.

REISIG, OTTO. *Deutsche Spielkarten*. Bibliographisches Institut, Leipzig, 1935.

RENSELLAER, Mrs. JOHN KING VAN. *The Devil's Picture Books*. T. Fisher Unwin, London, 1892.

RENSELLAER, Mrs. JOHN KING VAN. *Prophetical Educational and Playing Cards*. Hurst and Blackett, London, 1912.

ROSENFELD, HELMUT. *Munchner Spielkarten um 1500*. Deutsches Spielkarten Museum, Bielefeld, 1958.

SCHREIBER, Lady CHARLOTTE. *Playing Cards of Various Ages and Countries*. John Murray, London.

SINGER, SAMUEL WELLER. *Researches Into the History of Playing Cards with Illustrations of the Origin and Printing and Engraving on Wood*, London (Ed.), 1816.

TAYLOR, E.S. (Ed.). *The History of Playing Cards with Anecdotes of their use in Conjuring, Fortune Telling and Card-Sharping*. John Camden Hotten, London, 1865; reprinted by the Charles E. Tuttle Co. Inc., Tokyo, 1973.

TILLEY, ROGER. *A History of Playing Cards*. Studio Vista, London, 1973.

TILLEY, ROGER. *Playing Cards*. Octopus Books Limited, London, 1973.

*Fortune Telling with Playing Cards*. The United States Playing Card Company, 1923.

WAYLAND, VIRGINIA. *The Winstanley Geographical Cards*. Virginia and Harold Wayland, California, 1967.

WAYLAND, VIRGINIA and HAROLD. *Of Carving Cards and Cookery*. Raccoon Press, Arcadia, California, 1962.

WILLSHIRE, WILLIAM HUGHES, M.D. *A History of Playing and Other Cards in the British Museum Accompanied by a Concise General History of the Subject*. Edinburgh, 1876, reprinted by British Museum Publications, Ltd., 1975.

WHITING, J.R.S. *A Handful of History*. Alan Sutton, Gloucestershire, 1978.

WOWK, KATHLEEN. *Tarot Cards*. Stanley Gibbons Publications Limited, London, 1978.

In addition to the above-mentioned books are the journals published by the various playing card societies; in particular, the International Playing-Card Society *Journal* contains many authoritative articles on a wide range of subjects.

# Index